JOINED-UP SYSTEMS

SYSTEMS

BUILDING THE
INTEGRATED BUSINESS

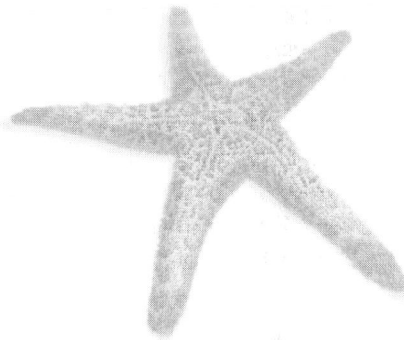

TREVOR ELLIOTT & DAVE HERBERT

Hodder & Stoughton

A MEMBER OF THE HODDER HEADLINE GROUP

Every effort has been made to trace and acknowledge ownership of copyright material but if any have been inadvertently overlooked, the publisher will be pleased to make the necessary alterations at the first opportunity.

Orders: please contact Bookpoint Ltd, 130 Milton Park, Abingdon, Oxon OX14 4SB. Telephone: (44) 01235 827720. Fax: (44) 01235 400454. Lines are open from 9.00–6.00, Monday to Saturday, with a 24-hour message answering service. E-mail address: orders@bookpoint.co.uk

British Library Cataloguing in Publication Data
A catalogue record for this title is available from the British Library.

ISBN 0 340 85054X

First published 2002
Impression number 10 9 8 7 6 5 4 3 2 1
Year   2007 2006 2005 2004 2003 2002

Typeset by Servis Filmsetting Ltd, Manchester.
Printed in Great Britain for Hodder & Stoughton Educational, a division of Hodder Headline Plc, 338 Euston Road, London NW1 3BH by J.W. Arrowsmith Ltd, Bristol.

M·C·A

MANAGEMENT
CONSULTANCIES
ASSOCIATION

Series Editor: Fiona Czerniawska, Director of MCA Think Tank.

The MCA was formed in 1956 and represents the leading UK-based consulting firms, which currently employ over 25,000 consultants and generate £4.3bn in annual fee income. The UK consulting industry is worth around £8bn, contributing £1bn to the balance of payments.

As well as setting and maintaining standards in the industry, the MCA supports its member firms with a range of services including events, publications, interest groups and public relations. The Association also works with its members to attract the top talent into the industry. The MCA provides advice on the selection and use of management consultants and is the main source of data on the UK market.

FOR MORE INFORMATION PLEASE CONTACT:
Management Consultancies Association
49 Whitehall
London
SW1A 2BX

Tel: 020 7321 3990
Fax: 020 7321 3991

E-mail: mca@mca.org.uk
www.mca.org.uk

CONTENTS

V

ACKNOWLEDGEMENTS

We owe a huge debt of gratitude to Sue Norris, whose drive, organization, professional ability and unflappability made this book possible.

We would like to thank Andy Mulholland, chief technology officer at Cap Gemini, Ernst & Young, for his ideas on adaptive architectures and his major contribution to sections of this book. We would also like to thank Clive Fenton for his contribution on risk, and Crea Mann for her efficient assistance with manuscripts.

We thank the Management Consulting Association for the opportunity to write this book and Fiona Czerniawska for her encouragement and support throughout.

And last, but by no means least, we thank our families for their support and patience.

FOREWORD

For the manager charged with changing or improving business systems, this book is a very useful and thought-provoking handbook. It reminds us of the real world problems, considerations, opportunities and failures. It adds considerably to anyone's vocabulary of considerations when planning and carrying out programs and projects. People with a technological bias can study it in order to broaden their outlook and to develop their understanding of how to make their technology succeed in real organizations. Project failure rate is embarrassingly high and the authors have given some explanation as to why.

Joined-up Systems is built on the long-term consultant experiences of several senior people and it exposes and reminds us of factors we might otherwise forget or fail to see, until it is too late. It clearly sets the challenge of joining up our business systems. Moreover, it keeps our focus squarely on the business and business results, not the changes and the programs of change themselves. It constantly reminds us to plan and manage the people, and focuses on the motivation, communication and morale aspects, which are so easily forgotten in large technology projects. It delivers a systematic framework for the change process so that we can judge our own current efforts and plans, and find our own black holes in time to prevent damage.

I took the weekend to read the book. I kept trying to scan rapidly but failed, since the text kept throwing such interesting logs on the fire that I had to slow down and read. I did not want to miss such good experience. I kept on admiring the authors' ability to make sense of the diversity of historical developments (resulting in legacy systems) and the diversity of technological innovation in the last decade. They manage to somehow paint a picture of the opportunities we have suddenly acquired in the last decade, along with clear warnings about what NOT to waste time doing. I felt like 'Have I been awake to all of this, or has it sneaked up on me?'

I am grateful to the authors for giving me a more complete grasp of the opportunities than I was able to assimilate from any other source. I shall happily recommend this book to my executive clients and my technical friends. They can both use the insights.

Here are some headlines I noted as I read the book:

☐ It articulates some of the real problems we have in making changes pay off and some of the subtle stuff we did not imagine would delay or kill the payoff.

☐ It makes the main theme of business evolution and architecture to support that evolution, clear and convincing.

☐ There are hundreds of practical observations and pieces of advice.

☐ This is a practitioner's view of the emerging techno and business culture changes in the last decade, with some practical advice on the consequences for your planning.

☐ You are lifted up to the whole system level of thinking, where the IT system cannot be the main point. Real achievement of the business results is the only point.

☐ There are great insights, not least with the help of surveys of the best thinkers in the world on cultural and social aspects that we need to consider when building systems.

☐ There are numerous useful case studies of real companies, both of author experience and international repute.

☐ The systematic sections on international communication, including video-conferencing and tele-conferencing, are pearls which I found useful reminders for my own practice.

☐ The risk chapter contains practical gems – refreshing compared to the too prevalent academic theory of risk management.

Enjoy the book. Share it with your team. Join up!

Tom Gilb, Consultant, Teacher, Author.
www.gilb.com
7 July 2002, Norway.

Author of *Principles of Software Engineering Management*,
1988, Addison Wesley.
and *Competitive Engineering*,
2002, Addison Wesley.

INTRODUCTION

❛We live in a moment of history when change is so speeded up that we begin to see the present only when it's disappearing.❜
R D Laing, *The Politics of Experience and the Bird of Paradise*, Penguin, 1990.

☐ **Fact** – In 1997, global finance companies predicted reductions in total operational costs of 6 per cent in 1998, rising steadily to 14 per cent by 2003, as a result of implementing e-business. The reality is that they achieved savings of 2 per cent in 1998 and 1 per cent in subsequent years. Why were the improvements so disappointing?

☐ **Fact** – Today, the strategic emphasis of business has shifted from how a company chooses to engage with its customers, to how customers choose to engage with the company. Yet, major global organizations have to spend $500,000 a day maintaining interfaces and 30 per cent of their Information Technology (IT) budget on integration solely to keep operations as they are. Can this be sustained?

☐ **Fact** – In a survey carried out in 2001, 81 per cent of respondent organizations said they would prefer to choose a full partnership as their desired long-term customer relationship when implementing major integration programs, such as those based around Customer Relationship Management (CRM) solutions. What does this mean in terms of the way we should be building and working relationships with suppliers?

☐ **Fact** – The Royal Bank of Canada claims a 6 per cent improvement in marketing cycle time and direct response rates that can exceed 40 per cent as a result of breaking down its customer base into 20,000 segments and employing a high degree of product customization. What has this done to its organization, its business process and technology capability?

Organizations today are chasing their tails trying to keep up with rapidly changing market pressures, customer demands and technology developments. Traditional ways of doing business are losing their relevance, forcing companies to seek new levels of flexibility in the way they operate. Predicting future threats and opportunities in the external market has become impossible, and the result is that enterprises need to be able to react to new events as and when they occur.

As organizations grapple with the question of how to achieve greater levels of market responsiveness, enhanced customer service and smoother, more productive supplier relationships, they are forced to look inwards at the complex array of rigid business processes, job functions and supporting IT systems they have amassed over the years, in an attempt to determine how these can be reworked to give greater business advantage.

At an IT level, organizations are trying to harness vast arrays of disparate applications in an integrated, holistic way in order to manage information coming into and going out of the

1

company. Far from being unified, these systems present a whole range of technical challenges. Legacy systems are juxtaposed with 'new-world' systems; applications in different departments have been implemented in isolation and do not interact with the systems of potentially complementary business units; and silos of information exist all over an enterprise, making it extremely difficult for the organization to build up a single view of the customer, the business, the market opportunity or the supply chain. Clearly this needs to change.

However, the sorts of changes that organizations seek to make today, in order to become more responsive to the markets they operate in, are much wider in scope than simply an IT challenge. Organizations seeking to be empowered rather than held back by their data assets and IT systems, find they need to conduct a radical review of their business priorities and their business processes if they want to see real improvements. They are having to ask themselves:

☐ Is the old way of tackling commercial opportunities the right way for the future?

☐ Are our staff currently deployed in the most efficient way?

☐ Are we poised to take advantage of new market possibilities, whatever these might be, even if we had more closely integrated IT systems?

It is in this context that the challenging subject of integration is tackled. This is not a technical book, but rather one which seeks to give business meaning to why an organization would want to attempt large-scale integration programs today, and how, strategically, this might best be achieved.

We have sought to simplify the issues, and deal with them in a pragmatic way. As practitioners, we believe in simplicity above all. Yet the integration of business systems can be a complicated affair.

THE THREE STRANDS OF SUCCESSFUL INTEGRATION: PEOPLE, PROCESS AND TECHNOLOGY

Technology developments for technology's sake rarely benefit anyone. Unless the goal of any system changes is to improve some aspect of business performance, the point has unfortunately been missed. Any serious integration program must consider the business process, people and technology issues in equal measure. The three cannot be separated, as each will affect the other.

Nevertheless, too often, organizations decide something must change, and begin planning a project based on just one or two of these three elements. Six or 12 months down the line, they wonder why business productivity has not improved. It is probably because they tried to apply new technology to an old process, or vice versa. Or perhaps they forgot to communicate the goals to, or retrain, the employees who would be affected.

CONTINUOUS CHANGE

Another common mistake is to see integration as a definable project with a beginning, middle and end. In today's fast-moving business and technology climate, it is no longer practical to plan huge, long-term technology programs which may take until the following year, or longer, to bed down. The chances are, if you do this, by the time you have reached final delivery, the technology will have advanced and the business goals will have changed.

Instead, the process of change should be seen as a continuous cycle. Successful integration does not have a beginning and end – it is a movable feast. Whether you are planning, building or running new systems, you need to keep your eye on the business processes, the people factors and the technology issues at every stage along the way, and ask yourself whether you are meeting each of their needs today, and whether you will still be able to meet them tomorrow.

Since predicting the future has become impossible, the only thing you can do to prepare your company is to ensure that any measures you take when developing and integrating your teams of employees, business processes and supporting IT systems are flexible and adaptable.

A PRACTICAL TOOL

This book is aimed primarily at the managers and practitioners of business systems implementation programs. A number of others may also find our ideas useful, such as the business executives who have to use the systems; managers responsible for business change; anyone trying to prepare a business case for new systems; those wondering how best to use external suppliers and those needing to gather business requirements across multiple countries, each with different business models. In short, people at the centre and on the periphery of business and systems change.

The approach here is to deal with real issues by bringing together some of the day-to-day challenges faced by practitioners and their organizations as they seek to deliver integrated business systems. We have also put together a set of practical, tried and tested approaches to deal with these issues.

'Joined-up systems' is defined as those business systems that carry out common business processes, supported by technology, which covers just about everything in business these days! These are the sorts of systems typically found in organizations worldwide. Coverage is restricted to the most commonly occurring business systems, such as sales systems, distribution systems, back-office administration systems and management information systems, but the principles apply equally to other, more specialist systems. Integration *programs* (the wider, more complex initiatives), and *projects* (more manageable subsets of the overall program) are differentiated.

The book is structured to make the content as accessible as possible, allowing you to dip back into specific content as the need arises. Since we are dealing with such a vast subject, which touches upon topics (such as business process) that are deserving of a book to themselves, the book is broken down into manageable sections, each of which breaks down further into a series of self-contained, yet connected chapters. The goal is to break down the integration challenge into logical areas.

Throughout this book, we have dealt concurrently with the three main dimensions of delivering systems – people, process and technology – reflecting our strongly held view that this is how these dimensions should be treated during each stage of program planning and delivery.

Visually, these three main dimensions of any change program can be represented as the corners of a triangle.

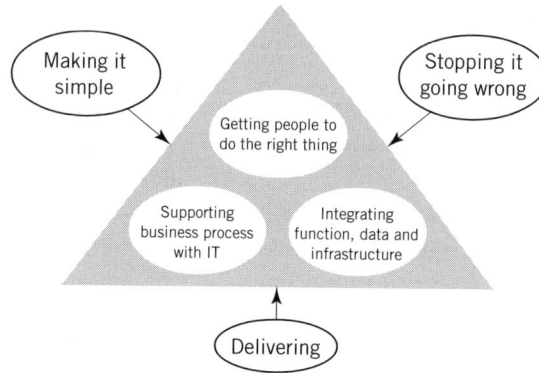

FIGURE 1: People, process and technology

Key issues are drawn out, relating to each of these three dimensions as follows:

1 **People** – Getting people to do the right thing: in order to deliver joined-up systems (in both the business and IT sense). Primarily, Part 2 deals with this theme, 'Creating the climate'.

2 **Process** – Supporting business process with IT: the main goal of joining up systems. This theme is dealt with in Part 3, 'Technology integration', and in the conclusion, 'The future of business process'.

3 **Technology** – Integrating function, data and infrastructure: essential in order to function as a business. This theme is covered in Part 3, 'Technology integration' and in Part 4, 'Delivering joined-up systems'.

On the periphery of the triangle, though far from being peripheral issues, there are three further considerations, essential in any integration program – how to break down the challenge into manageable projects; the various means of delivery; and how to stop programs from going wrong. These are covered in Parts 1, 4 and 5, respectively.

The book contents break down as follows:

Part 1 Understanding the challenge

Here it is established how program managers can attempt to reduce the apparent complexity of dealing with systems and their delivery. Chapter 1, 'Trends', sets the scene for the rest of the book by exploring some of the business and technology trends driving integration programs today and the issues they create.

Chapter 2, 'Managing complexity', continues to develop these themes, looking at the market pressures facing enterprises today, how these translate into business and IT challenges, and how organizations can sensibly contemplate the complexity that confronts them. This challenge is also the focus of Chapter 3, 'Eating the elephant', which examines how program managers can break down large, unwieldy integration programs into more containable, and manageable projects. Finally, in Chapter 4, 'Establishing the business case', we consider how to convince stakeholders of the value of essential systems integration work, particularly when infrastructure-based spend is required.

Part 2 Creating the climate

Here, the first point of the triangle, and the most important dimension of any business change is examined – people. In Chapter 5, 'Implications for people', we take a high level look at many of the issues impacting staff, their deployment and the organizations in which they work. The subsequent chapters consider the challenge of achieving business process and IT change in multicultural environments, and the important considerations to take into account when assembling project teams.

Part 3 Technology integration

This section deals with the next point of the triangle – technology – and focuses on the issues surrounding the integration of function, data and infrastructure. It also deals in part with the support of business process. The section has four chapters, each of which deals with a different aspect of the challenge, from how to tackle legacy systems in a modern IT infrastructure to the importance of taking an architecture-based approach to future integration.

Part 4 Delivering joined-up systems

Here, the focus is on some key practical approaches which have proven effective in delivering joined-up systems. The section is split into six chapters to make the information more accessible. Across them, information is provided in a broad spectrum of topics, from how to build an integrated architecture to what you need to do to improve your approach to testing. Each of the topics justifies a book in its own right, but enough information is given to guide you if you are a practitioner, or to let you know what to expect if you are about to put your business through an integration project.

Part 5 Stopping it going wrong

Things can and will go wrong with any complex integration program. This part adopts an unusual approach to the topic of risk and risk management. In Chapter 18, 'Things go wrong' a case study of a large multi-company (and multiculture) integration program that ran into difficulty is presented. We take a look at the corrective action applied and the results of this action one year on. In Chapter 19, 'Risk management in practice', the high level theory of risk management is bypassed and how organizations can avoid incurring risks on a daily basis is examined, seen through the eyes of a senior program manager.

Conclusion: The future of business process

The concluding chapter draws together the fundamental themes of this book by considering how companies' future business processes will differ to those employed today. Here, examples of enlightened organizations are explored. These businesses are visibly gaining market share today as a result of strategic integration that has given them more flexibility in their business processes, making them more responsive to new market threats and opportunities.

Before you go on to read this book, there are some fundamental issues that apply to all the topics covered in this book. Please take a moment to read through these. An approach to dealing with each of the questions raised here can be found in the book. We hope these questions prompt you to read on, and that the ideas and approaches assist you in framing your own practical responses to deal with the challenge of integration.

Fundamental issues

☐ The need for business and systems integration is growing. Companies are increasingly acquiring business advantage by becoming less and less vertically integrated. That is, companies are sourcing a wider and wider range of services from other companies and attempting to do less and less themselves. Working across company boundaries is just one of the factors that makes systems integration more complex. How can integration be achieved?

☐ Company agility is improving, and the speed at which businesses need to achieve systems integration is growing ever faster. Technological change both drives and is driven by this. The goal is to achieve the ability to combine and recombine elements or components at all levels of business and information technology. How can a framework for combining and recombining people, process and technology be successfully created?

☐ What are you striving to achieve in attempting a systems integration project? Does the end justify the cost?

☐ While benefit should be defined and measured, companies must know when to take a leap of faith. This can only be done within a defined business and technology framework. What does this look like?

☐ Large programs of change are doomed without effective sponsorship and visible leadership – everybody knows that. So why is it always a problem, and how can you make it less of a problem?

☐ While technology is a challenge, it merely creates a set of known or unknown constraints. It is the successful deployment and management of people and resources that is the most important and often the most difficult factor to get right. A 'team's' culture and attitude are driving factors, but how can you get these right?

☐ Knowing your customer and your stakeholders is key. But who are they and how can you make sure you put them at the centre?

☐ Spotting problems before they happen is an intuitive process and facing up to issues quickly is essential. Every manager needs to develop sensitive antennae and know when to trust their judgement. Recognizing typical problem areas will help, but what are they?

☐ Programs and projects are often risky. Yet this is not always obvious. The solution is not always obvious either. What can be done about this?

☐ A modern mantra is to 'be agnostic about technology, passionate about standards'. But in practical, implementable terms, what does this mean?

PART 1

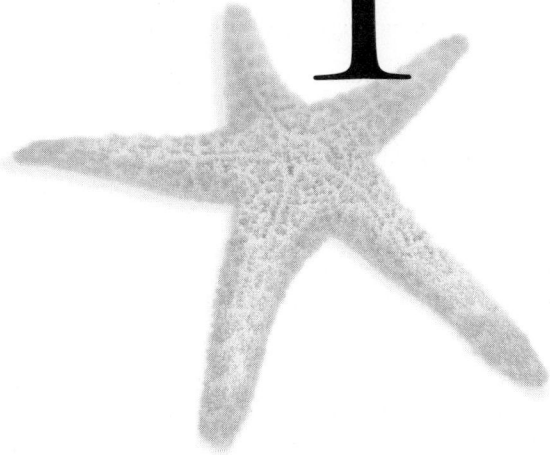

UNDERSTANDING THE CHALLENGE

CHAPTER 1

TRENDS

INTRODUCTION

There is no doubt that we are at a defining point in the provision of Information Technology (IT). Called upon to contribute to the performance and profitability of the business as never before it is no longer enough to merely cut costs. IT today must drive business change, help capture new markets and provide competitive customer service differentiators.

As a result, integration has come to mean so much more than simply bringing two or more IT systems together to ensure that they can share data. Without considering the reasons why those systems are being joined, projects are unlikely to produce that much sought-after return on investment. What is driving this frenetic need to join systems? Where should companies start, and how can they break down the gargantuan task that looms before them?

This will be the focus of the first four chapters, beginning here with an analysis of the various business, technology and people trends which are compelling organizations to rethink their development plans.

THE BIGGER PICTURE

The explosion of activity around integration among large companies results from a number of coincidental developments. At a macro-economic level, the last couple of decades have seen the increasing globalization of large companies, with brand names penetrating international markets on a wider scale than previously, amassing wealth on an enormous scale and using their growing power to impose their corporate cultures across whole continents (obvious examples are companies like IBM and Toyota).

Meanwhile, deregulation and privatization have facilitated competition by introducing new entrants into traditional markets. As a result, customers are presented with unprecedented levels of choice, raising their expectations about price and customer service and giving them more power as consumers than they have ever had.

The accelerating pace of technology development further intensifies the situation. Improved communications give customers access to more information and to more choices of service, driving down customer loyalty and putting companies under pressure to add increasing levels of 'value' if they want to retain market share in such a competitive commercial environment. As well as giving small and large companies alike the chance to bring new propositions to market very quickly, and to as wide a market as they wish to target, the internet raises the stakes for those that take up the challenge. Customers now expect to deal with companies through a choice of channels and around the clock.

As organizations work towards a clearer understanding of the direction they need to take to keep ahead in an increasingly competitive market place, key areas of concern emerge:

☐ How can we target our marketing more effectively?

☐ How can we exploit opportunities for cross-selling?

☐ How can we cost-effectively meet customers' needs for better service, around the clock?

☐ How can we provide a complete product experience or full service to the customer, while retaining focus on the profitable parts of our business?

☐ How can we become more responsive to customer demands without incurring higher operational costs or stockpiling inventory?

It is at the heart of these requirements that the need for strategic integration begins to emerge. These goals all have in common the need to capture, merge, analyze, share and exploit strategic business data – data that is currently scattered across an organization.

To make sense of that data and exploit it to commercial advantage, requires business systems to be aware of each other and to be able to interact. *This* is integration.

Viewing integration solely as a task of IT is dangerous. While organizations will need to be guided in their plans by the potential and the limitations of technology, they must give equal consideration to how business processes and the activities of people have to change. Otherwise, it is likely that any technological innovation will ultimately fail to deliver the required business benefit. A key theme of this book, therefore, is to emphasize the importance of working on technology, business process and people issues concurrently, as part of a single, continuous cycle of change.

TECHNOLOGY TRENDS

Technology developments are clearly contributing to the perception that the world is getting smaller. Technology is also responsible, to varying degrees, for the fact that competition is becoming fiercer, customers' expectations are growing, and employees are demanding new ways of working.

With the internet, IT has become a cause of business change, as well as its facilitator. It is now so pervasive that organizations can no longer choose to ignore it. Technology is no longer a 'nice-to-have' or a business support tool – it is as essential to doing business as electricity or telephone communications. Channelled correctly, IT has the ability to turn businesses around and generate new commercial opportunities. Realizing this, companies cannot afford to wait to exploit technology on a new level. They know that if they wait, their competitors will not.

With the continually falling price of technology and communications, most people can now afford to have a decent PC, laptop and/or Personal Digital Assistant (PDA) and access to the internet and e-mail, whether an office administrator, business manager or child consumer. Increased ease of use, improved performance of devices, faster data communications, increased portability of data and services, and the growth in standards and open systems, provide greater flexibility in how and when users can exploit technology. Workers can do much of what they used to achieve in the office while at home or on the move, and consumers also have unprecedented access to online services.

All organizations must adapt to this if they want to prosper in the long term. New ways of working and of spending leisure time, mean new opportunities – and threats – for businesses. Are customers still being reached in the most appropriate and efficient way, and with the types of products and services they really need? Is someone else doing this more effectively?

Old ways of doing things are being challenged, and it will be the companies with the freshest ideas and the ability to implement these quickly and ahead of the competition that stand to thrive while others founder; slowed down by traditional ways of working so that they are unable to respond to new opportunities. Innovative exploitation of new technologies will certainly help organizations to meet the substantial new challenges that face them, but IT alone is not the panacea.

Closer relations between IT and the business

It is only relatively recently that the direct correlation between IT and the performance of the business has been recognized as something that organizations should strive for. Before now, it has not been unusual for IT departments to be several steps removed from the wider business vision, introspectively working on innovations for innovations' sake, and unable to apply their skills to the pressures on the operational business.

Today, this way of working is no longer an option. IT costs have spiralled out of control as pockets of development activity have taken place in isolation, resulting in massive over-investment in commodity IT assets. At the same time, businesses have begun to ask themselves why planned projects have failed to deliver the business benefits they now so desperately need if they are to maintain and grow market share.

Whereas IT has always supported the business, it is now seen as being able to drive business. Consequently, it is now accepted that technology and business must work together towards common goals. Both the IT department and business management have started to realize that they have been guilty of poor communication, and that only by opening new channels of discussion will they avoid making the same mistakes when they tackle new projects.

For its part, the IT department is having to mature, demonstrating its value to the enterprise by producing better business justifications for planned investment. Meanwhile, business managers are now more likely to include the IT people in discussions about where the organization needs to be directing its commercial energy, so that they can differentiate between what is achievable and what is not.

Taking an enterprise-wide view of IT

As IT and the business become more closely integrated, so the possibilities for blending technology systems more closely with strategic business processes are becoming a reality.

Traditionally, IT projects have been initiated in response to a single, very specific business issue, such as 'We need e-mail', or 'The sales department needs a better way of storing customer and prospect details'. Typically, the objective has been an increase in staff productivity and ideally, a reduction in costs through greater working efficiencies.

The trouble with this approach has been that projects are tackled in isolation, with the result that business benefits have added up to no more than the sum of the individual parts. Sales teams have had their own contact management systems, accounts have had systems for invoice management, help desks have had systems to manage support issues, and telemarketing staff have had systems to manage phone-based promotional campaigns. Each department has been assigned its own data, and has needed its own software, hardware and storage.

This has resulted in substantial wastage – wastage in use of IT resources and wastage in people's time. Information has been recorded more than once, by different staff in different departments, in different formats and for slightly different purposes.

The rise of the internet and e-mail activities has only magnified the problem, creating even more data, which is being captured and stored repeatedly.

This has resulted in a backlash against IT. Calls for system upgrades and greater capacity at a time when the economy has not been buoyant, and market pressures have increased, with the continual shortening of product life cycles, the rise in competition, and the resulting squeeze on profit margins, has led to a clamp down on IT spend. Finance directors are refusing to sanction any more investment until tangible business justification can be shown.

Silos of information are no longer acceptable either. Organizations cannot afford to be extravagant in the number of people they hire. Staff need to be productive and accountable at all times. This means being able to access the information they need to do their jobs wherever they happen to be, whether working from home or on the road. As users become detached from their departmental desktops, information and technology needs to be able to follow them. They also need to be free to access information that has traditionally 'belonged' to other departments in the company, to help them to do their jobs more efficiently by empowering them to make more informed decisions and provide a better level of service.

BUSINESS PROCESS ISSUES

Business processes need to be more efficient too. The fact that customers are more fickle yet have higher expectations from suppliers, means that companies must work harder to win their business. Playing the lowest price game will not always be an option – rising competition and the level of choice accessible on the internet helps to drive margin out of commodity products and services. Organizations that only differentiate themselves on price will soon die.

Instead, organizations are forced into a battle of who can best serve the customer's needs. Knowing this, customers have in turn become more demanding, and are now more inclined to shop around to satisfy their needs, and so the situation continues to escalate.

As they seek to become more customer-aware and more customer-responsive, many organizations are turning to IT to help them track and analyze customer behaviour. In this way, they can adapt to meet customer needs and to stay ahead of the competition.

To achieve this ability, companies are having to rethink their business processes. These must now be supported across the entire enterprise. It is no longer acceptable for sales, marketing, finance and customer services departments each to have their own view of the customer.

Companies need to follow their customers' interactions with their organization from beginning to end to provide the most tailored marketing, full exploitation of cross-selling opportunities, and the most personalized overall customer service possible. This requires greater harmony between previously disparate departmental IT systems – that is, tighter integration, to facilitate greater information or 'knowledge' sharing.

Internal agility brings external adaptability

Above all, organizations need to be able to respond to opportunities as they arise, before their competitors. The internet has taught companies the importance of speed to market. Organizations have started to realize that the speed at which things happen on and through the internet requires a new approach to business innovation. Here, things happen too quickly for companies to predict what is coming next and to be ready for it. Adaptability – the ability to react to new opportunities as they materialize – has become almost more important than a company's capacity to proactively anticipate what is coming next.

However, for the larger organization, the pressure to remain slick and agile is a very real challenge. Some large corporations, perhaps with an old-world business mentality, intricate structures and unwieldy legacy systems, often find it difficult to adapt to new opportunities. Small companies, on the other hand, are typically much more flexible, and can respond more quickly to a market need.

In an attempt to become more adaptable, it is likely that large companies will begin to break down into smaller enterprises working with others in partnership.

In their book, *The Atomic Corporation*[1], authors Roger Camrass and Martin Farncombe argue that the days of the giant corporation are numbered and that these will be replaced with networks of smaller, smarter, more adaptable companies. They write:

> ‘As you can't be big and agile at the same time (the internal cost of movement is too high), fragmentation is looking more and more attractive. ’

They go on to argue that breaking up into smaller entities has never been easier because of developments such as the internet, which has substantially improved external communications and sharply reduced the cost of doing business.

The rise of supplier partnerships

Instead of being product- or service-centric, Camrass and Farncombe argue, tomorrow's corporations will be relationship-centric. The suggestion is that companies need to refocus on and reduce themselves to their core businesses, outsourcing peripheral activities to partners. Not only should this render them more agile, it will reduce internal costs, in turn improving competitiveness.

This does not necessarily mean the death of the large brand; rather there will be an extended supply chain sitting behind the brand in future. There are already cases where large, well-known names have become little more than brokers for other people's products and services – this is now happening in the insurance industry, the airline industry and has been happening in the retail and white and brown goods industries for a long time.

Moreover, while there are likely to be areas of dispute as companies fight over the more lucrative areas, there will be win-win situations, since one company's weakness is often another company's strength. This is why distribution channels exist, after all. By restricting what they do themselves and being prepared to open up to external partners, organizations

---

[1] Roger Camrass and Martin Farncombe, *The Atomic Corporation*, Capstone Publishing, 2001.

can make themselves slicker and more responsive. According to Camrass and Farncombe, it may be the only way companies get the results they're looking for:

> ❮ Firms have been trying to get sleeker and slimmer. They've re-engineered themselves, they've installed ERP [Enterprise Resource Planing] systems, and they've paid fortunes to stay ahead of the pack. But all they managed to achieve was a slight reduction in internal transaction costs and maximized efficiency of output. They missed the big prize because they looked at processes and information inside the firm's boundaries, instead of solving problems across the entire supply chain. ❯

If the premise of The Atomic Corporation holds water, the organization of the future will look very different from the large, unwieldy market leaders of today. Companies will need to adopt virtual business models. They will have to function as though their enterprise extends beyond their own company gates.

The advantage of a well-oiled supply chain

UK supermarket chain, Sainsbury's, now operates more like an atomic corporation than previously. The company recognized that its previous relationship with its suppliers was a contributing factor to the company losing its number one spot in its market. Thus, it instigated a complete review of its supply chain management processes.

In-store promotions had been a particular area of inefficiency. The supermarket chain would not talk to its suppliers about sales forecasts or about what it needed or wanted from the campaign. Therefore, when a promotion came around, the suppliers had to second-guess stock levels and where the displays were to be set up. The impact was either overstocking, or non-availability of the product at all. Since Sainsbury's was typically running 500 promotions in any one week, with a large variety of suppliers, it was making itself unnecessarily vulnerable to mistakes, especially given the relative unpredictability of promotional sales.

A pilot scheme, designed to tackle the problem, determined that poor supply chain communication was to blame. As a result of its findings, Sainsbury's implemented an application that would allow workflow management and data sharing over the internet – suppliers could access Sainsbury's sales forecasts and plan stock supply accordingly.

After a trial period, the supermarket chain found that its inventory pipeline had reduced to one week, compared with four to five weeks previously. Furthermore, because of the ability to perform 'What if' forecasting, Sainsbury's could also afford to be more ambitious in its promotions because it was less exposed to the risk of possible surplus stock.

What is interesting about this example is that the changes made have been as much process based as they are technology based. While it was new technology that provided the means for Sainsbury's to share the relevant information with its business partners, the heart of the problem had been poor supplier relationships. By rethinking its processes for managing promotional campaigns and then integrating its technology systems with its partners accordingly, Sainsbury's has achieved business gains as well as improved customer satisfaction.

PEOPLE ISSUES

For any major integration initiative associated with business reinvention to be successful, organizations need to be prepared to make cultural changes as well as technological changes.

This applies to the users of business systems as much as it does to the IT and business managers who have instigated the changes.

As IT's influence creeps into every aspect of business life, staff can no longer afford to ignore or resist its role in their working patterns. They must be prepared to use IT for research, for communications, and for inputting valuable information and knowledge, which can be used by others for the greater good of the business.

Yet, staff who are suddenly expected to be more open with their knowledge and data may feel threatened. Sales people are notoriously and understandably, protective of their customer contacts or business projections. If they are asked to share this information with other sales people or with colleagues in marketing, they are often reluctant. On a broader scale, whole companies can be resistant to working with partner organizations, fearful of losing customers to potential competitors.

These are all issues that must be overcome through a managed process of communication and education. If organizations want to realize the benefits of shared knowledge, they need to impress upon their staff why this is important facilitating the capture and sharing of their knowledge and providing incentives to encourage them to do this as part of their everyday job.

As organizations seek greater efficiency and improved customer service, they need their staff to be more productive during their working day. This means encouraging employees to use technology and communications while away from the office to receive and send information. Field sales staff and engineers need to be provided with the latest customer and product information while out on the road and with the means to send status reports back to base, to keep company databases up to date. Making this happen throughout the day, rather than relying on daily or weekly downloads once staff have returned to the office, saves time and ensures central data files are never out of date.

Furthermore, companies need to accept and adapt to the growing trend of employees working from home or spending more time away from the office, on customer sites or with business partners. Again, this means giving staff access to network and data resources so that they can do their jobs as efficiently as if they were at their office desktops.

All of this points to the need for a single, enterprise-wide approach to business processes and a consistent view of data. Far-flung team members can then participate seamlessly from wherever they happen to be. Indeed, as electronic communications continue to improve, many organizations find that a flexible attitude to working practices and the potential to join teams across distance is an attractive proposition, both when attracting new talent into the company and when assessing staff productivity against employment overheads.

The other side to this is being able to reduce unnecessary business travel, by enabling remote co-workers to collaborate virtually, using various forms of electronic conferencing. This will be made easier as companies address the integration and consolidation of their information resources.

IT staff

While business users are getting to grips with the spirit of flexible working, openness in information sharing and the importance of broader teamwork, the IT department has to tackle a further set of issues.

Part 2 explores in more detail the multitude of issues to consider as organizations embark on complex integration projects that have the business transformation goals highlighted above.

Outsourcing peripheral IT activities is growing in popularity too, meaning that IT staff now have to manage and work with partners just as the business staff do. These may be contractors or third-party organizations. Consequently, organizations look for different skills when they hire internal IT staff – people with commercial skills and with experience of working in inter-enterprise teams.

SUMMARY

A multifaceted challenge is emerging that now faces the majority of businesses. Being responsive to customer needs means being agile, unencumbered by disjointed technology, rigid business processes and blinkered staff. The challenge is to have a broad vision, end-to-end business processes, a flexible IT infrastructure and an openness to extend all of this beyond the confines of a single company.

1   Major trends such as globalization, deregulation, privatization and the use of technology are creating massive pressure for companies to change the way they do business.

2   To maintain control it is paramount that every business has an integration strategy in order that systems interact. This should consider every aspect of people and process integration and not just technology.

3   Technology development in the area of internet is bringing more opportunity for business. It is ubiquitous and as essential to doing business as electricity or the telephone.

4   Commercial organizations are waking up to the fact that information technology can create rapid revenue-generating ability.

5   Business processes within organizations are becoming more customer aware and are increasingly being linked across the corporation. In doing so internal agility of process and external adaptability to customers are the goals to strive for.

6   Extension of process outside the corporation and into partners and suppliers to reduce cost and increase focus, i.e. the adoption of more 'virtual' business models is an accelerating trend and has huge impact on process, people and systems integration.

7   It takes people to deliver joined-up business and systems. Working patterns, security of tenure, nature of business relationships are all changing, which in turn is altering how we create integrated business and flexible IT.

CHAPTER 2

MANAGING COMPLEXITY

INTRODUCTION

In this chapter and Chapter 3, the themes developed in Chapter 1 will be expanded, determining how recent market trends and developments have conspired to make the process of building an integrated business with joined-up systems so difficult. The aim is to define this complexity to make it more manageable.

The increasing power of the customer and the fact that one of the biggest challenges facing organizations today is how to respond to growing customer demands has already been noted. The issue is how to maintain customer loyalty in an environment where consumers are becoming increasingly fickle.

THE INCREASING POWER OF THE CUSTOMER

In the past 50 years, we have moved from a world where mass production was king, to one where the complexities of mass customization face every business. In the era of mass production, organizations chose between high-quality, high-cost niche markets or high-volume, low-cost mass markets. It was an either/or decision. The organization's infrastructure and workforce tended to be mechanistic and inflexible, with little regard for individual customer demand. Organizations were in silos and supporting technology tended to be aligned to those same silos, with the primary objective to automate process and de-skill the workforce. Applications building was focused on single goals in discrete areas of the organization, with little attention paid to whether or how systems could be integrated.

This mould was broken by the Japanese, led by Toyota. From the early 1960s, Toyota enlisted the help of its workforce to produce ever higher quality vehicles at ever lower cost, through the process of continuous improvement. The principles of continuous improvement tightly link cross-functional teams of people, which can be defined as those interacting in a known, consistent and predictable way, working sequentially in much the same way as the mass production model. The workforce is enabled to contribute to incremental, but continuous enhancement in order to satisfy the customer.

As in the mass-production organization, in continuous improvement the fact that the basic product is what the customer wants is not open to question. The supporting systems have to focus first on improving workforce capability and management knowledge. The workforce is trained in tools and techniques which help them to improve the tasks they perform. The processes and systems move from supporting vertical silos to being horizontally integrated, although not entirely – in most cases information is still passed up and decisions down.

Mass customization, however, is leagues away in terms of the demands it makes on organizations. Mass customization means developing and delivering a growing range of products and services, which are tailored to individual customer's needs. Yet costs have to be maintained at the levels usually associated with the volume production base of most mass production organizations. All processes, skill sets and workflows, as well as IT systems, have to be modularized so that they can be plugged together in a 'pick 'n' mix' way. Barriers have to be broken down between functions and an organization created that can grow based on the unpredictable and ever-changing needs of the customer and short-term, turbulent markets.

THE CHALLENGE OF BECOMING MORE RESPONSIVE

In today's world, the companies that will survive are those that successfully address seven key competitive edge issues:

1 Ever-increasing product or service quality.

2 A portfolio of functionally rich products or services.

3 High margins or low costs to give sales flexibility.

4 Low investment cost per unit.

5 Shorter quoted lead times.

6 Delivery to promise.

7 Leverage of the external market.

Driven by customer expectation and these competitive issues, organizations still need to pursue the process of continuous improvement. Nevertheless, they need radically different structures, business process, supporting infrastructure and systems. Market leaders are developing new learning methods for their workforces and better means of relating to their customers. The best organizations are structured around dynamic networks with processes that are linked together in a modular way rather than on a point-to-point basis.

The infrastructure that enables the business has to have no inherent added cost and be able to react almost instantaneously to new workflows, methods and process. The delivery and the product have to appear seamless to the customer. New ways of working in partnership with both the customer and third-party suppliers are being developed. Last, but by no means least, internal frictions have to be removed.

The key issues that have to be faced are how to:

☐ Accommodate flexible business objectives.

☐ Respond faster.

☐ Accommodate diverse and flexible organizational boundaries.

☐ Accomplish continuous re-engineering and productivity improvement.

☐ Improve knowledge and information management.

☐ Improve workforce capabilities.

CONTINUOUS IMPROVEMENT REPLACES SINGLE-STEP CHANGE PROGRAMS

It is no longer sufficient or economically viable to go through intermittent and massive single-step changes. Competitive edge rests with those companies that can continuously improve to the point of constantly reinventing themselves. Any degree of improvement or change inevitably meets with emotionally-based resistance at all levels. Therefore, there must be a major culture change, which affects the organization in its entirety:

☐ People.

☐ Process.

☐ Organization.

☐ Infrastructure.

☐ Technology.

☐ Knowledge management.

The reality for most organizations, other than start ups, is that they have large portfolios of systems and processes built over time, which continue to grow daily. These systems have many interdependencies and are uncoordinated. Technology is diverse in terms of platforms, operating systems, databases, languages and geography. There is, above all, a heavy dependency on legacy systems. Each new development or change in business direction causes further stress to current integration. As noted in the Introduction, in major corporations it is not unusual to find $500,000 per day spent on maintaining interfaces and 30 per cent of the total IT budget spent on integration issues. In one major engineering company, seven databases required 23 different technology platforms for data to be transferred between them.

Inevitably, there is a slow response to the need for business change. There are always many 'touch points' to be modified each time there is a change. There is overlapping functionality provided by different systems. Both finance and logistics packages and Manufacturing Resource Planning systems will have accounts payable and receivable within them.

With multiple entry of data, re-keying and no ownership of data quality, there follows a huge problem with data integrity. Depending which database the user is interrogating at any one time in the differing work cycle, he or she will receive a different answer.

Every move to disentangle, improve or change this environment becomes high risk because of the many interdependent interfaces. Even the simplest of changes or upgrade can have unforeseen and far-reaching consequences. This leads to high costs when changes are made or because there is a continual invention of 'work-arounds' and 'make-dos'. The whole organization becomes inflexible, either through fear of the consequences of making any changes, or through lack of capability. Every day that passes compounds the problem.

The question is how to move from the spaghetti environment of today, to the modular, plug-and-play world of tomorrow, without incurring massive incremental costs and totally disrupting the day-to-day business and today's balance sheet. The answer is to understand, first of all, just how much of a problem there is.

MEASURING COMPLEXITY

Faced with such a major problem, it is important that the correct decisions are taken right from the start and that action and management approaches are appropriate.

Initially, there are four dimensions with which to assess the complexity of any integration task, so that complexity can then be managed. These are: scale, impact, diversity and geography. It is the combination of these four dimensions that defines the degree of complexity and will help to quantify the risks involved. Measurement in these dimensions can be used to ensure that the appropriate management framework is in place.

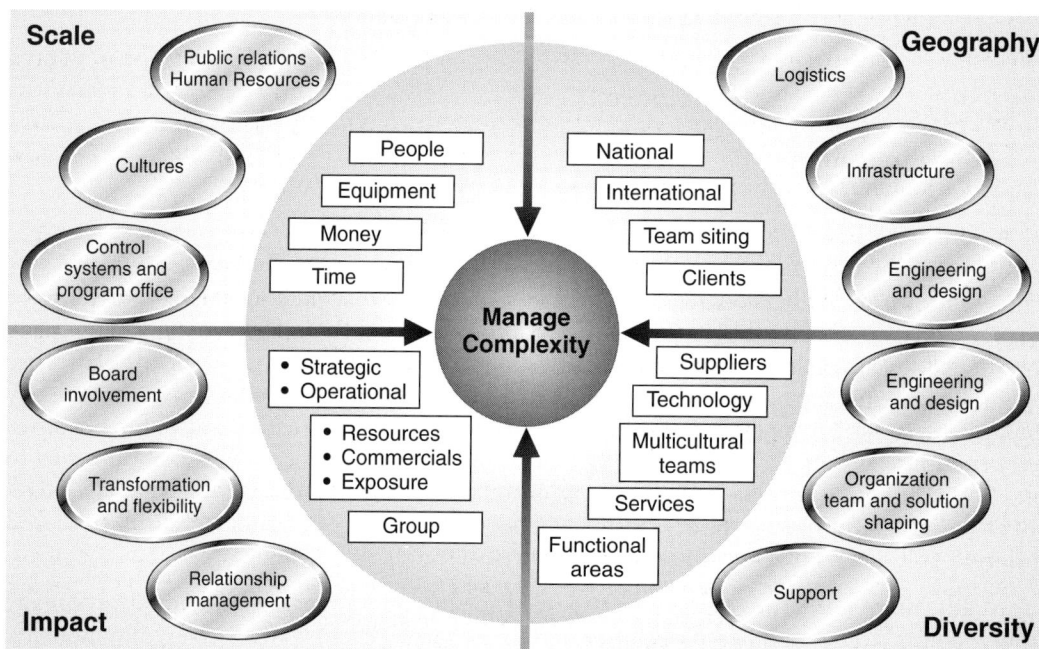

FIGURE 2.1: The multiple dimensions of complexity and their impact

Scale (size) is relative. Measures, such as the numbers of people affected by the project or change, can be applied. If one were to look simply at the raw numbers, what is considered large by a company of 1000 employees would pale into insignificance for a major multinational, like General Motors. It is far better to estimate in terms of percentage of employees involved against the total number of employees or, if appropriate, particular skill sets or roles. The percentage number of processes affected, technology platforms involved and budget committed.

Impact is also quite straightforward to assess. Is this a strategic or an operational change? Does it affect many departments, or just one? What are the commercial consequences and what is the company's exposure?

Diversity can be measured in terms of the number of functional areas involved in the change and how many different services will be affected or required. What is the size and number of the multicultural teams required? How many different technology platforms will be affected or required? How many suppliers need to be involved?

Geographical measures or considerations are the location of teams affected by or affecting the change. Where are the delivery bases of both clients and suppliers? Will this be purely a national or an international change?

The scale measures will influence which control systems need to be put in place and how much effort will be required to provide the governance. What attention should be paid to culture, and how will public relations and human resources be handled? Impact defines the amount of board involvement required, how much time and effort needs to be spent on relationship management and how performance and business benefit are measured. Diversity dictates the shaping of the delivery team, the shaping of the solution and the engineering and design of the delivered solution, as well as what support will be required. Geography is the key factor that drives logistics, infrastructure and communication.

There is a fifth dimension – the stability of objectives. This is vital and needs to be measured on a separate axis to the other four dimensions. In a mass-customization world, no one can know exactly what the next customer wants or what the company's next product will look like. If the company needs to be dynamic, you need to begin to think differently about how you manage integration projects, depending upon their planning horizons.

By determining where on the complexity-stability scale the change comes, you can ensure that the appropriate delivery and management framework is applied. What needs to be in place if you are to stand some chance of success? What are the fundamentals that need to be recognized and the ground rules? Part 4, looks in some detail at the delivery approaches and frameworks you will need to apply these ground rules successfully.

TOTAL CHANGE MANAGEMENT

The cycle of continuous improvement and the needs of mass customization have been well explained in terms of business needs for a number of years. However, integration delivery has not generally recognized the demands this puts on project delivery. Organizations still seem to be split in terms of development of the new and servicing the existing, whether that be application, networks, infrastructure or operations. There needs to be a joining up of the change process, both in terms of the linkage between business process, technology systems, people and organization, and the total change cycle. There are three distinct phases in the total change cycle:

1 Strategic planning and design.

2 Development and deployment of change.

3 Operational or 'concurrent improvement'.

Strategic planning and design begins with the articulation of business direction and the organization's strategy for change. It includes the processes to define the strategic plans for organizational development and resource deployment, and the creation of the strategic Information Systems (IS) or IT plan, with which strategic plans must be aligned. Strategic planning extends into the process of proposition development and business alignment,

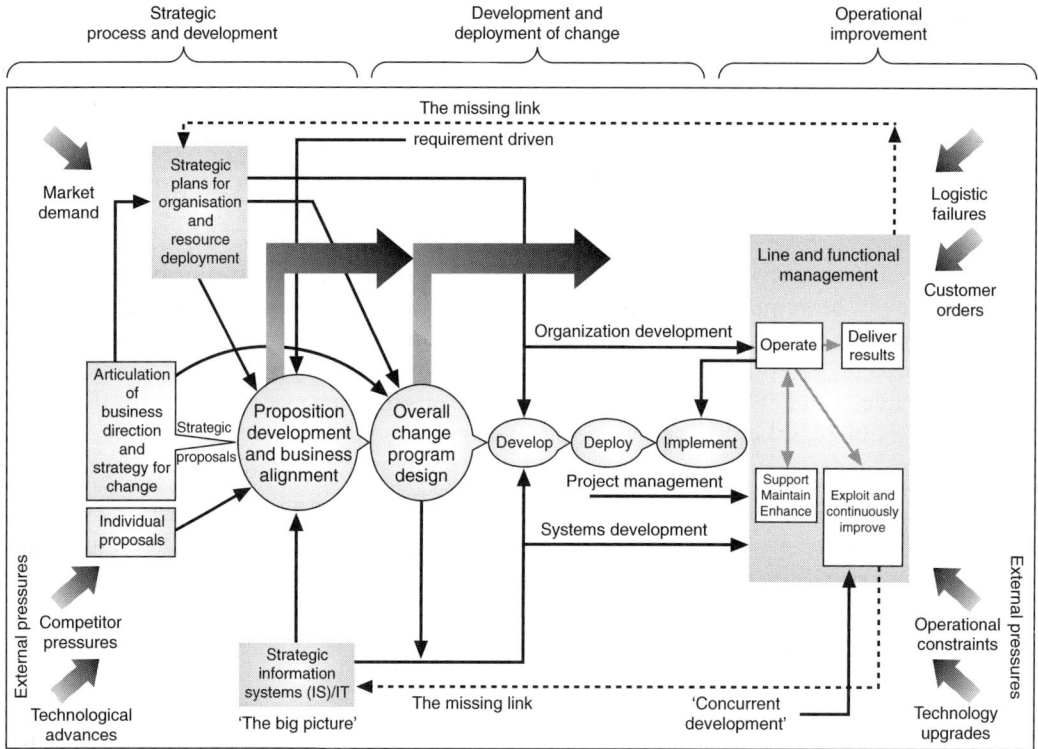

FIGURE 2.2: Total change cycle

selecting how the business will move forward. What are the priorities? What is the business case? How feasible is it? The phase concludes with a design of what the scope and shape of the overall change program(s) should be, with an indication of timelines, deliverables, benefits and opportunity windows.

For many companies that have undergone or are undergoing major transformations, this is not an unfamiliar set of steps. It is usually a cathartic but rewarding exercise, where the Executive gets a fresh hold of the business and gives it, themselves and their employees new direction. However, subsequently the energy all seems to dissipate, direction and urgency are lost from that point on. Why? Before answering this question, let's consider the next two phases in the cycle – development and deployment, and what we have called operational improvement.

Development and deployment and operational improvement are all about delivering required changes and improvements. This involves breaking down those strategic needs into real business requirements and also deciding how the projects that are set up to deliver them should be defined. What are their boundaries? How will they interact? How should you sequence them? From where should you source the expertise? How should you procure the resources? How should you mobilize both the organization itself and a whole tier of suppliers to deliver? How should you put together the teams required and make them effective?

RECONCILING CHANGE WITH THE DAY-TO-DAY BUSINESS

Since, until now, change has been at best sporadic, if not a one-off, every time you go through the exercise you have to invent and reinvent the processes to some degree. No wonder lead times are long and all the energy created during the strategic thinking begins to dissipate.

Once the change has been made, it is handed over to the day-to-day business team. Line and functional management are then responsible for delivering the predicted benefits from the organizational change, technology upgrade, or new processes and systems. They have to operate and deliver results, working very closely with the support and maintenance team to exploit and continuously improve. In the majority of cases this is carried out using different teams and different sets of processes and relationships to those put in place during development and deployment. Time is taken to transfer knowledge and transition the new into the current system (which has frequently moved on during the time taken to design, develop and implement the change).

At this point, the Executive can really begin to lose control. Daily decisions will be taken by the line management to 'improve' the operational systems. While each decision in itself may look justifiable, over time there is a great danger of drift away from the vision and direction. The organization takes a deep breath and another major change process is instigated!

CHANGING THE WAY CHANGE IS IMPLEMENTED

It does not have to be like this. The problem is that the organization is impacted by change pressures of different orders of magnitude and at all levels. At the highest levels, business direction is defined by market demand, macro-economic forces, competitive pressures and technological advances. On a daily basis, operational management responds to individual customer needs, workforce capability, financial constraints, legacy infrastructure, and systems and technology upgrades. Some simple changes need to be made to tie these two sets of change pressures together.

To provide the missing link, the daily reaction to change needs to be connected to the strategic planning. The planning cycle needs to be a constant process. Planning horizons have to be shortened so that delivered change becomes proactive, not reactive. Processes put in place for development of all things new have to be the ones used for the day-to-day business environment.

Mobilization for one-off change programs in the organization and its suppliers has to be eradicated, and transition and deployment phases radically reduced. Crucially, the development and delivery time-scale has to be accelerated and 'de-risked'. Change has to take account of the day-to-day business and the day-to-day business has to take account of change. Therefore, line and functional management have to take responsibility for it, and must not have it done 'to them' or 'for them'.

All this means not only a radically different and dynamic organization in itself, but also a radically different and dynamic relationship with the company's integration and technology suppliers. It indicates contracting a number of key suppliers for collaboration at the strategic level, who then work closely within that framework to deliver specific individually defined packages of change. This is not a new idea. Look at how the car makers contract with Tier 2 suppliers (key suppliers who are not part of the same immediate Group), and how suppliers are involved at the strategic planning stage of new models in order to shorten development life cycles and effect 'delivery to promise'.

BECOMING YOUR OWN SYSTEMS INTEGRATOR

To be successful, the customer-supplier relationship needs to be much more open than has been traditional. Suppliers need access to the strategic thinking and business case development of their clients. Clients need access to the costs and capacity management and organizational processes of their suppliers. This dictates some fundamental changes to contractual relationships.

Initially it may be necessary to outsource much of the change skills and experience of major change. This should only be done on the understanding that the change consultancy or integration practice role is to begin by driving change and then gradually hand over responsibility, not only for the program but for the ongoing process of change.

The supplier of key change skills and planning must indeed be prepared to deliver its crown jewels. Knowledge transfer of how to effect change must be part of the partnership with the client. It should be appreciated that there will be a continued need to provide specific skills and there will be ongoing packages of work to effect specific changes. Both client and supplier organizations require a solid, documented business case that they share, based on this understanding.

In the same way, the client organization should look closely at what it needs to do itself. It needs to turn the organization into its own systems integrator. It should do this by retaining control of the strategic phase and the delivery of its brand into the market, but looking radically at the outsourcing of many processes of the business, which have until now been considered an integral part of the organization.

Proof that technology is only part of the problem

The following example of a successful business re-engineering program was recognized with a Quest Award from *Datamation* magazine in 1996.

Express delivery company, DHL, had a global problem with their systems department. The express package delivery model, in which the originating point (sender) always pays for shipments, was being supplanted by one which sees the delivery point (recipient) often initiating, tracking and paying for the service. Furthermore, many accounts wanted their business with DHL to be centrally negotiated and invoiced. The existing information systems simply could not cope.

DHL decided to seek outside help. Interestingly, the consultants that won the contract to re-engineer the systems did so largely as a result of suggesting that the process of integration would be only 20 per cent technological, but 80 per cent organizational. Creating and sustaining an internal IS organization capable of delivering integrated solutions in perpetuity was deemed to be the real issue.

In their analysis of DHL, the practitioners noted a lack of structure to link the company's executives and the people in charge of the business processes with the technologists supporting those processes. The result had been overlapping development of silo applications and many conflicting priorities.

The consultant's proposal included the establishment of the following:

☐ A business process management group.

☐ A meeting infrastructure to ensure effective communication between and within functions.

☐ A quality program.

☐ A training strategy and program.

☐ Methodologies, including a central electronic library for procedures and documentation.

☐ A full set of descriptions for the job required to deliver integrated systems.

At the beginning of the project, the practitioners played most of the key roles in the new IS organization. However, as the new integrated applications were developed, DHL staff worked closely with the external staff in order to achieve the transfer of knowledge required to take over all key positions.

The re-engineering of DHL's IS group yielded a number of benefits. The evolution of a common business model provided the whole organization with a single view of the business. Much efficiency was gained on the IS side, as related developments were combined or realigned. Data quality improved, resulting in increases in revenue from more accurate billing and reduction of re-work. Efficiency was increased too, because data now enters the systems only once. Customer retention improved as DHL became easier to do business with. The systems are now more flexible, allowing DHL to respond more quickly.

KEEPING IT ALL TOGETHER

Throughout this book, the need to manage the integrated business, keeping business processes, technology systems and people and organization closely aligned is stressed. Maintaining continuous change in step across the whole business, its supporting systems, and its people requires the skills of a dedicated manager. If change is to be part of the day-to-day business, just as IT has become transparent to the business, there has to be a line function or role of 'change manager'. This does not mean that responsibility for change is not part of the function of every manager. Rather, it means that you should treat change management much as you do human resource (HR) management. In leading companies, line managers are expected to pay much attention to the management and development of people, while still having a HR function responsible for ensuring that the correct strategies, frameworks and processes are in place and adhered to.

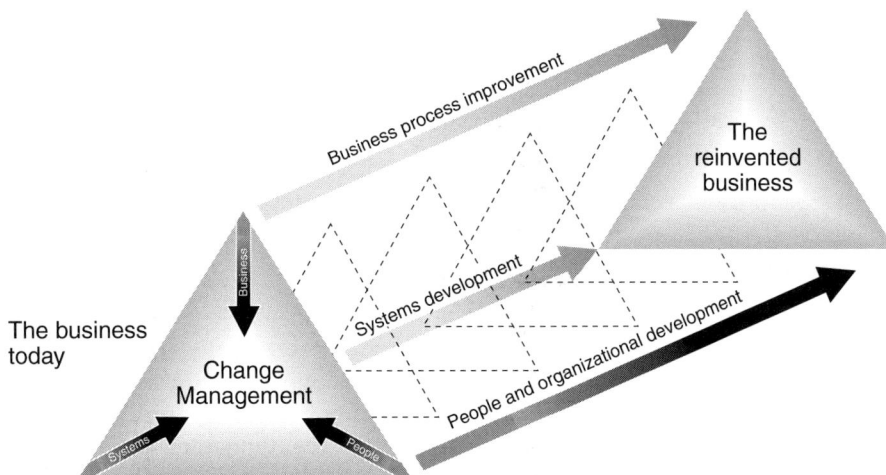

FIGURE 2.3: Achieving continuous change

OVER-ARCHING ARCHITECTURE

In order to keep all of the change processes together there needs to be an over-arching architecture – a view of the bigger picture. Few people would attempt to put a several thousand piece jigsaw puzzle together without reference to the completed picture on the outside of the box. With a wider perspective, it becomes easier to choose the correct priorities and to deliver continuous change in an evolutionary way.

Architecture provides the required insight into and the understanding of, complexity. It is only through comprehension that one can make adequate decisions and integrate multiple projects running in different timelines but all focused on the realization of strategic goals. Architectures serve many different purposes. They will help you to:

- ☐ Define structures.
- ☐ Mitigate risks.
- ☐ Exploit new technology.
- ☐ Integrate with partners.
- ☐ Integrate systems.
- ☐ Develop processes and method.
- ☐ Identify gaps in business alignment.

The architectural view is not about the design of content. It aids this and ensures correct solutions. However, architecture focuses on behaviour within a context. How does each department interact with its environment? How does each process-flow fit into the business? Its objective is to provide a way to design a solution combining context, behaviour and structure. By doing this, architecture bridges the gap between strategy and design. It enables coherent execution of both business and IT investment.

In effect, by having an architectural view, along with a dynamic journey plan or transformation map, you will produce the necessary reference models. These, in turn, enable you to become proactive and to anticipate events.

CHOOSING THE RIGHT PRIORITIES

In their books, *The Goal*[1] and *The Race*[2], Eliyahu M Goldratt and Robert E Fox pointed out, in the context of continuous improvement, that:

> ❲In any organization a very small number of constraints govern the overall level of performance. If these few constraints can be relieved, the performance of the entire organization will be raised significantly. ❳

The initial step is to identify exactly what these small number of key constraints are, and to alleviate or eliminate them. There are numerous ways of analyzing these 'pinch points' in the business, such as value-chain analysis. However, few, if any, examine these critical areas of technology, business process, people and organization in unison. An approach has to be found to do this in order to understand correctly what are the real fundamental underlying pinch points.

[1] Eliyahu Goldratt and Jeff Cox, *The Goal*, Gower Publishing, 1993.
[2] Robert E Fox and Elihayu M Goldratt, *The Race*, North River Press, 1998.

EVOLUTIONARY DELIVERY

Most projects and programs today aim towards a final delivery date. For a project, that may be fairly easy to determine both in terms of its goal and the length of the planning horizon. In programs, we talk about delivering the vision, and are much more inclined to plan in sub-phases or tranches of work.

This evolutionary delivery program approach has taken much from the teachings of Tom Gilb, author of *Principles of Software Engineering Management*[3], who expressed the basic principles as:

- [ ] Delivering something early to a real end user.
- [ ] Measuring the added value to the user in all critical dimensions.
- [ ] Adjusting both design and objectives based on observed realities.

The problem is that, usually due to the complex interdependencies, any phased plan still has deliveries arriving in substantial releases. The major constraint becomes the business's capability to cope with the absorption and implementation of change every three to four months, while sustaining its focus on meeting key business-as-usual objectives.

This is a fairly typical scenario and is brought about largely for two reasons. Firstly, because in terms of the total change cycle, line and functional management do not own the change responsibility, but have it done *to* them. Secondly, the whole planning cycle tends to focus more on what is being delivered, rather than on how well it will perform or what value it will add to the business.

We have already argued the case for change management as a line management function to overcome the first problem. If the principles of evolutionary delivery are correctly applied, they should overcome the second problem. Gilb, in *Principles of Software Engineering Management*, defines the critical concepts as:

1 Multi-objective driven.

2 Early, frequent iteration.

3 Complete define, design, build, test in each step.

4 End-user orientation.

5 Systems approach.

6 Open-ended architecture.

7 Result not process orientation.

LEADERSHIP, NOT JUST MANAGEMENT

Leadership is probably the most critical factor in determining the success of today's complex integration projects.

As business has changed over the last five to ten years, so the demands on project leaders have changed. In the mid 1990s, to be successful it was sufficient to have the skills to set demanding targets for the team, be energetic to the point of being aggressive, and have a good knowledge base in terms of both IS/IT and the enterprise in which the project took place.

[3] Tom Gilb, *Principles of Software Engineering Mangement*, Addison Wesley, 1998.

Today a successful project leader has to thrive on dealing with complexity and chaos. It is vital that he or she has the capability to be a constant lighthouse for the team in the raging seas of complexity. The role has fundamentally changed to one where the leader must both motivate and inspire through coaching and mentoring, and create the context for the achievement of excellence by the team. Personal integrity and excellent communication are essential skills for this position.

The project leader's role is to create the correct environment within which the team can deliver. Without the leadership to interpret the frequent changes of direction that are bound to occur, the team will lose its way. Without the leadership to deliver value to the business, the team can easily become self-absorbed in producing the 'best' deliverable. Without the leadership to create the context for team members to develop and learn, there will be no knowledge base on which to build an enduring and self-improving delivery process.

SUMMARY

1 Mass customization puts new demands on organizations beyond continuous improvement, and affects all parts of the organization. Any improvements in delivery of integration projects are lagging in dealing with these added complexities.

2 To survive, organizations need to be able to continually reinvent themselves, their direction, how they fit together, what and how they produce, while driven by a fickle market. Therefore, they cannot afford to outsource the change process or treat it as a sporadically occurring event.

3 The change process has to be inherent and integral within the organization, creating the need for a change management function in the same way that most companies have a human resources function.

4 New ways of involving integration partners at strategic phases and new ways of contracting with suppliers are required.

5 Managing complexity requires understanding and a process of measurement. This alone will enable the correct management and delivery frameworks to be used.

6 There needs to be a total change cycle, which links daily operational change back to the strategic direction and planning cycle, so that executives can maintain control.

7 The cycle of change needs to be speeded up.

8 Most organizations are paralysed by their existing spaghetti systems and processes. They need a way to break free without disrupting their current balance sheet.

9 Putting a new 'plug and play' organization in place demands a major culture change to overcome the innate emotional reaction to change as much as it requires alteration to physical systems and processes.

10 To be effective in this new environment of chaos and flux requires effective leadership and direction more than management process.

CHAPTER 3

EATING THE ELEPHANT

INTRODUCTION

A great deal of the improvement in US productivity between 1995 and 1999 was generated in just 6 of 59 sectors, according to consulting group McKinsey in a 2001 report. The report concluded that the improvements in those sectors were generated by improvements to business models and not to new technology, and that most of the $1400 billion investment by US companies in this period failed to generate a return.

There are those who would refute this conclusion, arguing that technology enables business model change, or that everybody now has technology so it is unlikely to be a sole differentiator anyway. Whatever, it is now very clear that the greatest commercial returns are gained when companies create maximum synergy between technology, IT and business strategies and organizational structure. Organizations need to tackle the evolution of their business by addressing all these elements.

At the same time, the need for a tangible business return from IT investment is causing organizations to reassess how they tackle large programs. It is becoming increasingly difficult to justify the cost of large initiatives. Now, the onus is on IT managers and business sponsors to realize tangible results in an acceptable time frame.

This does not mean a shift to isolated integration programs, however. As highlighted in the previous chapters, this would be a precarious step backwards. On the contrary, real business benefit will be achieved only if change is approached on a continuous, evolutionary basis, where each project undertaken is considered for its upstream and downstream effects on other aspects of the business. Meanwhile, IT changes must be approached in the context of a consistent, flexible overall architecture, which allows systems to be easily joined up.

It is imperative, then, to be able to keep in mind the wider picture (the program as a whole), yet be able to meet mid-range targets (subsidiary projects) along the way, which each have their own set of business goals and success measures.

Think of it as trying to eat an elephant. The overall challenge is large, and the whole may not be entirely visible. It will also move as you go along. Organizations need to begin by working out where to start, how to break the overall challenge down into manageable chunks, and how to establish the feasibility of the intended change.

The focus of this chapter is to reduce the challenge to a series of manageable tasks, before we consider in Chapter 4 how to translate defined projects into something that business management will be able to understand and appreciate from a 'business benefit' point of view.

Some questions to ask yourself at this stage include:

- ☐ What benefits do you need?
- ☐ How can the overall aim be broken down into achievable initiatives?
- ☐ How will the costs and benefits flow?
- ☐ Is what you need feasible?

Unless you attempt to address these questions, the success of your integration program could be in jeopardy. As we saw in Chapter 2, the challenges facing organizations today are many, and complex. There are as many internal challenges as there are external ones. Taking an initiative from concept to fruition and getting it to continue to deliver benefit will depend on a complex brew of politics, motivation, communication, alignment, buy-in, mobilization and risk management, as well as making the technology work. We will revisit the intricacies of delivery approaches and risk management in Parts 4 and 5.

LOOKING FOR BENEFIT

A key theme of this book is the need for organizations to be more flexible, so that they can adapt and respond to new business opportunities as they arise in the marketplace. As the e-business boom demonstrated to so many companies, speed to market is everything and it is getting harder and harder to predict and plan for customers' changing demands.

An ability to rapidly innovate and change their internal processes and, therefore, their systems, in order to respond quickly to changing and new markets, is becoming increasingly essential for organizations, yet traditional IT systems have not allowed this. Managers have had to respond to business need by commissioning systems on a piecemeal basis. Since IT is still considered by many companies to be a cost rather than an opportunity, budgets for 'grand plan' programs have been hard to secure.

It has often been the case that the systems with the cheapest initial cost have been implemented to address a pressing, departmental business need. This has been regardless of the future impact on the cost of running systems, whether these fit in with the company's wider strategic direction, or whether they further erode the company's flexibility to deal with new business opportunities. How can organizations manoeuvre out of this position and argue the case for the bigger picture when financial directors are (understandably) demanding a rapid, tangible return on investment?

KEEPING SIGHT OF TANGIBLE BUSINESS GOALS

Many businesses strive for tangible outcomes but do not continue to measure the success of an initiative. No wonder so many programs head off track and fail to deliver the expected results. It is imperative to define the business goal and link all initiatives to achieve this. However much you break down the wider program into manageable chunks, it is essential never to lose sight of the overall direction you are following.

Companies often embark on large programs out of a desire to increase or protect market share and profitability in response to the marketplace. Nonetheless, some rush ahead without clear knowledge of their financial starting point. Having an adequate understanding of the financial cause and effect in a business, including both revenue and cost drivers, is critical to the ultimate business case. Without this understanding, it is difficult to define valid opportunities for improvement.

If you need to improve customer acquisition and retention, you may find that your distribution and customer servicing capability is inadequate. Perhaps the company's existing call centres are inefficient and under-utilized. Investing in a new multi-channel contact centre (able to deal with website access and e-mail enquiries as well as telephone and paper-based transactions) and closing down the existing call centres may provide a double opportunity to boost business. This would bring up efficiency levels and reduce operational costs but also improve customer acquisition and service, enabling market share to improve.

This is enough of a business justification for what you are about to do. In IT terms, this translates into an investment in the creation and implementation of a new IT architecture. Additionally, an opportunity may be spotted to reduce the cost of back-office operations. This will require the re-engineering of the constituent customer support and customer service functions. It will also require the reorganization of Information Systems (IS). The logic of these opportunities is shown in Figure 3.1, which has some examples of each opportunity's contribution to investment cost, increased value and revenue improvement.

From this point it is possible to break each high-level opportunity into subsidiary initiatives and define the projects required to achieve each initiative, as discussed in Part 4 which deals with the planning and design of program and project delivery in some detail.

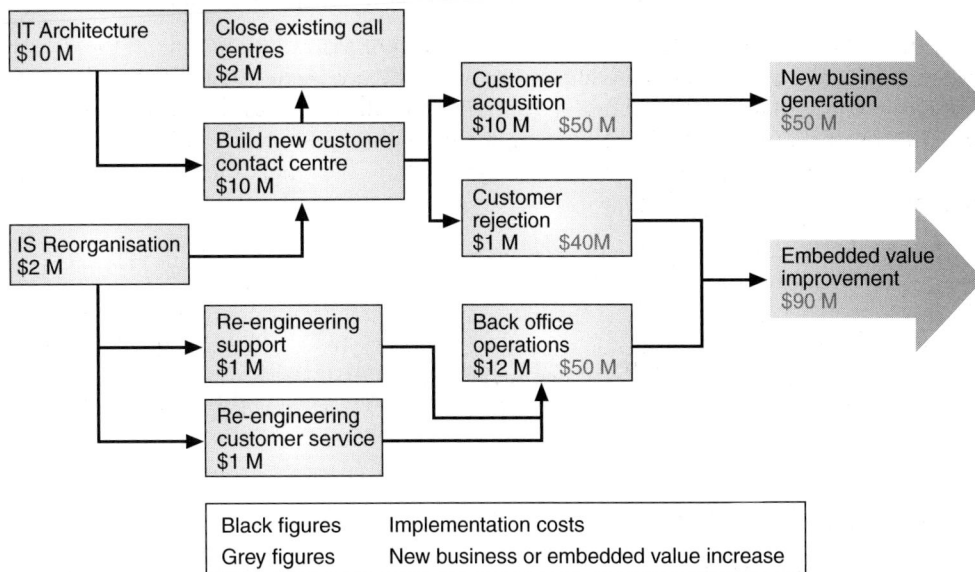

FIGURE 3.1: Flow diagram showing opportunity breakdown and its relationship to overall business

Another consideration when taking stock of what you plan to do and how you will measure success, is whether the goalposts are likely to change as you roll out your initiative. This is often the reason why more traditional integration programs run aground. They are so extensive in their scope and take so long to implement, that by the time they are halfway complete, the business objectives have changed making the program redundant.

This is another reason why it is essential to balance shorter term initiatives with longer term intentions. The agile company needs to be able to change what it is doing while it is doing it – that is, achieve the fine balance of transforming while performing.

It is vital to be clear about which benefits will be felt when, as a result of which initiatives and how they inter-link. Moreover, factors such as feasibility which includes achievability and particularly the time frame over which these will be achieved, need to be known.

INTANGIBLE OUTCOMES

Firstly it is important to explore the 'intangible' outcomes likely to arise from an integration program. These outcomes, which seem difficult to predict with precision, could be as critical to the company's future performance as some of the more visible and direct outcomes. The investment markets now increasingly value companies based on non-financial assets as well as on more tangible measures of success. Ernst & Young[1] showed that 35 per cent of investment allocation decisions were now attributable to non-financial measures, and that these are widely taken as leading indicators of future financial performance.

What intangible benefits might you look for when planning an initiative or set of initiatives? The increased agility of an organization is certainly one. Conventionally, organizations have relied on their ability to predict market trends and to develop suitable products which appeal to customers, to keep them in the game. In the new world, however, the emphasis is shifting to be able to do this almost in real time, without the element of prediction. As market opportunities arise, the agile company, with the right IT infrastructure in place, can respond to these immediately by establishing new processes – and new products and services.

Increasingly, the business opportunity defines the company's response, instead of the company's IT and process capabilities defining what the company is capable of. It is easy to see how the ability to be more responsive to market demands in today's fast-changing, highly competitive business world might be a desirable intangible objective.

ESTABLISHING FEASIBILITY

Despite the original focus of a business systems program, it is not uncommon for the intended business benefits never to materialize. Therefore, it is essential to ask yourself some hard questions about your organization before you go too far. Often failure occurs because the goals of the program were not feasible to begin with. It is wise to establish realistically whether an initiative or a program is achievable. As desirable as it might be to achieve an agile organizational structure, there will be a mountain of issues to overcome first.

The main dimensions to consider when examining a program's feasibility are:

1 Political feasibility.

2 Capability.

[1] Ernst & Young, 'Measures That Matter', 1997.

3   Operational feasibility.

4   Economical feasibility.

5   Technical feasibility.

Political feasibility

Will the program achieve the political support in terms of vision and buy-in that it needs across the company? In global companies, political differences driven by commercial power can cause difficulties. Perhaps the head office's IT function needs to develop a global set of applications. It then goes on to define a set of processes and applications that have a certain amount of global capability, but may not be adequate for all the regions that the application will need to operate in. It is not uncommon in these circumstances for the new applications to be met with local resistance.

Indeed, it is the country-specific companies that typically hold the power, since they are the sales arms of the company. If they do not accept the new application for their needs and the organization does not see the importance of spending enough money and time on getting buy-in and alignment from the end users it serves, major problems can arise. The roll-out schedule could double in length as end markets are persuaded to join in, business benefit may be lost as markets are late coming on-stream and the initiative could end up costing much more than was budgeted or be halted altogether.

Capability

Does the organization have the skills and resources it needs to achieve the goals set out, and has this sort of project been undertaken before in the organization? Personnel capability is a large topic dealt with in Part 2, however a few comments are appropriate here. In people terms, consider the speed at which the organization needs to achieve the initiatives and the range of parallel initiatives that will be needed. Moreover, bear in mind the availability of key management skills. All too often, those directly involved with delivering projects are insufficiently aware of the benefits they are expected to deliver. Some project managers blatantly disregard the link between the initiatives they carry out and the benefits they purport to deliver. Even more catastrophically, some disregard delivery of the benefits (as set out in the business case) early in the delivery cycle, as the difficulties of delivering the business or system change start to overwhelm both them and the organization. Therefore, consider whether you have people available who can keep sight of the original direction and purpose of the program. If not, it will not be long before you hit trouble.

To establish feasibility, the use of resources will need to be prioritized. It is vital to offset cost against capability. It is pointless to attempt any change without the right critical skills in technical and business areas. If you do not have the skills, do not go any further because your initiative will surely fail. Aim for a balance where you buy in external assistance, either use a third party to build part or all of the solution and/or bolster your own resources with contract staff. Focus on initiatives with the ability to achieve the outcome and prioritize these ruthlessly. It is by far preferable to complete a couple of things than to fail to deliver many.

Operational feasibility

How radical is the level of process innovation? Is the initiative simply maintaining the current business process by implementing a new system, while leaving existing processes untouched? If this is the case, why bother? To create business benefit, it is necessary to achieve a level of process change – either to make existing processes cheaper or to enable very different processes. Yet, is it feasible to expect the business and IT to be able to achieve this level of change?

What effect will this have on existing business operations – can operations gear up to support the new set up? What measures will be needed to ensure this is the case? Is it realistic to expect this to happen successfully?

Examples exist where there is conflict between strategic programs and service delivery. In large IT departments, the formation of a perceived elite to deliver change and a lack of attention paid to getting new systems and process into service, can cause delay or the cancelling of projects.

Realistically appraise the likelihood of people in the organization recognizing what the benefits are and of them continuing to achieve these. Frequently, the first flush of strategic direction gets blown away by the practicalities of running newly introduced systems, however strategic they may be. Once the main strategic investment has been made, the organization lapses back into its old mentality of cost control and investment starvation. Ensure that you assess whether it is likely that adequate budget for handover and for future running costs can be secured and that good relationships can be established.

If business users are not adequately prepared for the process changes, the whole program could be in danger. If users do not have sufficient training and support in those crucial first days of operation, the best systems can fail to produce the expected business benefits. Again, it is essential to assess the true nature of relationships with the end users and other factors, such as their ability to spend time, in addition to their daily roles, on contributing to the success of the program.

Economical feasibility

Does the business case stand up? Having an unrealistic view of the potential benefits of new systems is dangerous. Beware of relying too heavily on supplier claims for the benefits you might derive from a new software package. How this is implemented and used and the processes it supports is down to the implementers and users and the marrying of technology with people and process. Is there a way to do this within cost?

Costs always go up during an initiative. This leads to scope being cut or the costs being swallowed and the business case being only partially achieved or the project cancelled. Be ruthless and cynical in assessing the likelihood of increased costs and, if possible, get a feel for cost sensitivity – how much increased cost can you afford before you threaten the benefits case? You should know this in order to assess feasibility.

How rapidly will the business drivers change? Are you automating a sales force only to see it closed down? Does this make the project economically feasible?

Technical feasibility

Is the potential technical solution viable within a reasonable cost? Is an adequate architecture in place, or does the project require a significant amount of new technology investment – can this be achieved in the time-scales?

The more common current technology challenges are discussed in detail in Part 3. Suffice to say here that establishing the feasibility of whether an initiative is technically possible is a balancing act. Most things are possible; the key thing to consider is at what cost?

Take the example of analysis and reporting requirements. A simple business need for a standard set of business key performance indicators each month is likely to require investment in data integration, data transformation and storage, analysis and reporting tools. It will also require a delivery infrastructure for the reports and training for end users. Consider the additional requirement for an ad-hoc reporting capability, to drill down from the top-level reports into any source data required, for all users. While this might be possible at a cost it is almost certainly uneconomical.

Assess whether an initiative adds to the complexity of the systems and business processes you possess as a company. It may be feasible now but downstream it may create too much complexity and ultimately mean that systems and processes become impossible to change. It is, of course, legitimate to consider a tactical implementation based on an urgent business requirement, for which there is an urgent revenue or cost imperative, but make sure that downstream impact is minimized. Total cost of ownership is often overlooked when organizations make tactical implementations. It is all very well for companies to be frugal and aim for a low cost of upfront development but as project cycles become shorter, immediate paybacks and low cost of ownership should become as important as upfront expenditure.

SUMMARY

1 Consider the approach you need to adopt in order to establish how feasible the overall initiative is. Do you need outside help? As businesses get leaner, you almost certainly do. What will this do to your potential costs, and does it make the benefits impossible to achieve?

2 Make sure you design a balanced set of initiatives and establish their feasibility early on. Organizations need to assemble a set of initiatives, which ensure that the three core elements to the program – people, process and technology – are catered for in appropriate amounts. Make sure these initiatives are as self-sufficient as possible and as small as practical without compromising the aim.

3 Think of each initiative as a number of component projects that are integrated and that address people, process and technology – culture, infrastructure, support services, customer-facing functions and benefit delivery. Previously each initiative might have taken a year to implement, but today, the emphasis is on fast delivery. Individual projects need to be kept small and manageable, ideally taking no longer than six months to deliver. Have a journey plan and allow/disallow initiatives and projects against this. Assess their feasibility realistically.

4 It is possible to get carried away with too much detail and you can end up trying to over-engineer the solution. If you want to see business benefits within an acceptable time frame, it is probably more important to get something established early on – it can be refined and improved later.

5 Don't set your goals too high. In Part 4 we discuss how to move towards adaptability and the creation of an architecture and infrastructure that enables continuous change. Undertaking too much in one go, even if massive overall change is required, can fail to deliver benefits.

CHAPTER 4

ESTABLISHING THE BUSINESS CASE

INTRODUCTION

Having identified the integration projects that will take your organization closer to where it wants to be, the next stage, to move things forward, is to gain senior management buy-in for the proposed initiatives. This may not be as straightforward as it sounds, particularly if your goal is to persuade the board of the merits of infrastructure-level investment, which at face value may not appear to promise immediate, visible results for the business. In addition, future business systems planning will be characterized by the need to invest in the ability to adapt to as yet unknown market opportunity, rather than in the capability to meet a known market demand.

There may also be existing projects in progress which run counter to the aims of the new business objectives. As well as conflicting with your new aims, these may tie up important resources that you ideally need to exploit in your new initiatives. How will you handle this?

Even if you believe you have a business case that holds water, how can you convince key stakeholders that this is an appropriate investment and a journey worth making? Have you adequately considered the alternatives? And how will you maintain stakeholder buy-in and involvement to make sure the benefits get delivered?

Finally, how will you measure and monitor the success of your initiatives to ensure that those benefits do indeed come to fruition?

This chapter provides some answers to these challenges.

MAKING THE BUSINESS CASE

You have established the breakdown of initiatives, the flow of benefit you are aiming for and overall feasibility, as discussed in Chapter 3. There is now a need to translate these into a formal business case. If the planned projects are infrastructure-based, you will need to present these in terms of tangible (and intangible) business benefits, showing what sort of business return can be expected, how and in what time frame. The imperative behind most system and business investments, after all, is to create a financial benefit for the organization, which will maintain or improve the current state of the business. Making a good, solid business case is, therefore, the touchstone that will drive decisions throughout the planning and roll-out of the intended projects.

As with any other business proposal, you should seek to set out the baseline you are starting from and a set of clear objectives for the implementation. Success can then be measured against milestones. The most effective business plans prioritize the opportunities and allocate effort accordingly. To ensure maximum support, they set out a portfolio of benefits that will be achieved – intangible, tangible and with short-, medium- and long-term impacts. Thus, the business can appreciate when and how it will see a return on its investment over time. All of this should be measurable.

It is often not appreciated that the business case is both a critical project management tool and an enabler of the change process, if used correctly. The measures of success form the basis for key performance indicators (KPIs) and scorecards – both elements should be monitored regularly. If a project starts to run over its budget, it is natural for the project manager to attempt to correct the error. However, if a project starts to fall short of its benefit delivery, how often is it corrected? Indeed, how often is this even measured? Frustratingly, not very often. The business case must be used to establish unequivocal measures of change against which success or failure can be judged and managed. A monthly alerting and reporting mechanism should include an assessment of benefit delivery and be used as a lever to communicate and reinforce actions in order to make an initiative successful.

Business cases vary from organization to organization, but the best ones incorporate the following:

1　The current status is discussed, describing both problems and opportunities. Comments are made sensitively, so that existing processes and systems are not seen to be undermined, for example, 'The current situation provides good foundation for…'.

2　Business objectives are defined in term of outcomes required, using the type of reasoning and logic covered in Chapter 3. The solution is described in *business* terms, but includes a description of the full range of changes needed to process, technology and people.

3　The financial case describes certain key measures based on predicting cash flows over the intended lifetime of the project – an initiative is generally deemed to be worthwhile if it pays back the investments over a relatively short period. The most useful measure is 'net present value', which forecasts the profit of a project or initiative and gives a consistent view of the value of future money, bringing it back to today's value. The 'discounted payback period' is also an important measure and gives an indication of the amount of time taken to repay the investment. Other important measures include the 'internal rate of return', which is used to judge the risk to the investment – the higher the rate of return, the lower the risk to the project.

4　The required investment is broken down in detail, ideally expressing the investment required aligned to the services that will be created.

   ☐ **Functional services** – Typically people and process-oriented projects where new functionality is required.

☐ **Maintenance services** – Usually administrative or back-office change, for example, provision of backup and recovery services.

☐ **User services** – Commonly provision of services, such as desktop applications or network resources.

☐ **Infrastructure services** – The creation of, for instance, adaptive architectures.

This leads the management to think in terms of services, which increases appreciation for the cause and, therefore, buy-in. This is particularly relevant for projects that may have a high technical or infrastructure-led content.

5 The benefits are set out in some detail, related to the overall business objective and quantified. A good business case will assign real numbers to any intangible benefits being brought in – cultural and capability change may be hard to measure and manage but they could be the biggest discriminators of future value. Highlight any financial benefit-based initiatives that also create a non-financial benefit, for a double win.

6 The cost of doing nothing will be set out as a point of comparison. Here, the business case forecasts costs and benefits over the life of the existing system's suggested replacement, and compares these with the forecasts if the existing system remained in place. Doing nothing may decrease market share, for example, and some projects can be justified purely on the basis of market share (i.e. investment and running costs are outweighed by revenue lost by decreased market share).

Doing nothing may also reduce efficiency through increasing the running costs. For instance, an elderly back-office system may have been subjected to increasing change during its lifetime, making rapid change to configuration, code or data (e.g. to launch a new product) too slow and expensive. If competitors, by contrast, have more modern, adaptive systems, this could mean losing business advantage. Absolute or relative decrease in efficiency must be calculated as part of the 'do nothing' option.

7 A thorough business case will also identify and address any risks to the likely success of the project or initiative, providing a sensitivity analysis of these and their possible impact on the project. (Risk management is discussed in detail in Part 5).

8 An implementation plan will also be included, detailing the overall journey that must be made and picking out key milestones to mark where benefit will flow. These will be linked, as much as possible, to the services that will be delivered.

CONSIDER THE ALTERNATIVES

When developing your benefits logic (we explore benefit scenarios in more detail in Part 4), always consider whether there is a more pragmatic route to the desired solution, since you will have to justify your case against this. There may be simpler, less cash-hungry ways to achieve the same outcome over a slightly extended period of time and it may be worth considering these alternative courses of action, if only to be able to argue against them.

As Part 3 argues, adopting an adaptive approach, based on a flexible, integrated IT architecture, is a highly desirable goal to work towards to bring long-term agility to a company's operations. Yet this is an ambitious proposal for any organization. A blend of pragmatism at this point may be best, to enable you to establish a feasible program, which the board will buy into.

CONVINCING THE EXECUTIVE AND STAKEHOLDERS

The process of securing senior management support for any new initiative must start before the business case has been submitted. Alignment of goals as the benefit logic is being shaped and the feasibility of the project or initiative is established, needs to be an ongoing process. Work with all the stakeholders to ascertain how realistic the desired outcomes are and attempt to bring any disagreement back to what is possible. Propose and agree measures of success and how the delivery of benefits will be approved. Lack of communication or miscommunication is a common area for discord and mismatched expectation.

In many companies, stakeholding departments will be very wary of signing off benefits and the delivery mechanisms because this will affect their operating budget for the following year. Whether cost reduction or revenue improvement, this will fundamentally affect these departments as they will have to deliver the proposed benefits. Your project is more likely to be successful, therefore, if the stakeholders are supportive of what is being done, rather than reluctant collaborators.

Hold stakeholders to account and get them to buy in to the levels of benefit that will be realized, how these will be measured and how they will be delivered, and ask them to agree to own the realization of the benefit. Effort at this stage will be repaid a thousand-fold and it is worth getting the CEO to ask each and every stakeholder 'Do you agree? Sign here' (further tips on this can be found in Part 4).

'Selling' initiatives is an essential activity throughout but particularly at the business case stage. While this might be relatively easy at a business application level, where the likely benefits are more immediately evident, this becomes a slightly different story where less tangible assets, such as the overall infrastructure, are concerned.

Frequently, the business imperative has a short-term view. Infrastructure and the creation of services, are often sidelined in the interests of short-term cost containment. We have all seen the less desirable results of this, as short-term decisions to implement systems at an application-by-application level have led to a world of incompatible systems linked by point-to-point interfaces. Avoiding this relies on being able to persuade the organization to move from a departmental, application-based view of IT, to an enterprise-wide vision.

JUSTIFYING 'ENABLING' OR INFRASTRUCTURE PROJECTS

How can you persuade the business of the merits of this type of investment, when rapid, tangible business benefits appear to be the board's main priority?

Traditionally, infrastructure-level investment decisions are the domain of the IT department. Yet, as organizations need to achieve greater flexibility and responsiveness in their business processes and product and service offerings, their goals are more closely aligned with those of the IT department than they might first think. Business decisions (albeit indirectly) now drive the choice of technology, and not the other way round. Business and IT departments should, therefore, be considering their options in partnership. With the advent of service-based architectures, which we will cover in more detail in Part 3, many more essential functions are implemented within an infrastructure architecture.

Part of the problem when trying to secure senior buy-in for enterprise-wide, infrastructure-level investment, is that the initial costs associated with this type of project are perceived to be much higher than those incurred through the more traditional approach of buying or developing local applications that fulfil an immediate need. Nevertheless, this does not take into account the long-term cost of ownership of the systems, which will almost certainly be higher with the latter approach because companies seek to maintain disparate systems or develop point-to-point interfaces when they later try to integrate these disjointed systems in order to share data between them.

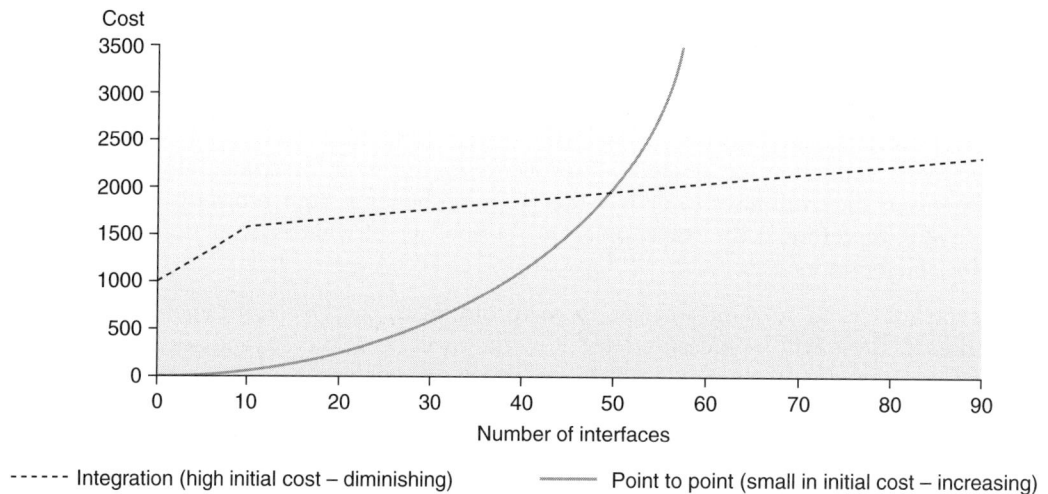

FIGURE 4.1: Integration infrastructure

In the medium to long term, the cost of maintaining an adaptable architecture, rather than a series of disparate, stand-alone applications should be lower. Thus, focusing on the cost of ownership and the cost of *not* having adaptability is a way to sell your new initiatives. This is where bundling initiatives into categories of service – functional, maintenance, user, infrastructure – may help.

Approach those stakeholders who will benefit the most first. Functional services are usually the easiest to sell and these will generally be driven by the appropriate business group. At the other extreme, infrastructure services are the most difficult to promote and buy-in from as far up the organization as possible should be sought. In particular, illustrate how the infrastructure, especially with the use of Enterprise Application Integration (EAI) and web services to link the back office, front office and ecosystem, are critical elements to the business strategy (these services are discussed at more length in Part 3). The return on investment can also be expressed in terms of better service levels, which are measurable, taking the focus away from the technology.

For maximum effectiveness, the sales message will need to be tailored to the particular audience. Financial directors, for example, will respond best to terms such as investment, variable versus fixed cost, discretionary versus non-discretionary spend. Hypothesize if necessary, although you must say what your assumptions are and link any benefits back to these assumptions.

'Hot' business applications such as e-business or ERP (Enterprise Resource Planning) depending on the bandwagon of the moment, where there is a greater perceived business imperative are a good way to link and position the benefits of a flexible infrastructure.

ALIGNING EXISTING INITIATIVES WITH YOUR NEW PROPOSALS

Dealing with inflight projects, which may be pet projects of key stakeholders, will always be an issue when aligning the organization to achieve adaptability. There will, of course, be those projects that are entirely tactical, that do not align with the adaptive direction, but are critical to continue. These might be projects aimed at staving off a sharp drop in market share or those which are required for legal or regulatory reasons.

However, if the organization has existing projects that are going off course or have little adaptive alignment, these should be reviewed for benefit generation and for strategic fit. If they appear not to be delivering, ruthless action is required to cull these projects. If they do not deliver benefit, do not allow them to carry on. They will only diminish your ability to deliver business systems that are aligned and deliver value to the business.

Those projects that do appear to deliver benefit, meanwhile, should be assessed in the light of direction, timing and how they fit into the overall strategic plan. You may of course want to slow them down or speed them up. Try to demonstrate the extent of their value creation (or otherwise) when trying to convince stakeholders that they need adjusting. Emphasize how stakeholders will gain value from initiatives elsewhere if you want to stop or change their projects.

Moreover, a pragmatic view is not to tinker too much with projects that are running successfully – allowing these to complete without hindrance may give critical quick wins.

MEASURING AND DELIVERING APPROPRIATE BENEFIT

Once you and your organization are clear on the business benefits you are striving for in your new initiatives, these can be used as a measure for better management and leadership and to monitor successful delivery.

At the end of each stage in a project, make sure you review the benefits at the same time that you are reviewing system design. Although this might sound like obvious advice, this tends not to happen and it is more likely that benefit cases only get revisited when a change occurs.

Any system implementation is most effective when a measurement framework is central to the management process; evidence of success is a great motivator and evidence of any short-coming can prompt motivation where it is needed. Measurement is a tool to create alignment of people who are focused on achieving a desired outcome – if you can measure it, you can manage it.

Although performance against financial goals is a common and obvious way of measuring success, companies have experimented with new measurement frameworks as non-financial measures have grown in importance. These include the balanced business scorecard.

Change should be measured across four key dimensions: financial, customer, business process and people. It is important to adopt the measurement of key performance indicators within a framework that works across these categories in order to achieve a balance of success, which stands more chance of being sustainable than if only a single dimension was attempted.

The challenge is to identify which measures within a framework matter to the program and to the company and adequately reflect the desired outcomes, thus creating value. Individual projects will have basic KPIs, such as cost and effort status against project milestones. If there is (as there should be) a direct value attributable to the project, for instance, cost reduction or revenue enhancement, this KPI should be measured, forecast and managed along with the more conventional project delivery KPIs.

If there is a larger program, KPIs for each project should 'roll up' or at least be linked to the top-level business change balanced scorecard.

An example of such a top-level scorecard, taken from the pharmaceuticals industry, is shown in Table 4.1. You will need to adopt a measurement framework and a set of KPIs that are expressed at an appropriate level for your goal. Nonetheless, the principle remains – objective measurement aids decision making.

Once measurement is established, the progress of a venture against its milestones and measures needs to be communicated to everyone involved and affected by the project. This is in the interests of keeping people informed, managing the successful outcome and maintaining everyone's motivation and support.

SUSTAINING BENEFIT

Responsibility for managing the realization of benefit will pass from program or project management to line management, probably at the point of project completion. If the measurements put in place begin to show that the projected benefits will not occur, it is critical to take action. Do not be afraid to make changes to project scope after the benefits case has been agreed and while the project is in progress.

Each project is a learning experience for everyone and further potential improvements will emerge at each stage of the project, especially in the design stages. It may turn out that the benefits cannot be delivered as envisaged. If this is the case, changes may need to be made, for example cutting scope and investment or altering the delivery mechanism.

If the marketplace that you are attempting to address, changes, do not allow people to continue to try to drive initiatives through (many attempt this even after it has become obvious that the business needs have changed). A number of companies implemented sales force automation solutions during the late 1990s, for instance, only to find that economic conditions dictated that the companies should divest themselves of their sales teams and adopt a different channel strategy. The answer was not to blindly continue, but to coordinate the systems changes with the planned business changes in order to avoid needless investment in new systems.

Joined-up systems is not just about integration, but also describes the art of adopting coordinated initiatives linking business with technology.

Once an initiative has been completed and the business system delivered, along with its constituent people and process parts, it is generally handed over to a service delivery organization to manage. Not unsurprisingly, such organizations run along very different lines to investment programs and tend to be cost-managed rather than 'benefit' managed. Decisions are generally made by local managers under strict budgetary control.

As a rule, there is no process to ensure that local decisions made in service delivery do not compromise overall benefit delivery and, worse, strategic direction. Therefore, ensure that part of the hand-over of responsibility for benefit delivery includes the specific measures of benefit delivery and their status. Make these part of the normal day-to-day business's operational targets and measures. Ensure that the business case includes sufficient investment in the

PERSPECTIVE	STRATEGIC OBJECTIVES	MEASURES	TARGETS	OWNER/ ACCOUNTABILITY	INITIATIVES
Financial	☐ Shareholder value ☐ Profit ☐ New revenue	☐ Operating margin ☐ Revenue from new services	☐ Top 10% of FTSE companies each year ☐ Retail Price Index X% annually ☐ 25% in three years	☐ Finance director ☐ CEO ☐ Business development manager	☐ Implement EVA*
Customer	☐ Differentiation ☐ Strategic alliances ☐ Customer service	☐ Value for money ☐ Profits from alliances ☐ Customer satisfaction	☐ Number one customer rating ☐ $x million in five years ☐ Number one customer rating	☐ Marketing director ☐ Business development manager ☐ Marketing director	☐ Create customer segmentation model ☐ Redefine channel strategy
Business processes	☐ Productivity ☐ New product development ☐ Segmentation	☐ Revenue/work hour ☐ Product development cycle time ☐ Number of initiatives targeted at profitable segments	☐ Best-in-class within five years ☐ Reduced by 50% in two years ☐ 60% within one year	☐ Chief operating officer ☐ Research and development manager ☐ Marketing director	☐ Re-engineer new product development process
Learning and innovation	☐ People policy ☐ Alliance management ☐ Customer focus	☐ Management span of control ☐ Number of learning partnerships ☐ % management time interfacing with customer	☐ Triple in three years ☐ 10% in five years ☐ 20% in two years	☐ Human resources director ☐ Business development manager ☐ CEO	☐ Develop new HR strategy ☐ Implement performance-based manager compensation program

TABLE 4.1: Example of a balanced business scorecard showing measures across four main dimensions

service delivery organization or in the service bought from a supplier or partner to enable the adherence to strategic imperatives and consequent benefit delivery.

SUMMARY

1 Drafting and presenting business cases, is becoming harder in the changing business and IT climate. As organizations become more ambitious in their objectives, so they must be prepared for greater complexity in the implications for their integration programs.

2 If you are the person briefed with translating the company's changing business needs into IT systems which support both what the enterprise is trying to achieve today and where it wants to be tomorrow, it is up to you to sell the resulting initiatives back to the business.

3 Continuing to compromise by taking short cuts is no longer an option. Companies are already strangled by legacy systems, which restrict their flexibility. If you continue to build on the complex legacy created, you will only succeed in taking the company further away from where it wants to be. Program and project managers must stick to the vision that they have been charged with delivering.

4 Having broken down larger initiatives into definable chunks, establish their feasibility with a pragmatic and slightly cynical viewpoint.

5 Be realistic about what the organization can achieve, given that day-to-day business operations must be allowed to continue undisrupted.

6 When selling the business benefits in the business case and in any presentations, use business language and highlight benefits that the audience can identify with.

7 Focus on both tangible and intangible returns for the business and those which will materialize in the short term as well as the long term.

8 Work on generating buy-in from stakeholders at an early stage and continue talking to them – ensure that you know who all your stakeholders are, from business to service delivery. They all have a key role in delivering benefit.

9 Measure what you want to achieve at all stages.

10 No ambitious integration problem will succeed unless people, process and technology changes are recognized as being equally important and are dealt with concurrently.

PART 2

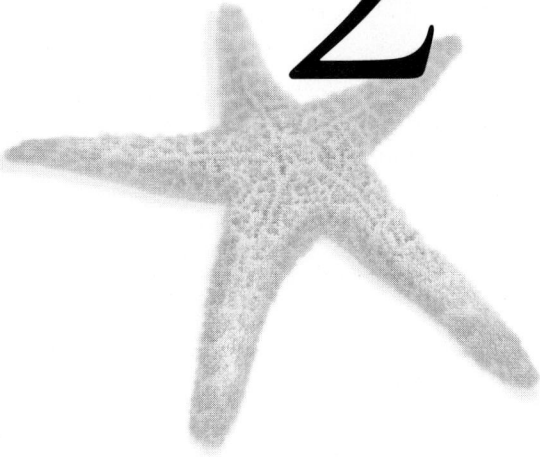

CREATING THE CLIMATE

CHAPTER 5

IMPLICATIONS FOR PEOPLE

INTRODUCTION

This section examines the various people-related issues facing businesses as they make the leap from traditional, hierarchical, department-based company structures to a scenario where business processes are extended across and beyond the organization.

By discussing the people issues first, the intention is to emphasize that successful integration, of the scale we are advocating, depends as much if not more on human factors and business practices, than it does on having the right technology in place.

In this chapter, the scene is set by examining the various ways that new market developments and business pressures affect companies' workforces, both IT and operational. Chapters 6 and 7 look at the dynamics of the multi-company, multicultural workplace and how organizations can build and manage harmonious, productive teams within the current volatility of the business environment and the wider market.

THE CHANGING WORK ENVIRONMENT

The Introduction explored some of the ways that businesses are likely to change in the future, as they attempt to respond more efficiently to customer needs.

One major trend is that organizations are likely to reduce their areas of focus to those where they genuinely add value and can create profitable growth. This could lead to large corporations breaking down into much smaller entities, leveraging partners to complete their offerings, instead of insisting on remaining self-sufficient with all the associated costs.

A second substantial change is that organizations are trying to try to improve the speed with which they respond to changing markets and customer needs, in pursuit of greater agility.

As these two changes come together, companies find that their business processes and staff responsibilities need to broaden in scope. Organizations need an enterprise-wide view of their business processes, their markets and their customers. As they increasingly engage with partners to provide complementary services, they also need to extend this business, market and customer view along the entire supply chain.

The implications for the workforce are that staff can no longer afford to wear blinkers. As hierarchies and departmental barriers are broken down, employees need to be made increasingly aware of the bigger business picture, not just where it begins and ends with their defined role. This trend is mirrored in the currently popular IT applications, such as Customer Relationship Management (CRM), and knowledge management. They are about turning data into meaningful commercial information, which can be shared and exploited across and beyond the enterprise – again, to build that bigger picture.

Staff are called upon to share what they know and to exploit knowledge gained from elsewhere, in a way that will benefit the business, for example, through better customer service, or a more in-depth perception of market developments. Sales staff are now expected to share knowledge with marketing and customer services departments, so that each has a complete view of the customer. As sales and customer information are also shared out to partner suppliers, the need to share knowledge and follow the business process are extended even further. As a result, employees are expected to multi-task, and to collaborate in multiple, virtual teams.

PRESSURES ON IT STAFF

Many of these changes are magnified for IT staff. As technology and business processes become tightly woven, the pressures on technologists become substantial. It is no longer enough for companies to employ technical geniuses. Although project teams will need the finest blend of new world and legacy system skills, they also need the business knowledge that will enable them to apply their expertise to a rapidly changing and highly pressurized commercial environment and to communicate effectively with business managers and business users.

Businesses have often been frustrated by the service they have received from their IT departments. These may have seemed to focus on technology for technology's sake, often taking a long time to deploy solutions, while business units have been guilty of failing to harness planned IT investments to achieve tangible results for the company. Instead they have gone out and procured systems and services from external suppliers on a needs-must basis, leading to a piecemeal approach to systems development and a breakdown in relations between IT and the business.

One way that organizations have tried to address this has been to appoint managers, who are accountable for IT services to particular parts of the business. Extended project teams have also been created to manage the various parties now involved in technology decision making, to make business users much more involved in and accountable for the success of projects.

THE CHANGING SKILL REQUIREMENT

With every new technology innovation, new skills are amassed, presenting organizations with quite a challenge when it comes to recruiting and retaining the right balance of skills.

There are still many old, legacy software systems in service today that do a perfectly adequate job and require older skills in languages such as Cobol to keep them ticking over. The ongoing role of legacy systems is covered in Chapter 8.

At the same time, new technology will always necessitate new skills and technical staff will need to be up to date in order to keep themselves marketable.

It is here that the need for a close relationship between IT and the business becomes more apparent, as development and integration shifts from being based around bespoke applications to packaged applications, such as Siebel, which start to take technicians closer to the business and away from the machine. This is particularly the case when organizations begin to move beyond package solutions and into web services, where fluidity is key and the business process and technology become almost indistinguishable.

Skills in integrating business processes within and across enterprises and deploying the technologies that enable this, are clearly becoming critical too. This is a consequence of the growing need for an enterprise-wide picture of the business and the move towards virtualization as companies seek to plug gaps in their own businesses by working closely with partners.

We have begun to see a shift in recruitment emphasis, from the need for highly technical systems analysts to a preference for technically-literate business analysts. Since most organizations are already overstretched when it comes to the size of IT department they can sustain, they are now having to prioritize the most strategically important skills.

As a result, some organizations consider outsourcing to address their legacy needs. Where older systems exist and are deemed to have continued value to the business, yet not at a strategic level, it can prove a more cost-effective option to have a third party provide the maintenance and upgrade services. This frees up internal teams and budgets to focus on more leading-edge developments that will directly affect productivity and customer service.

THE OUTSOURCING OPTION

The increasing availability and use of outsourcing services, such as application management and service delivery, is playing a part in the shift in IT skills that organizations require today.

Advances in technology and communications allow companies to move parts of their operations to more cost-effective locations. For example, organizations may wish to consolidate their data centre activities into a single European location. They may wish to organize help desks into regional centres, perhaps located in Kuala Lumpur, Sri Lanka or Brazil. Or they may like the idea of concentrating applications management in India or the Philippines, where the work can be done just as well but where labour is cheaper.

An increasing number of companies are doing this. These tend to be organizations that operate in multiple markets around the world. Consumer goods and retail companies have shown a particular take up of these kinds of remote services, while companies with higher value products, such as financial service companies, tend to be lagging. Many of these still have vertically integrated capabilities within the countries they operate in, with their data centres, help desks and application management teams all located in high cost centres close to the markets they serve. These companies too are likely to change in time influenced by macro-economic factors which make offshore services a feasible option.

The growth in outsourcing, either within a country or where the business or IT function is taken offshore, will have consequences for domestic employees. They will either be outsourced and then find themselves working for other clients, or be made redundant. Knowing this, IT staff are having to adapt their capabilities before their value diminishes.

THE IMPACT OF CHEAPER INTERNATIONAL LABOUR

As organizations buy into the idea of outsourcing, leaving them to concentrate their internal resources on business-critical development, the availability of services from cheaper labour markets will change the market for skills in systems delivery and support.

Changing economic conditions also mean that cheaper markets exist today for higher value business services skills. Countries like Spain, Australia and New Zealand provide a range of near-shore services, such as Java programing and web-based development. In addition, the range of offshore services offered to Western companies by countries such as India, has grown significantly in recent years. While Western markets have drawn on cheaper labour markets for IT services for more than a decade, the scope of what is outsourced has become more sophisticated recently – skills levels and quality of processes around the world have matured.

For example, India now has government support and multinational agreements to cooperate in software development. The value of its software exports is currently doubling every two years and is forecast to continue to at least double every three years in the immediate future, according to NASSCOM, the National Association of Software and Services Companies. What's more, in 2000, there were more firms accredited at SEI CMM level 5 (Software Engineering Institute Capability Maturity Model[1] – a quality accreditation) in India than in anywhere else in the world, according to the Carnegie Mellon Software Institute (2000). While companies have traditionally provided primarily application support and maintenance services offshore, an increasing source of additional revenue generation will be through application development services and consulting services.

When take up of these higher value services grows, this will affect the working patterns of people in Western markets, who will have to adapt the type of services they provide, focusing on higher value skills and the ability to manage third parties. Approaches to management may need to vary according to the country from which the services originate, since some working cultures prefer to work on their own initiative, while others require more defined instructions.

The outsourcing option does not apply solely to technology services either. Multitudes of organizations have already outsourced their call centre activities to remote, more cheaply run facilities, for example. As organizations become more focused and more virtual, they are likely to outsource more and more of what was originally deemed to be part of their core business. Banks will outsource credit rating services, for example, while manufacturers will continue to farm out more and more of their production line activities, until what is left as their competitive edge is little more than a brand.

CHANGING EMPLOYMENT TERMS

While organizations continue to outsource peripheral activities to third parties, this leads to a reduction in internal employment and a rise in the use of contract staff. Again, this applies to business services as much as to IT services. Increasingly, organizations strive to achieve a balance of variability in their labour cost base by employing contract staff and third parties for more 'commodity' services.

Organizations are increasingly concentrating their recruitment energies and budgets, on people with higher value skills as they offload non-core activities to third parties. This will have an impact on the sorts of skills that workers seek to acquire in future when going through education and training. In the meantime, organizations may find themselves fighting over staff with higher value skills.

[1] NASSCOM, 'IT Software & Services in India', *Strategic Review*, 2000.

At an IT level, for instance, many companies already find it difficult to ensure the availability and security of critical resources, such as managers, analysts and designers.

Finding the right management skills is a particular challenge, given that some internal IT departments now use contractors for as much as 60 per cent of their workforce, with some contracts now as little as a month long. This is often a deliberate policy – in order to deliver business systems, organizations increasingly maintain a cadre of skilled managers and designers and buy in everything else. The sort of manager that can coordinate and motivate such a transient workforce can prove hard to find.

For those with more mainstream skills, for example, developers and support staff, the changing workplace dynamics mean a lack of stability compared with when a good technician could be guaranteed a job for life.

Now technology graduates are emerging into a much more dynamic, volatile job market, and find that they need a broad range of skills, rather than a core specialism, in addition to that all-important commercial experience. Today's technical staff, even if they prefer permanent positions, discover that they need to adopt a mind-set more like that of contractors, becoming more versatile and ready to move around to ensure they have a portfolio of up-to-date skills to offer future employers.

Indeed, individuals must now take personal responsibility for the currency of their skills instead of falling back on their college educations or expecting a long-term employer to train them in the skills they need for the next few years.

CONTRACTS

Employers need to change the types of contracts they offer if they want to draw upon skills that exist outside of the company as a means of keeping internal costs down.

When organizations become more choosy about the types of people they take on as permanent staff and the job market becomes more volatile, people's loyalty ties will change. While outsourcing grows in popularity and organizations become more virtual in their make-up, employees may begin to wonder who they actually work for.

Consequently, it is likely that employment laws will have to change. Already, these vary from country to country, with certain countries in Europe (particularly southern Europe) more resistant to outsourcing because of its implications for staff terms and conditions when transfers of operations take place.

Yet, at the same time, organizations will need to ensure that they retain access to good people, even if those people are no longer on the payroll. One option is to offer flexible contracts to associate staff – consultants they may want to hire for short periods at a time. This allows organizations to rely upon a wide range of excellent skills, treating the consultants as employees, but without a binding long-term agreement.

Where key skills are found to be in short supply, companies will find themselves having to take the work to the people, instead of bringing the people to the work. This will drive the market for offshore labour, since there is no longer any reason for overseas talent to be imported. This applies as much to commodity business skills (for instance, call centre operations) as it does to IT. Home-working is likely to grow in popularity for the same reason.

Organizations bear in mind, when attempting to attract highly prized people, that employees today are not necessarily motivated by the same things that drove people in the past, such as job security and predictability, technical challenge and a reasonable level of pay. Today, employees are much more likely to be attracted by the opportunity to work from home, sabbaticals and flexible working hours.

People also need more recognition and autonomy and good training and development, over and above high salaries and a secure job. As a result, management hierarchies are giving way to matrix management and more fluid reporting structures. In this way, staff have a chance to show creative flair while working in teams with peers.

THE IMPACT OF TECHNOLOGY ON WORKING HABITS

Remote collaboration, enabled through the widespread growth in the internet and e-mail, is having a substantial impact on working habits. In fact, this book was developed collaboratively via teleconference and e-mail instead of face-to-face meetings.

This collaboration can take place across countries and time zones overnight, without developers or the client or end user leaving their workplace. Each can still work in their teams, actually or virtually. This increases the speed of development and testing by the users, reduces time to market and means that many systems can be developed anywhere in the world, enabling organizations to tap into the cheaper skills markets, such as India.

This sort of technological development also means that global applications can be cost-effectively supported through web-based systems from a small number of locations (or even one location). Users can register faults on a website, which are then allocated to support engineers who will correct the fault and post the patch to the website. Users then download the patch, apply it and distribute it. The process is limited only by the speed taken to fix the fault. World time zones no longer have a bearing and are increasingly used to advantage. Faults found overnight in one time zone can be fixed in another time zone, to be applied the next day. This has a significant effect on building and supporting systems globally.

SUMMARY

1 It is necessary to have an enterprise-wide view of business processes and, increasingly, one which extends beyond the company boundaries.

2 There is a need to share knowledge with and work alongside colleagues from other departments and companies.

3 People must be versatile, to continue to provide value to the business.

4 There is a necessity to be multi-skilled and to take responsibility for keeping those skills fresh and marketable.

5 People must think and act increasingly like a contractor.

6 For the organization, there is a need for a change of culture. If versatility is the goal, companies need to establish working environments where people are encouraged to become multi-skilled; have an enterprise-wide view of the business; collaborate in virtual teams, in smaller, geographically dispersed groups than previously and to share knowledge, even across company boundaries.

7 As Albert Einstein famously said, 'It has become appallingly obvious that our technology has exceeded our humanity.' Today, this is truer than ever, and organizations that ignore the human factors of integration do so at their peril.

CHAPTER 6

MANAGING MULTIPLE CULTURES

INTRODUCTION

As organizations pursue their goal of greater agility and market responsiveness, they need the buy-in of their employees and of any contractors and partner companies. True integration will not be achieved unless the people, as well as the IT systems, are joined up and working towards the bigger vision. It is evident from Chapter 5 that achieving the change in mind-set from a blinkered, departmental perspective to an enterprise view of the business and where it needs to go, is essential for the entire workforce.

When workers regroup across departmental, geographical and even company lines, they will encounter different cultures and different approaches to working. Sales staff often have a different mind-set to marketing staff, for example, which is different again to the perspective of financial staff. Even within departments, differences in people's backgrounds and training can dictate different expectations and practices. Cultures also differ from region to region, and clearly from country to country.

Cultural differences are considered in this chapter, with a view to determining, in Chapter 7, how managers can best harness these differences and build cohesive teams to deliver business integration at the level that organizations require today.

SYSTEMS INTEGRATION IS PEOPLE INTEGRATION

The role of culture takes on particular importance as teams are formed to deliver all aspects of integration, due to the scope and complexity of work tackled now and the diversity of people that will be involved. As Chapter 5 highlighted, this is likely to comprise staff (internal, external and contractors) with a range of legacy skills, packaged software skills, new world technology skills (such as Java, HTML and web services), program managers, risk managers, business managers and departmental staff, both nationally and internationally.

In *Principles of Software Engineering Management*[1], Tom Gilb claims that, when it comes to the failure of software projects, 'the real problem is communication between people'. Gilb's solution was a Bill of Rights, designed to improve internal communications by empowering people to know what they were doing and what they could expect from the company. This is an American approach. Gilbs example promoted the right of individuals to challenge and question. In some countries accepting this could be a challenge.

Whatever people's background, nationality or personal skills, everyone has a set of filters in place that they use automatically when communicating with each other. These alter not only the way in which we speak and act but also the way in which we receive messages and perceive the actions of others. These communications filters, as well as people's values and attitudes, are the product of the individual's cultural heritage.

LAYERS OF CULTURAL DIFFERENCES

Research by Geert Hofstede, professor of organizational anthropology and international management at the University of Limburg, Maastricht, suggests that our cultural make-up is acquired like layers of an onion skin[2]. At the core are behaviours we learn in childhood from our immediate family. These are the most difficult cultural norms to change or cut across. Next in importance is nationality followed by class/caste, specialism/profession, organization and, finally, marketplace. Of these layers, marketplace is the most easily changed. This is essentially because individuals can usually reorientate themselves to market changes, much as companies do, without compromising their basic values and cultural principles.

It is important to understand this cultural paradigm because it affects not only individuals and how they operate, but also companies and governments. It dictates organizational design, leadership style, management style, business structures and practices, processes and procedures, staff motivation, customer service and quality. It is crucial to the way meetings are managed, and information presented. It helps explain how decisions are made. Most importantly, cultural make-up is the catalyst for building successful relationships.

We do not have to go abroad to experience different culture. It is easy to identify different values, customs and practices in the different companies we come into contact with. McDonalds and Ikea are good examples of distinct cultures. For anyone that needs to work where outsourcing and offshore operations become the norm, it is vitally important that they understand the impact of cross-cultural issues.

Historically, the emphasis in IT management practice has been on command and control. High-profile project failures have created the belief that success can be achieved only by the heavy, hands-on management of linear projects. Yet integration projects do not always lend themselves to this way of working: they may be too complex, involve too many different activities, and have groups working in parallel. The managers of an integration project, therefore, need to find other models for what they do, recognizing that people deliver successful integration projects, and that people tend to like people who are like themselves. People like to work with and buy from people who they like. The key to success must be to find those elements that people have in common, while recognizing and exploiting their differences.

This applies at all levels of the cultural 'onion', whether it is bringing people together from different national or ethnic backgrounds or creating joint teams from different parts of an organization, third-party software suppliers and consultancies. Cultural management is the key to the way that teams are built and motivated.

[1] Tom Gilb, *Principles of Software Engineering Management, Op. Cit.*
[2] Geert Hofstede, *Cultures Consequences: International Differences in Work Related Values*. Beverly HIlls C.A. Sage Publications 1980.

ACHIEVING TRUST

All relationships, whether between organizations, teams or individuals are built around trust. There is much talk in business today about working in partnership rather than as 'clients' and 'suppliers' but the partner relationship is one that is earned, not established by contract. It is earned by each party demonstrating that they have the capability to perform their expected role and that they have the goodwill to apply their skills.

Trust is built up through a number of elements, as shown in Figure 6.1. An individuals cultural perspective emphasizes the use of one or more of these elements as more important than the others.

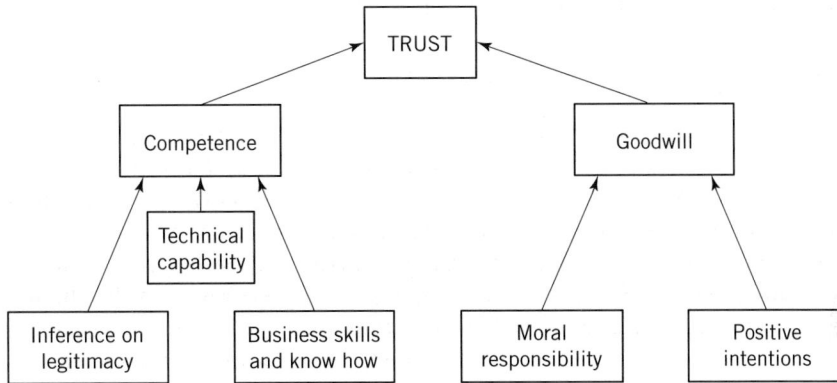

FIGURE 6.1: Trust

This model can be applied to all relationships. A consulting firm demonstrates its competency by proving that it is legitimate, that it is not exaggerating its capabilities. This is often done by use of customer references, publishing facts about the economic health of the company or by talking about well-known organizations it has worked with in the past. The consultancy also needs to show its technical capability by publishing case studies, arranging company visits and exchanging the CVs of key personnel.

Nevertheless, without the feeling that this competence is going to be deployed for mutual benefit that there is 'goodwill', the feeling of 'understanding needs' will not develop. There has to be a feeling that each partner has both positive intent and will be morally responsible and that each partner is committed to the joint project and keeps promises. This is not only crucial in the first stages of a relationship, but essential to manage through the inevitable crises that beset all complex ventures. These crises are discussed in detail in Part 5.

People's positive intentions are signalled both on first impression and by their ongoing behaviour and support. To ensure that there is no room for misinterpretation, it is vital that there is an early development of similar goals: 'We are both in this to make a profit'; 'We both want to expand our businesses'; 'Only together can we survive'.

Without these practical demonstrations of competence and goodwill, it is impossible to move 'trust' and 'partnership' from concepts and aspirations into practical application. Unfortunately, all those layers of the onion act as a filter, affecting all the communications vehicles used to demonstrate competence and goodwill.

CULTURAL MISPERCEPTION

Consider the story about the Anglo-Saxon salesman who was kept waiting days for an appointment with a Middle Eastern businessman. Once the appointment came, the salesman, driven by his need to achieve a sale, launched straight into a product demonstration. His motivation for doing this was the Anglo-Saxon business tradition of showing competency first, to earn the right to a business relationship. Yet the Arab buyer, more interested in establishing moral responsibility, responded by asking seemingly aimless personal questions. His objective was to see if he wanted to do business firstly with this person and secondly with the company, as was the norm in his culture. Only after establishing this, would he be interested in determining the strength of the solution.

This culture clash is also apparent at more subtle levels. The vast majority of the signals that people send to each other when they communicate are through body language, but body language can give problems. How firm do you expect someone's handshake to be? What do you think if someone looks you straight in the eye? How do you feel if someone turns away from you while you are talking to them?

Depending on your cultural background and the context of the exchange the answers can be different. In Italy, it is acceptable to begin speaking before someone else has finished. In Britain this would be considered impolite. Yet in Britain it is considered acceptable to leap in without a pause once the other person has finished talking. Indeed, most Europeans are embarrassed by silences during a conversation while in Japan one should leave a polite gap before beginning to speak, in order to give due consideration to the ideas which have just been expressed.

Nancy Adler of McGill University in Montreal, Canada is a well-known and respected researcher of international organizational behaviour. She has done much work around the subject of effective communication when the double barrier of differences of language and culture are put in place. She talks about the 'mis' factor – how mis-perception leads to mis-interpretation and ultimately to mis-evaluation.

She demonstrates how culturally determined perception can distort, block or even create what people choose to see and hear. In an experiment she set up, some Mexican and American children were shown pictures of a bullfight and a baseball game very rapidly and mixed together, so that they saw each picture only for a fraction of a second. When questioned afterwards, the Mexican children only remembered seeing the bullfight, while the Americans, despite seeing the same juxtaposed images, only saw the baseball game.

Although Adler was looking at international issues, it is worth considering how many times you have had meetings with people from different companies and assumed that they would see things in the same way that your colleagues would do. For example, you assumed that they would 'get the point' or would understand company-specific behaviours.

In the cross-cultural setting, whether international or just cross-group, there is another common factor at work. Most people have a tendency to make sense of the world by putting people and things into categories and by forming stereotypes. This leads to misinterpretation and errors of judgement.

Cross-cultural stereotyping involves using your own cultural values and norms to understand the behavioural norms of another culture. This is very evident at an international level but it can be equally disastrous when inferences are made about other organizational or social groups.

Stereotypes can be helpful but more often lead to negative or defensive behaviour. The behaviour of strangers can indeed seem strange, even threatening from the perspective of one's own value system. The most firmly held stereotypical views are often those that have been laid down in early life and are subconsciously believed. These are evaluative and tend to be confirmed rather than changed on further observation and experience. The positive results of this negative stereotyping are that they are usually founded on the differences in values. These differences can provide a useful raw material to build mutual understanding.

So far, we have considered the differences between co-workers in terms of values and the impact in terms of communication. However, for the impacts to be as wide-ranging as they are, there have to be other dimensions. The current, standard way to define these dimensions is the result of some work done by Hofstede, originally in the 1970s, then later updated.

NATIONAL DIFFERENCE IN VALUES AT WORK

Having established the 'onion skin of culture' concept, Hofstede used data from employees of IBM around the world to establish key attitudinal differences. In IBM, he deliberately chose a company with a strong sense of its own identity and culture, which it imposed on its employees. He was also able to study people who not only worked in the same marketplace and organization, but shared the same profession and could be expected to be from similar social classes. The only cultural variables, therefore, were nationality and family.

Hofstede discovered that differences in values and attitudes at work were better explained by national culture than by position, profession, age or gender. He identified five main dimensions:

1 **Power distance** – This measures how acceptable an unequal distribution of power is to the least powerful members of a society or organization. Is the boss right because he or she is the boss (high power distance) or only when he or she demonstrates that they know the right answer (low power distance)?

2 **Uncertainty avoidance** – This defines how threatened people feel by change or by lack of clarity, trying to avoid situations where there is a lack of stability as a result. They attempt to create sets of formal rules to govern every behaviour, they reject ideas and behaviour which is not 'normal'. Countries where there is high uncertainty avoidance tend to have more centralized structures and less flexibility.

3 **Individualism/collectivism** – This relates to how closely knit a society is and whether members of that society believe their first duty is to themselves or to society. Looking at success in sport aptly demonstrates the differences between Americans and Europeans. In both Germany and the UK, team sports are highly thought of and the success of the national football teams can change the way the country, as a whole, feels about itself (collectivism). In the US, athletes are highly prized (individualism), while team sports are largely restricted to domestic competition.

4 **Masculinity/Femininity** – This contrasts those societies where there is a greater emphasis on competitive values and career success to those when quality of life is more important. This could be expressed as materialism versus concern for others. The masculine/feminine elements come into play here, because those societies which emphasize career success tend to more rigidly define men's and women's roles. Scandinavian countries strongly emphasize quality of life. They expect women to work, and lead the way in giving fathers

the option to care for newborn children. In Austria however, career success is of great importance and women are expected to stay at home and care for the children.

5 **Confucian dynamism** – The long-term/short-term view. Being willing to accept that returns on investment, whether investments of effort or financial investments, will be reaped at some time in the future or immediately.

Hofstede and his colleagues mapped some 60 countries against these dimensions to look at the differences between national cultures. Not only does this produce interesting league tables, plotting the relative positions of countries on two of the dimensions at a time gives rise to a potential explanation of the stereotypical antipathies we are all familiar with.

The renowned difficulties when the French (FRA) and British (GBR) work together becomes easier to appreciate, for example, when one looks at the relationship between the dimensions of power distance and uncertainty (see Figure 6.2). Culturally, the French accept much more difference in the distribution of power than do their British counterparts, while the British are more comfortable with uncertain and unstable conditions.

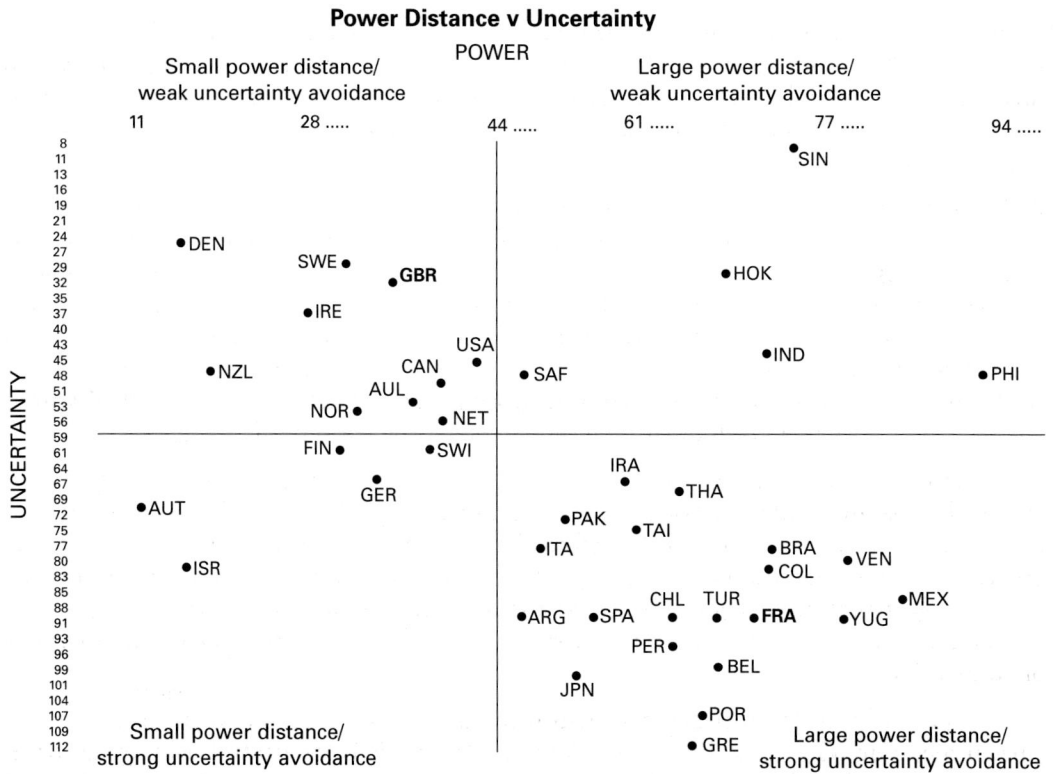

FIGURE 6.2: Differences between national cultures (Hofstede, *Cultures and Organizations*, 1996. Reproduced with permission from the author and copyright holder).

So how is this translated into business behaviour and management style? While the British, with most other north-western European countries, have a democratic and inclusive style to their business management approach, the French typically have a much more hierarchical command and control structure, which in turn leads to a much more directive organization. Also, the

French typically deal with uncertainty less effectively than their British counterpart: they try to create sets of formal rules to govern every behaviour, and they reject ideas and behaviour which is not 'normal'. The French have a codified legal system, while the British have 'common law', which is built up by setting precedents as each new case arises. The French, in describing the British historically as 'perfidious', 'hypocritical', and 'vague', are, in fact, describing a lack of a general model or theory and a preference for a more pragmatic, evolutionary approach.

By working together the French may see that there is usually no ulterior motive behind a British colleague's vagueness but rather a capacity to adapt to circumstances. Similarly it is only through close cooperation that the British come to realize that, far from being 'distant', 'superior' or 'out of touch with reality', their French colleagues' concern for a general model or theory is what lends vision, focus and cohesion to an enterprise or project.

MULTICULTURAL TEAM DYNAMICS IN PRACTICE AT CGE&Y

This may appear fine in theory and it is easy to see how it explains our stereotypical views of each other but what about in practice? Consider an example of multicultural teamwork.

During 1999, engineering conglomerate Asea Brown Boveri (ABB) was in the process of rationalizing its process control and logic (plant automation) software provision. It wished to divest itself of a highly skilled team of 40 people. By the end of the year, it had agreed commercial terms to outsource its team to CGE&Y, with the latter taking over the assets and personnel, and selling back their services.

Although the team had been together for almost ten years, it had been through a series of four takeovers and mergers during that period, but always involving engineering companies. This frequent change of ownership had helped to form a very close-knit team of like-minded German engineers who had responsibility for delivering a software product to internal customers. They were used to working in a 'factory' environment and used to standard engineering production techniques in the way they designed, built, tested and supported their single software package. This was, therefore, a well-drilled, small team that worked within well-defined boundaries without the external pressure to make a profit.

The decision to farm out the operation to an external IT services company, which was externally, customer and profit focused and used to working in a project-oriented culture, was agreed at senior management levels, before the team became involved in the outsourcing process. Consequently, the initial feelings of the personnel were ones of great uncertainty, triggered by factors such as new business sector and drivers, new company culture, new ways of working and new colleagues. This combination would be unsettling to anyone, regardless of cultural influences.

The purpose of bringing together the ABB team and a team from an external consultancy (specifically Cap Gemini's UK-based General Motors delivery centre) was to create a common approach to delivering software, using 'factory' rather than 'project' organization and principles (the differences in these approaches are explained in Part 4). This was to be the first step in expanding the UK model on a worldwide basis through the cooperation of teams dedicated to servicing the General Motors account. Once the concept was proven in Germany, it would be rolled out in Detroit in the US.

The UK team was given the responsibility for this, in full knowledge that the IT services company's existing structures, organization and rewards system would not support the initiative. Although, at the most senior levels, there was recognition of the need to create such a transnational model, the team had to develop the working organization through networking and persuasion. The team knew that they would be breaking new ground, with only tacit senior management approval during the initial stages.

The first objectives for the UK team were to assist the transitioning of the German team and to create an operation that could help to deliver IT application development and support to Opel in Frankfurt.

The difficulties that can be encountered when working at a distance were well known. Experience indicated that there was a need to create a 'team' approach early on, through building trust and common respect and to leverage this goodwill to deliver some concrete advances in a short time-scale. Lastly, it was necessary to have an inclusive decision-making process supported by persistent communication. Therefore, initial priorities were to establish trust and to begin a creative process.

Some of the challenges that lay ahead can be explained by Hofstede's research into national cultural differences. This research, while finding some remarkable similarities between the Germans and the British (and indeed the Americans, who would now be part of the equation at the Detroit base), also shows up some clear differences, which are highlighted in Table 6.1.

	BRITISH	GERMAN	AMERICAN
Power Distance Indicator (PDI)	35	35	40
Masculinity/femininity	35	65	44
Individualism (high number)/collectivism (low number)	89	67	91
Uncertainty avoidance	65	35	44
Long-term orientation	25	31	29

Hofstede used a mathematical formula to look at the relative importance of the various cultural factors to different nations. The numbers themselves are not important, other than to highlight the differences between the countries.

TABLE 6.1: Key cultural comparisons

The main difference for the British compared with the Germans and the Americans, for example, is in uncertainty avoidance. Additionally, there was likely to be some friction for the Germans, with the more individualistic approaches of the British and Americans.

The power distance indicator (PDI) factor would suggest that UK experience may be adequate in terms of how 'democratic' the managerial style should be, regarding decision making and challenging managerial decisions. With a low PDI, one might expect a preference for interdependence between managers and subordinates and that, as with the UK-based team, subordinates would quite readily approach and contradict their bosses.

Again, with the close scores between the UK and Germany on masculinity/femininity, it would be reasonable to assume that both teams would have similar expectations with regard to earnings potential, recognition for a job well done, opportunities for promotion, and achieving a sense of worth through rising to a challenge. All of these could be important to motivate the combined team.

The management of the team in Germany would differ with the individual versus collective approach. One could expect the differences to be even more marked once the US contingent was incorporated in the team.

German employment law and the close relationship in terms of collective bargaining of government, industry and workers, has been a secret to stable growth and economic success over the last 50 years. While all three nations are very close in terms of the speed of success (Hofstede's long-term orientation measure), it was accepted that the US contingent would be more prepared to accept change and the probability of future success than the Germans, with the British sitting somewhere between them.

In summary, in these five elements of cultural make-up (value placed on authority, on oneself, on other people, on certainty and on time), the divergence would be most marked in terms of the attitude towards uncertainty. This was likely to manifest itself through higher levels of anxiety, but the anxiety could be channelled to deliver success. The area of most concern would be the British antipathy towards the need for rules and regulations.

According to Hofstede's principles, the German workers could be expected be more abstractive in their thinking, more analytical, basing decision on logical principles, and more scientific. This would be underlined by their educational and working background as engineers. As a result of this kind of analysis, it became possible to 'sell' the software factory concept to the Germans as a standardization of skills, to the Americans as standardization of output and to the British as being flexible and mutually supportive.

SUMMARY

1 While it is easy to discuss culture at a theoretical level, the example demonstrates the complexities of culture in the workplace, particularly in the future. These are more likely to involve dynamic teams made up of people from different departments, different companies, different work patterns, not to mention different geographical locations.

2 It has become more important than ever for managers to be aware of the dynamics at work between colleagues thrown together to form new teams. Unless managers address the 'people' issues associated with closer business integration, it is unlikely they will get the results they are looking for.

3 Cultural differences need to be recognized openly and developed to create new best practice.

4 Culture affects employees' expectations of what they want from their job and how they approach it.

5 Culture can have a profound impact on how co-workers interact and, unless recognized as a cultural difference, can lead to misinterpretation and a breakdown in working relationships.

6 Trust is central to any working relationship, but different people have different ways of judging and demonstrating trust.

CHAPTER 7

BUILDING TEAMS

INTRODUCTION

The aim of this chapter is to explore the factors that managers need to take into account when putting together successful, harmonious teams to implement and work within the new, integrated enterprise. As organizations strive to make more effective and cost-efficient use of their workforce, which now comprises their existing staff alongside contractors and external third parties, managers need to ensure they are pulling the right strings to get the best possible performance from this multicultural mix. This means recognizing and working with people's differences and can dictate how well co-workers understand each other and how effectively they will cooperate.

In Chapter 6, we looked at the differences in culture between different countries that can affect the effectiveness of international teams. Yet, as we noted, it does not take a country divide to introduce potential cultural clashes in the workplace.

DIFFERING COMPANY CULTURES

Every company has its own culture, for example, its own business priorities and its own working practices. Some companies may be employee-orientated, showing more interest in people development than the tasks they do and their deliverables. Other companies may be more 'customer-orientated', focusing their energies outwards on the marketplace rather than on the quality of internal processes. Table 7.1 sets out how different company values can affect a business.

The idea of the virtual enterprise is gaining credibility. Organizations are beginning to work in partnership or use outsourcing arrangements rather than do everything themselves. So the significance of inter-company cultural differences takes on a new level of importance. Until recently, the main effects of differences in company culture have been on recruitment and forming business relationships, rather than building multicultural teams.

	OPERATIONAL EXCELLENCE	CUSTOMER INTIMACY	PRODUCT LEADERSHIP
Key business processes	☐ End-to-end supply chain efficiency ☐ Reliable and convenient basic service	☐ Customized product creation and/or personalized basic servicing to achieve best fit ☐ Premium service to achieve a total solution	☐ Technology invention ☐ Product commercialization ☐ Market exploitation
Organization and skills	☐ Central authority, low level of empowerment ☐ High skills at the core of the organization	☐ Empowerment close to point of customer contact ☐ High skills at boundary of the organization	☐ Ad hoc, organic and cellular ☐ High skills abound in loose-knit structures
Management systems	☐ Transaction profitability ☐ Command and control, standard operating procedures (SOPs) ☐ Quality management	☐ Customer equity measures, like lifetime value ☐ Satisfaction, share management	☐ Rewarding individuals' innovative capacity ☐ Risk and exposure management
Information and IS	☐ Integrated low-cost transaction systems ☐ The system is the process	☐ Granular customer databases, linking internal and external information ☐ Strong analytical tools	☐ Person-to-person communication systems ☐ Technologies enabling cooperation
'Rules' and norms	☐ Process-driven ☐ Conformance, 'one size fits all' mind-set	☐ Customer-driven ☐ Variation and 'have it your way' mind-set	☐ Concept, future-driven ☐ Experimentation and 'out-of-the-box' mind-set

Source: Treacy and Wiersema *Discipline of Market leaders*, HarperCollins, 1996.

TABLE 7.1 Company values

Trying to build a collaborative and cohesive team, where partner organizations are focused on different value sets, can lead to some interesting conflicts. Imagine attempting to establish a common set of objectives if one company is focused on operational excellence and the other is focused on customer intimacy, without recognizing the different value sets. How can trust be built up, when all the demonstration of competency will be focused on things like customization and flexibility on the one hand and reliable basic services and 'one size fits all' expectations on the other?

CULTURAL EFFECTS ON ORGANIZATIONS

Nancy Adler of McGill University claims that the first goal of cross-cultural management is 'to describe organization behaviour within countries and cultures'[1]. What might one find by using cultural insight to look at a company and to analyze its behaviour, style and structure?

For example, let's examine a typical US-based company that has a global presence. Testing this organization against cultural expectation, one would find motivational style which expects small power distance (see Chapter 6 for an explanation of terms). There is a high degree of peer competition, key performance indicators (KPIs) are set through a bargaining process with management and management itself challenges and sets up conflict situations. People within the organization at every level are expected to take care of themselves, the attitude being 'We only employ adults'. While this presupposes small power distance, it also emphasizes individualism over collective good – sometimes to the detriment of the company as a whole and therefore the

[1] Nancy Adler, *Op. Cit.*

individual. The objectives set for and by management focus on achieving individual performance within a narrow scope of control and it is rare to find any that are focused on integration.

Leadership is not strongly apparent. There may not be a clearly communicated overall view of the company as a corporate entity. There is more emphasis on growth through local achievement. The positive side of this, if you have weak uncertainty avoidance, is that there is great flexibility for local management because there is an expectation that drive and direction should be given at a local level.

However, this can lead to frequent changes of direction, since the company has to operate in a reactive mode, influenced by global events, its changing marketplace and competitors that have more vision. Organizationally, it has become a federation of local entities managed as profit centres. There is much local product and service variation and it is extremely difficult for it to manage global business because its business systems and processes are incapable of handling simple things, such as profit distribution for global business across participating countries.

Managing integration within such a corporate culture is bound to be tough. It is essential that the strains that appear are countered by the way that project teams are put together and a culture change program.

Although each business, regardless of marketplace, carries out the same set of generic functions: acquiring business; creating and maintaining products; delivering to customers and managing the business processes. Each of these functions requires different and specific skills. Even within companies the people best suited to each of these areas will have developed sets of organization and occupational practices. The accountant can be expected to be driven by well-defined processes and attention to detail, while the salesperson will be open-minded and search for user-friendly solutions. They may use a different vocabulary to express themselves. Then there are personal differences, based on upbringing and education and age. This can also affect use of language and general attitude. Culture is everywhere.

FORMALIZING THE PROCESS OF BUILDING TEAMS

To meld this culturally diverse group into a single cohesive team requires a seven-step approach:

1   Information gathering.

2   Building mutual understanding.

3   Finding the bridges and defining common objectives.

4   Leveraging the cross-cultural differences.

5   Building a unique team culture.

6   Creating momentum.

7   Becoming self-sustaining.

The foundation for the first five steps needs to be accomplished prior to the initiation of a project. The mobilization phase of the project needs to focus on the cascading of the cross-cultural foundation to all stakeholders and the creation of momentum is key.

To ensure that the five steps have been completed, it is advised that the project management holds some form of workshop or meeting, initially with the key management team and decision makers. A typical framework for such a session is shown in Table 7.2. It is essential that this process be carried out before the project begins and on a face-to-face basis, regardless of circumstances, geography and time-scales. Time and money spent at this stage can easily be cost-justified by immediate improvements in productivity. The critical day is the first one, which focuses on flushing out those cultural differences in a way that can make use of best practices from the different inputs. 'Working with' rather than 'doing to' must be the mantra.

Day 1: Awareness
— Know each other
— Team building
— Cross-cultural awareness exercise
— Cultural differences assessment
— Soft skills wrap up

Day 2: What are we supposed to deliver?
— Project/program presentation
— Expected deliverables
— Company knowledge
— Business case

Day 3: Logistics
— Resourcing
— Accounting
— Reporting
— Personal Ts and Cs (Terms & Conditions)
— Joint project delivery best practices
— Organization benefits and concerns

Day 4: How we deliver
— Planning
— Organization
— Methods, tools, communication strategy
— Change management
— Risk mitigation
— Issues resolution
— Escalation processes

Day 5: Next steps
— How to get organized
— Responsibilities, authorities, stakeholder maps
— Action plan
— Commitment
— Benefits and concerns

TABLE 7.2: Mobilizing as a multicultural team

COMPETENCIES FOR MULTICULTURAL WORKING

Those who contribute to an integration project are often chosen for their technical skills, rather than their ability to perform effectively in a multicultural environment. This is an oversight. Recent research has been directed at defining and measuring a set of core personal competencies that can be identified as pivotal success factors for working on a multicultural project. The work, still in its infancy, is beginning to provide a useful set of tools to help individuals develop appropriate skills and attitudes for transferring their technical and managerial skills into the international arena, and to become effective as quickly as possible in unfamiliar cultural settings.

These tools have been created by WorldWork, a company based in London, which is dedicated to helping individuals and organizations identify and fill the specific gaps they face when transferring management and leadership skills to an international context. They see this 'gap' effect to be based on three factors.

1 The added challenge of managing a deep-lying multicultural diversity in values, beliefs and ways of working, often involving working across a number of cultural divides simultaneously.

2 The tendency for managers, regardless of how experienced they are, to feel increasingly uncertain and lacking in confidence as they become small fishes in larger ponds.

3 The lack of provision, in terms of tools, to help individuals build transferable skills to work across cultures that are specific to the demands of their role.

WorldWork has created two tools. The International Competency Set (with ten competencies and 22 associated skills, attitudes and areas of knowledge) defines the special capabilities required to transfer professional skills to an international context. The International Profiler (TIP), a psychometric tool, provides managers with structured feedback in terms of the energy, emphasis and attention they bring to the International Competency Set.

WorldWork has also created a licensing process to help consultants and human resources professionals to use these tools to provide structured feedback to individual managers, both one to one, in groups and over the telephone. The TIP feedback provides:

☐ Awareness of potential gaps in a person's international competence.

☐ Linkage to individual roles, required working style and appropriate attitudes and approaches.

☐ The rationale for development and initial action steps for gap closing.

The ten WorldWork competencies and their associated dimensions are defined as follows[2].

1 Openness

To be effective when operating in a global business environment, it is necessary to be open to the way your international partners think and behave. Openness comprises three dimensions – new thinking, welcoming strangers and acceptance.

People who are open tend to be receptive to new ideas and are keen to build relationships with people different from themselves. They also accept the way others do things, even when attitudes and behaviours are very different from their own.

2 Flexibility

An important element of adapting successfully to an unfamiliar environment is the ability to change behaviour and to modify assumptions to work more effectively with people from the new cultural setting. Such flexibility comprises three dimensions – flexible behaviour, flexible judgement and a willingness to learn languages.

At a simple level, behaviours that show good manners and respect for other people vary considerably from one country to another and if a visitor is unable to change his or her behaviour, misunderstandings or offence can easily be caused. At a deeper level, those who are flexible can also use each experience of people from a different culture to question assumptions and modify stereotypes about how they operate. Moreover, to learn and use the language of a host country is a clear demonstration of the wish to adapt to the new culture.

3 Personal autonomy

When working with international partners, especially if they are from countries with cultures unlike your own, it is easy to lose focus and a clear sense of direction. Those partners may have very different priorities, see different things as important and want to achieve different goals. It is easy to find your own personal autonomy becoming diluted or compromised. Personal autonomy comprises two dimensions – inner purpose and a focus on goals.

[2] © WorldWork 2002, The WorldWork Partnership, 6 Porter Street, London W1U 6DD Tel: +44 (0)20 7486 9844

Personal values and beliefs provide individuals with a consistency or inner purpose, like a gyroscope that enables them to keep their balance when dealing with unfamiliar circumstances or when facing pressures that might make them question their own judgement or sense of worth. Such individuals must also retain their determination to focus on goals associated with their professional assignments, even when, in certain cultural contexts, it is both difficult and stressful to do so.

4 Emotional strength

Being surrounded by people whose behaviours, habits, values and customs are unfamiliar can be draining and stressful. To learn and make progress in such an environment it is necessary to have a certain emotional strength. This comprises three dimensions – resilience, a coping mechanism and a spirit of adventure.

A certain resilience in attitude when immersed in an unfamiliar cultural setting is critical, particularly as gaffes or inappropriate behaviour are inevitable and this in turn could lead to embarrassment, isolation or stress. To learn and progress in such a situation, therefore, requires not only a readiness to experiment but also an ability to bounce back when things go wrong. The stress of living and working in a new cultural setting also requires a well-developed coping ability, whether through physical exercise, relaxation or relying on friends or family for social support. A spirit of adventure is about searching out and enjoying new experiences, even if they are unpredictable and outside the normal scope of your competence.

5 Perceptiveness

When people communicate with each other, only some of the understanding comes directly from the meaning of the words spoken. Often the words will have hidden meanings, which arise from a shared history and culture. Colleagues and business partners will be able to read between the lines to understand the full meaning but it will be much less apparent to outsiders. An even more important element of understanding comes from the interpretation of subtle aspects of the speaker's tone of voice, body movements, facial expressions and eye contact. In our own cultural setting, we all make these interpretations at a sub-conscious level but a set of clues which indicate one thing in one setting, may mean something quite different in another. People with perceptiveness pay attention to these verbal and non-verbal cues when communicating, and quickly learn to interpret them in the context of other cultures. Such perceptiveness comprises two dimensions – being attuned and having reflected awareness.

People who are 'attuned' are focused on observing other people's demeanour and behaviour to better understand what they might be thinking or feeling. Those who have reflected awareness are attentive to how their own behaviour may be perceived, interpreted and evaluated by others.

6 Listening orientation

The ability to focus on another person and really pay attention to what they are saying and communicating is a vital business skill in any setting. In the face of language and cultural barriers, mutual understanding with international partners can only be achieved by an active listening strategy. Active listening is based on the understanding that mutual comprehension and common agreement at an international level is a special challenge. Even when the simplest of words are understood across cultures in a common language, they carry different associations and meanings that can create misunderstandings and reduce trust. Active listening is a proactive strategy that aims to check and clarify by paraphrasing and exploring the words that they use and the meaning they attach to them, rather than to assume understanding of others.

7 Transparency

Conveying information and communicating intentions clearly in an international context is a particular challenge for both native and non-native speakers of English. Simple messages conveyed with the best of intentions often lead to misunderstanding and even mistrust. One key skill for any speaker anxious to minimize the danger of miscommunication is transparency, which can be described as a lower risk and more explicit mode of communication. 'Transparency' has two key components – clarity of communication and exposure of intentions.

Native speakers of English and non-native speakers who have reached a high degree of fluency in the language, are often unaware how difficult their less fluent, non-native-speaking business partners find it to understand and process their natural style of delivery. Some are able to adapt their use of English to meet the needs of non-native-speaking partners. They achieve this by adopting where necessary a 'low risk' use of English, involving words, phrases and a style of delivery which are in little danger of being misunderstood. Regardless of their fluency in the language, effective communicators in English are also aware that to build and maintain trust in an international context, they need to ensure that their intentions are signalled clearly and explicitly.

8 Culture knowledge

There are special challenges involved in transferring our professional skills to working with international partners whose values, attitudes and style are very different from our own. We can often break trust and cause offence by acting normally. There is often a gap between our intentions, which are often positive, and the negative impact we unknowingly have on others. One of the key competencies for reducing or repairing this gap is cultural knowledge. This can be seen in terms of two dimensions – valuing differences and information gathering.

Valuing differences is about sensitivity to how people see the world differently, a desire to explore what the benefit of a different perspective may be and also a keenness to communicate respect for such diversity to the international partners involved. Such respect is not possible without the basic skills and motivation necessary to find out about a specific cultural context.

9 Influencing

One of the great challenges of working in an international context is to get others to follow you, despite the cultural and linguistic gaps that need to be bridged on the way. The ability to influence people internationally comprises three dimensions – rapport, range of styles and sensitivity to context.

Building a sense of rapport with key international partners at a personal level through building common ground and winning trust, is essential for a productive working relationship. It helps take the sting out of the inevitable misunderstandings that arise when managing tasks across cultures and/or at a distance. However, rapport alone is only a beginning. To lead your partners in the direction required, and with their potentially very different motivations and values in mind, it is necessary to draw on a range of styles of working. Does the cultural context favour a fairly hard sell based on business benefits, for example, or a lower trust building style based on the importance of a long-term relationship? Finally, any attempt to influence requires a sensitivity to context within organizations, particularly the cultural variables affecting decision making and distribution of power.

10 Synergy

Problem solving in a multicultural context is fraught with difficulty, but provides the opportunity for more creative and effective outcomes. This will not happen by chance. It requires a careful and systematic approach to ensure that the different cultural perspectives are not suppressed, but are properly understood and used in the problem-solving process. This approach to create synergy can be described as creating new alternatives.

A WORD ON TECHNOLOGY

Culture also affects people's acceptance and use of technology. It is therefore important to pay close attention to this aspect in terms of progressing delivery of complex integration projects, and the design and implementation of the end product, the business processes and the supporting technology.

Today, many integration projects need to be managed over distance. Teams of developers are rarely located in the same place and frequently the implementation demands roll-out to multiple sites. Moreover, with the growth of home-working and the coming of age of offshore software development, the old style of management – walking the shop floor – has become impossible and irrelevant.

This creates two stresses – an increased need to communicate and a higher reliance on technology, rather than personal presence to deliver direction and give leadership. Under these circumstances, the demands on leadership are high. To be successful, the project manager or program director must be able to communicate so clearly, that even when he or she is not present or is unavailable, the team can second-guess his or her decisions.

The more common methods of collaborating over distance – the telephone/teleconference, fax, e-mail and videoconference – pose some risks to the effectiveness of the communication. This can be particularly true where cultural differences between co-workers are already in play, since contextual/non-verbal information surrounding the communication will have been removed to some degree, even with videoconferencing.

To create an atmosphere of universal acceptance of change, even continuous improvement, managers must make it easy for teams to work together. More than this, they must make it easy for business managers and users to follow the development process and use the delivered product with minimum disruption.

The use of technology has developed. From the point of merely aiding mechanistic organizations, where the primary use was automation and deskilling of the workforce, technology now delivers systems that augment workforce skills and knowledge and automates where it makes sense. This is a move to empower the workforce and to allow management to draw upon workforce capabilities to service the customer in new and flexible ways. This empowerment must take account of the issues raised by these cultural dimensions of power distance, uncertainty avoidance and personal achievement versus group benefit. With careful forethought, both basic technology design and implementation programs can be modelled to facilitate the acceptance of change instead of trying to crush opposition.

SUMMARY

1 The cultural issues affecting team dynamics should not be underestimated. A key factor in the success of any complex integration program will depend heavily on the relationship between fellow workers as they proceed towards a common goal.

2 Once the people issues associated with creating an integrated business are settled, organizations can move on to think about how technology can aid integration. Organizations that skip straight to the technology are missing the point and stand to be sorely disappointed by the fruits of their attempts at business re-engineering.

3 If the technology is joined up, but the people are not (i.e. changes in people's attitudes and job roles have not been considered and addressed), true integration will not be achieved.

4 In a global business environment, which depends increasingly on the collaboration of remote teams even across multiple companies, interpersonal skills and an appreciation of different cultures and working habits are becoming essential.

5 Managers wishing to harness cross-cultural teams, whether these are inter-department, inter-company, inter-region, or international, must take responsibility for identifying interpersonal skills gaps and potential attitudinal problems. They should tackle these by clearly communicating the company's new objectives, and through a formal program of education and retraining.

6 Cultural differences can and need to be assessed at all levels, from organizational to personal.

7 Relationships at all levels are built on trust. Understanding culture allows trust to be built more effectively and more rapidly.

PART 3

TECHNOLOGY INTEGRATION

CHAPTER 8

CONTINUOUS LEGACY

INTRODUCTION

Organizations adopt the right mind-set for integration by identifying the ways in which they want the business to change and then rethinking the role that will be played by people as the company remoulds itself. Then it is time to consider the extent to which technology can help.

Technology clearly has a fundamental role to play in integrating a company's business processes and it has advanced to a point where a great deal more is possible than ever before. However, it is not without its limitations. Organizations need to be careful that they do not over-extend their expectations beyond what is feasible or find themselves entering a cul-de-sac which they cannot reverse out of later.

One of the most substantial developments of the last decade has been the simple emergence of common, accepted, open standards, which enable any user, device, or system to communicate in the fullest sense of the word. This is having a profound effect on how organizations plan their IT strategies.

Companies are no longer restricted in their business creativity by legacy systems and incompatible applications. They have the freedom to connect diverse networks of users so that these can work together on a range of business processes, wherever they happen to be. Co-workers do not even have to work for the same company to benefit.

How easy is it to exploit this new way of working to commercial advantage? Technologically, what is involved? Does it, for example, require old systems to be thrown out in favour of new, more modern computing methods?

In this section of the book, the considerable technological challenges involved when companies attempt to embrace new business processes and the new systems to support them are explored in the light of the developments in IT and communications.

Here are just some of the challenges you may be wrestling with in your attempts to marry your more traditional IT infrastructure with the type of IT architecture demanded by today's business requirements:

☐ Large organizations need to connect their internal structure and functions to externally valuable processes that maximize their competitive strengths.

☐ Smaller organizations need to become connected as outsourcing of non-core activities becomes the norm, in order to offer their value in focused areas.

☐ Back-office legacy functionality needs to be maintained and reapplied in support of the new front-office value propositions.

☐ The shift to support online multimedia interactive processes (as opposed to off-line, function-centric support) primarily through data integration.

☐ The need to support and proactively take part in continuous processes or value chains, which lie across the enterprise and require integration with other enterprises and users.

☐ The provision and management of an increasing number of users and presentation formats, covering everything from PCs and mobile phones to interactive television (iTV).

☐ The move from content to transaction as the true value in the new processes, imposing needs to provide, authenticate and audit transactional actions.

☐ The need to do things fast, at minimal cost or impact to the rest of the enterprise, remaining flexible and uncommitted to any single technology.

☐ Above all, the need to support continuous change, carried out rapidly and cost-effectively to address the constantly changing and increasingly volatile external marketplace.

Any one of these is a significant challenge in its own right. Add to this the need to both put new technologies in place and support old systems' functionality, simultaneously and without disruption, and the challenge intensifies.

If this sounds like a series of insurmountable hurdles, it may be so with the technology and architectures that organizations have been working with to date. However, consider the argument that the only effective way of rising to the challenges of the new world of externally facing communications, is to refocus IT investments at an architectural rather than a system or application-specific level. It is only by doing this that companies stand to achieve the flexibility and responsiveness that they now require. Predictability and rigidity are out; today's energies must be devoted to process rather than function.

Enlightened companies are already making this their goal for joined-up systems. They have begun to recognize that the old way of doing things does not buy them the speed to market required to keep them ahead of the competition. Instead of being able to predict future market trends and knock up applications to support this in record time, forward-thinking organizations are investing at a technology infrastructure level, enabling them to respond to new market opportunities on an almost ad hoc basis – creating processes in real time as new market drivers emerge.

Technologically, this is demanding and this will be explored in detail in Chapters 10 and 11. In this chapter and Chapter 9, the role played by legacy systems in the modern IT environment is examined. Most sizeable organizations are still challenged by the need to match up old, yet trusted mainframes with the latest technology to fulfil new market demands while protecting previous investments. Does the new world of the internet and extended supply chain still have a use for legacy systems and, if so, how can you establish what that use will be?

Legacy systems did not stop with the mainframe era. From mini-computers to 'open systems', to desktop computing and now internet-based, pervasive computing, IT departments have found themselves amassing new 'legacies' at every stage. How can companies harmonize these disparate systems to meet business challenges and at what point (if ever) will we see the end of legacy systems?

LEGACY SYSTEMS: WHAT ARE THEY AND WHAT IS THEIR ROLE TODAY?

Let's start by challenging the term 'legacy', which is a rather negative way of viewing a current business asset. 'Legacy' sounds as though its usefulness is past. Those who become caught up in the connotations of legacy may be too concerned with the limitations of their older systems. They should focus on what these systems still offer them. After all, no one would hang on to these systems if they were redundant.

Legacy systems, particularly those based on mainframes, are considered by many IT people to be the most stable and reliable systems they have. They have a strong track record, the internal IT people understand them and know how to manage them and they support long-established, core, repetitive business processes, rarely needing to be changed. In short, everything we seek from new systems, except flexibility. Organizations, therefore, divest themselves of these prized assets at their peril.

Furthermore, legacy systems represent a company's differentiation. They contain the core of the business – financial data, sales data, staff data, information on how the business is performing and what it needs to do in future. They provide a depth and richness that no new, process-based applications could claim to match.

The challenge is to retain all that is good and valuable about these systems, yet connect these assets into new world applications. The two can and must co-exist. Imagining that they somehow compete and that one is better than the other is to miss the point.

True, as stand-alone systems, older machines would not be able to do half the things that companies need them to today. They are usually constructed with data and function too tightly integrated, for example, which jars with any desire for greater flexibility of working. Nevertheless, legacy systems rarely function in isolation anymore, which means their perceived limitations are misplaced. Since today's legacy systems typically form part of a wider patchwork of supporting IT systems, their limitations can be addressed – compensated for – within the infrastructure as a whole.

A useful way to differentiate between the role of legacy systems and that played by more modern applications, is provided by the terms 'front office' and 'back office'. These are relatively modern terms. Back office generally refers to legacy applications and indicates systems whose role is to support internal functions. Therefore, it does not really matter if these systems are proprietary, provided they are standardized across the parts of the organization that use them. 'Front-office' applications, on the other hand, tend to deal with more specific business functions and often involve connectivity to the external world.

Think of your company's complete IT infrastructure as an integrated transport system. In this context, legacy systems (back-office applications such as Enterprise Resource Planning) can be seen as a rail system – privately owned and carrying pre-defined quantities of traffic to predetermined destinations at pre-defined times. Elsewhere in the system there are roads, providing more flexibility in how and when they are used, but creating chaos because of their lack of predictability. It is not possible and does not make sense to run the traffic from one transport system on the other. Both have their place and to be successful means understanding how to balance conflicting requirements with capabilities.

Appreciate and accept the difference between the relative roles and merits of front- and back-office functionality. This will enable you to maintain all that is good and worthy about your existing, reliable legacy systems once you enter an architecture-based integration model. You will be able to address the demands of the fast-moving marketplace, using open standards provided by the internet and application integration protocols, such as XML (which allow disparate enterprises to communicate and share data), but you will not have to part with systems that you have invested heavily in and which underpin your whole business.

This gives companies a whole new freedom. They no longer need to feel pressurised to change their legacy systems to integrate them with more current and largely external business demands. On the contrary, legacy systems generally should be treated as stable systems to be left alone, with the rapid process changes created at a front-office level, where newer and more flexible technology can be used.

MULTIPLE LEGACIES

Nevertheless, it is probable that you will have multiple legacy systems across your organization and not all of these will be appropriate for the new, flexible IT infrastructure you aim to build. Consequently, how do you assess the value of your various legacy systems and establish their role in your new architecture?

It is no mean feat to determine the business value of legacy systems when companies have tens or hundreds of these older machines. They may run different business applications in different departments and probably spread across different geographical locations. Achieving an overview is just the first step. Only with a clear picture of these assets, can an IT department decide what is of genuine business value, with a long-term future.

There are three main factors to consider when planning and delivering an integration program – people, process and technology. When establishing the value of legacy systems, you must take these same three factors into account. You need to understand, for example, who needs to use the systems, what for, and what data will be involved. An additional factor to consider is frequency of change. If the demands placed on a legacy system are likely to change frequently and rapidly in future, you may have no choice but to consider a technology refresh and replace the system in question.

DO THE ORIGINAL PURPOSES OF LEGACY SYSTEMS OFFER ANY CLUES?

One way to establish the value of legacy systems in any future paradigm is to consider their original purpose.

The earliest computer systems were designed to reflect the office environment at the time and this was largely organized into departments, each with their own tasks and filing cabinets. Computer systems were set up without questioning these business models, to simply capture and automate existing tasks.

Then, the work being computerized tended to be numerical in nature, such as automating purchasing functions. Mainframes provided the computational power – typically via single machines in isolated data centres, run by experts, and with no direct touch by the end users (many IT managers wish we could revert to those days!). Changes to systems were rare, and this was acceptable, since the processes that had been computerized were long established, stable and predictable.

However, the machines were expensive and it was common for systems' processing time to be shared across similar tasks for multiple parties. In retrospect, this could be seen as an early iteration of managed services provision (MSP).

Gradually, companies began asking the machines to perform increasingly complex tasks. Before long departments, for example, accounts, were given direct connections, using terminals or 'green screens' that enabled them to perform basic queries. The user interfaces had been made intelligible enough for someone other than a technician to be able to use, paving the way for the later development of the true GUI (Graphical User Interface).

The next significant leap came in the early 1980s, when the scientific/academic world came up with the notion of departmental computing, employing 'mini-computers', which could be applied to specific tasks without sharing processing power with other applications. Freed from the constraints of sharing one set of resources with other applications, users had more flexibility in the way they used the machines; they did not have to wait in line to carry out their tasks. This era also heralded the introduction of the first networks – resources began to be shared across multiple computer systems, which were not interdependent.

The natural progression from this point was to bring adaptability to an individual level, empowering each user to work on their own tasks at their own pace on their own machines. This is where the desktop PC made its appearance.

Nevertheless, there was a substantial difference between the early view of desktop computing in the late 1980s and the vision of the PC in the early 1990s, during which time the industry experienced a mind shift in how it regarded computing. This mind shift holds an important lesson for the issues that many organizations face today.

IT IS NOT PERSONAL BUT NETWORKED PRODUCTIVITY THAT MATTERS

In 1988, the vision of desktop computing involved users empowered to work on a personal level, in relative isolation, solving individual problems. The move away from shared resources towards individual working patterns was considered to be a leap forward rather than a step backwards. Little thought was given to the role that the PC would play in the enterprise as a whole. In short, PCs were used to solve isolated problems and were not properly integrated into the company network.

By 1993, things had moved on somewhat and the industry had come to realize that a more important aspect of empowering users was to enable them to be productive on both a personal and group level – allowing co-workers to communicate and share knowledge electronically. Organizations began to see the PC's role as part of the business's aims. The same lesson is now being learned with the internet – that its real usefulness is in the wider connectivity and knowledge sharing it allows, not in its ability to support isolated websites or processes.

This heralded the ascension of 'standards' up the IT agenda. The realization dawned that the importance of IT was not in the computing, but in the information, which became more valuable when shared and communicated. When computing was primarily back-office based, standards mattered far less. Organizations could pick a platform and, if all the computers serving that part of the business followed the same rules, operations would not be hindered much by the existence of other, non-compatible systems.

Yet, as the model of departmental computing gave way to matrix models of working, which extended beyond single departments to other parts of the enterprise, the issue of standard means of communications between disparate systems began to raise its head. With the rise of e-mail from 1995 onwards, standards became even more important – the rigid procedures of the past were breaking down and people were starting to work over e-mail. Today, when businesses ask themselves whether they are 'e-business' ready enterprises or not, they should consider whether they could permit e-mail to be turned off. If the answer is no, they are an e-player – no question about it.

The internet was the final stage in arriving where we are now. It introduced the magic ingredient for the sharing of knowledge and resources, inexpensively and increasingly interactively. This applies both internally and externally. What is the internet, after all, if not a standards-based communications infrastructure that seeks to overcome many of the problems embroiled with legacy systems? It allows multiple, disparate systems to be connected so that they can communicate with each other.

However, the lessons learnt during the early years of the PC must be applied to the exploitation of the internet age. Many enterprises are already making the mistake of treating 'e'-based projects on a one-by-one basis, to answer a particular departmental need, exactly as they did with the PC. This will turn out to be as expensive and time consuming as in the early 1990s, when many of the isolated investments in PCs had to be replaced with a common architecture once the true role and value of the technology were recognized.

SUMMARY

1   Many legacy systems still offer high levels of value to companies. They encompass years of investment and improvement, they are stable and robust and contain a company's most intimate and valuable corporate data – its crown jewels.

2   Organizations that attempt to replace these highly reliable systems with something more modern and 'open' have missed the point. It is more important for back-office systems to be reliable and secure, than highly functional and modern.

3   Versatility, functionality and advanced integration should take place at a front-office level, leaving legacy systems to do what they have always done – store and process data securely, at a low level.

4   Connectivity, communication and interaction are the essential aspects of the internet revolution. Organizations that exploit web technology on a departmental or website-specific basis are making the same mistake as the early adopters of the PC.

CHAPTER 9

CONNECTING THE UNCONNECTABLE

INTRODUCTION

The internet is making many things possible in technology terms, yet it is creating some phenomenal business challenges for organizations across the world, regardless of their market focus. The authority of doctors is challenged as patients attend their daily surgeries armed with research from the internet, for example. Sales assistants are challenged as customers begin to demand better terms, equipped with competitive knowledge on current market values.

How can the right meld of legacy and new, customer-facing applications help organizations to square up to these challenges? Half the battle is recognizing that we have arrived at this point – customers today are intelligent and have more power and more choice. The challenge is how to respond to this.

USING IT TO BECOME MORE RESPONSIVE TO MARKET TRENDS

If we look at where we have come from, we begin to get a better idea of where we need to go next.

Organizations had automated simple, existing business functions in the early days of computing and they soon began to look for other ways that computer systems could make them more efficient – by stripping costs from their operations and making staff more efficient.

Before long, business managers' expectations started to rise, causing them to demand a tangible contribution to the business from their IT systems. Companies sought to remove any duplication of effort from their operations. They used computers to handle data strategically and to help with efficiency and resource planning, as has been seen over the years through the growing sophistication of Enterprise Resource Planning (ERP) systems.

Initially applied at a departmental level, resource planning systems gradually expanded in scope, to streamline business processes across an enterprise, using a complex blend of accounts, materials and staff data. Using front-end tools, such as business intelligence/ reporting applications, organizations have gone on to use this sophisticated data to build profiles of their business, identifying hot spots and weak spots, past and future.

Taking this a stage further, using increasingly sophisticated front-end applications software, organizations are now able to analyze their business by customer, using this business intelligence strategically to market existing and new products and services to their clients, based on previous buying habits and indicated preferences.

From a technology perspective, this evolution of business needs has placed huge demands on companies' IT systems. In the days of back-end number crunching, systems could be left to do their thing, with performance and reliability the only factors of real importance. Now IT is intimately involved with people and business processes. Its performance is an extremely visible element of business success.

However, as the business becomes more involved with defining its needs from IT systems, insisting that these systems contribute proactively to the business's performance, the demands on IT managers intensify. It is not enough to be able to empower workers or groups of workers operating in isolation. The emphasis is on ensuring that valuable commercial data is available in a robust, up-to-date, single central source, to be accessed by anyone who needs it. This places a resounding emphasis on efficient, secure communications and interoperability of disparate systems.

Moreover, it does not stop there. As organizations look beyond their own companies for the next level of business efficiencies, enhanced competitive edge and superior customer service, these open communications must now extend outwards.

THE WAY FORWARD

In 1997, Cap Gemini (now Cap Gemini Ernst & Young), established a business model to define the next stage of business and technology models beyond ERP, with the purpose of projecting the likely impact of technology-enabled business change. By analyzing past patterns of change in response to changing technology capabilities and comparing with future technology capabilities, a pattern could be identified. The result allowed a prediction to be made about future business models, based on a business/technology hybrid.

The premise was that the next business model would be built around the use of networks in order to extend resource planning outside the current boundaries of the enterprise. This conceptual business model, originally christened Network Resource Planning (NRP), defined an 'adaptive architecture' – one which allows for much flexibility and almost instantaneous support of new business processes, which can be put in place in response to new business opportunities as these emerge.

It is worth examining the progression of business models that led to this conclusion, and to the subsequent development of thinking about Dynamic Responsive Processes (DRP). The conclusions, now borne out in the early adopter market, led to the creation of the term 'adaptive enterprise' (coined by Cap Gemini Ernst & Young). This describes a business which has grasped and implemented IT and cultural change to take advantage of the increasingly more volatile, external market conditions that the internet, and in particular the world wide web, has created.

Adaptive enterprises can rapidly create solutions in response to new opportunities emerging in the ecosystem (i.e. the marketplace). They can implement these in their businesses by the rapid building of processes in the front office, using stable connections via an overriding IT architecture to connect to their back-office capabilities. This concept is shown in Figure 9.1. (We will return to this topic in more detail in Chapter 10.)

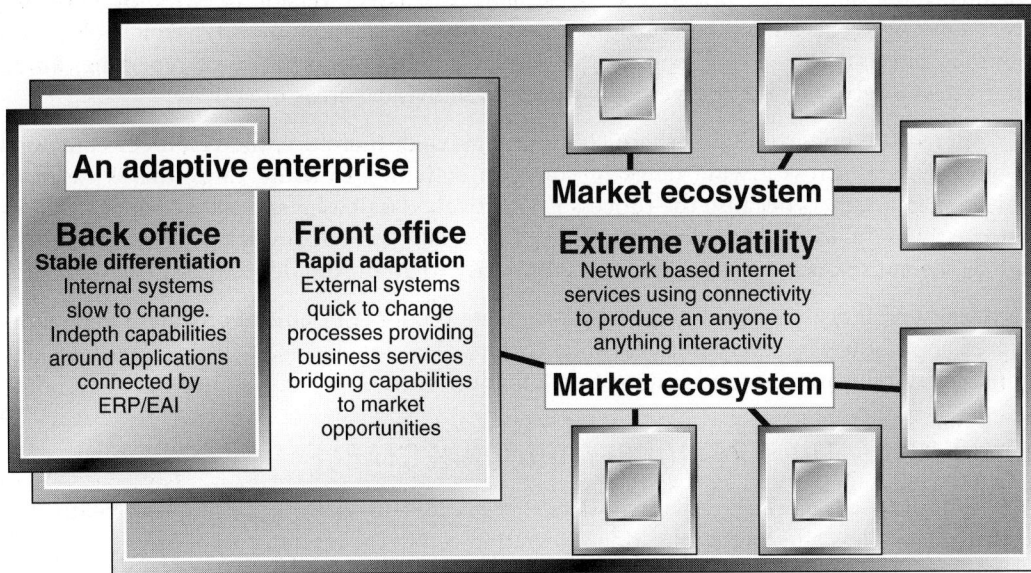

FIGURE 9.1: An adaptive enterprise

THE GROWTH IN COLLABORATION

In Chapter 8, we sought to identify the ideal role for legacy systems in the new world of externally facing communications and systems integration. To make this process easier, we suggested looking at those systems' original purpose to help determine where their true value lay. At this point, it is useful to revisit other significant changes that our industry has been through, since there are important lessons to be learned from past mistakes. One of the most relevant of these lessons concerns the role of collaborative computing.

The arrival of affordable, networked personal computers in the early 1990s allowed organizations to think in terms of collaborative/work group computing for the first time. Teams of workers had the flexibility to use their own applications for their own purposes but, instead of working in isolation, they could now share data (knowledge) with colleagues.

As a result, suites of applications could be used to link together the various, previously isolated functions in an area of the business, such as manufacturing, to allow a complete picture and, most importantly, optimization of the activity. The capability to plan and use all the resources in a manufacturing operation in a coherent manner by sharing and communicating common data between the functions was called Manufacturing Resource Planning or MRP.

In other industries, similar approaches to core areas were adopted and still form the basis of several valuable business models, for instance Supply Chain Management (SCM) or even, some would argue, Customer Relationship Management (CRM). Whatever the title, it all comes down to connecting and facilitating data between various functions in a common activity area to improve overall competitiveness.

AN ENTERPRISE-WIDE PERSPECTIVE

As the various parts of a business became transformed in their effectiveness, the spotlight shifted to the overall efficiency of the entire enterprise. The technology of networking delivered more and so the possibilities of supporting a larger version of MRP, covering the entire enterprise, became more obvious. Hence the progression to ERP, which offered a common data integration between all the activities, with the promise of repeating, on an enterprise-wide basis, the improvements gained in individual areas of activity.

ERP offered the opportunity to share common data and, therefore, the resources contained within the data, across a wide range of common activities. In some cases, this is easier to achieve than in others because the process is effectively data-based and self-contained. This is particularly useful for financial information, but when applied to complex process integration, such as the entire business value chain, it is less easy to attain the desired results.

It is asking a great deal to expect a single ERP software vendor to be able to provide, individually-tailored applications for every business area. Nevertheless, the legacy of ERP is important and forms a vital foundation around common data that can be used to support new areas.

CONNECTING THE PREVIOUSLY UNCONNECTABLE

The ability to accomplish effective data integration in core activities, but with the consequence of less effective application integration, led to the opening up of proprietary ERP technology to allow other applications to be integrated to the data flow. This new technique, known as Enterprise Application Integration (EAI), was pioneered by a number of new suppliers such as SeeBeyond and Mercator, who offered tool-kits and adapters to allow other non-ERP applications to be integrated to the original ERP implementation.

Best-of-breed and niche applications could now be selected to extend coverage to individual business functions or existing legacy applications with value, while still maintaining the benefits of integrated data. EAI offered the capability to align applications to the various parts of the business process and to provide a common data flow. This technique lowered the cost, increased the coverage of the common data integration model and, if an investment was made in workflow, could achieve a highly effective process.

In some businesses, the cost and time taken to achieve this has diminishing returns, making the final steps unattractive. A further complication is the degree to which increasing integration efficiency is offset by increasing inflexibility. At a time when the impact of the internet was starting to be appreciated, this was a contributing factor to place further investment in integration on hold.

Application integration remained a costly, yet highly desirable goal to increase business effectiveness. This was especially true in business functions that needed to coordinate activities, which lay at least partially outside the enterprise, but would benefit from cohesive interaction between a number of activities or tasks.

EXTERNAL COLLABORATION – LETTING THE TASK DRIVE THE PROCESS

A task-driven environment is described as one where the activity is not logically structured to fit within an existing set of applications. Obvious examples of this have been the recent breed of CRM and SCM applications. Here, the task is defined by external factors and circumstances and must be capable of responding to these. A customer has a requirement and should not care that the internal applications require the information to be processed.

Task-oriented working (TOW), as we might call this, is the natural development of the promised collaborative working models that started to appear with the PC in the early 1990s. Unfortunately, it does not address the key question of a genuinely interactive process that lies across the enterprise, with external clients or suppliers requiring access. Furthermore, it is not only a matter of access, it is also a matter of process integration between their systems. Process integration has become the new goal for efficient working.

Before the internet and its associated technologies, it was literally unworkable to even consider this. It would mean all parties in a business relationship undertaking to use the same ERP vendor or entering into the joint development of an EAI-based process (which would be expensive and limiting).

The only successful answer for connecting one company's processes to another lay in certain specialized, high value/throughput areas, which could justify Electronic Data Interchange (EDI), a costly interpretation of this requirement based purely on data integration.

EDI requires all members of a specified value chain or process to agree to adopt a data format for communicating among themselves. The simple data protocol covered in the various EDI standards requires an extensive business model to be put in place. Service organizations acting as third-party agents to the members supply this.

While high-volume manufacturing in the automotive industry can and does benefit from EDI, it is far removed from the goal of application integration, let alone the flexibility that process integration provides. Consequently, the goal of the adaptive architecture business model was to determine exactly the business requirements and benefits for an extended process model. This model would be used to join internal business divisions to provide new value to the integrated market proposition, as much as to join and connect customers, suppliers and partners in new external value chains and propositions.

EMBRACING THE INTERNET

The new technologies of the internet were the key factors underpinning the proposal of an adaptive architecture. These offered a common communication infrastructure both internally and externally, together with the common desktop display of the browser, which could be used by anyone, regardless of other applications and systems.

This is the ability to be 'reactive' to the fast-changing business world, to capitalize on customer, supplier, product, or even external changes, which occur at an increasing rate making it impossible to predict them and develop applications and processes proactively.

When considering this new model, now recognizably emerging as business exchanges, consumer portals and other so-called e-business models, it soon became apparent that the static fixed nature of business value chains (imposed by the limitations of current communications) would rapidly dissolve. Competitive advantage would lie with obtaining the optimum chain at the critical moment, making value exist in the speed with which the response could be generated, not only in the capability to communicate and negotiate online interactively.

Bill Gates subsequently called this 'doing business at the speed of thought', and, along with other strategic thinkers, redefined competitive advantage as resting with the speed in which relationships could be exploited. Sun Microsystems' CEO, Scott NcNealy, defines success as belonging to the person who dies with the most valuable contacts in their address book, believing that knowing and using the market ecosystem is driven from relationships.

Given the overall pace of change that the 'e' factor is bringing, it seemed inevitable that this would be a requirement of market leaders within a very short time frame. In fact, the only amendment to the original predictions has been to collapse the time period for the adoption of these new business models from five to three years, as the pressure to embrace the new has accelerated the rate of adoption.

This line of thought led to a further change to the adaptive architecture business model in order to cover the advantage described as 'velocity'. This factor has to seamlessly join with the adaptive architecture model, possibly as it is being rolled out within an enterprise.

The new processes have to use business intelligence, to decide upon the response dynamically, at machine speed and without the need for human intervention (though possibly with the need for human approval). Again, this is already a recognized approach to fast-moving business problems where speed in itself is a requirement for success.

The challenge is to use the new technology to provide dynamic responsive processes and, in so doing, to define what knowledge would be required to drive which capabilities within the processes. This means drawing together all the parts of past, current and new technology in a single architecture, delivered by new methods and valued in a different way, to support an increasingly dynamic business model. The technology industry identifies this model generically as 'grid' computing, connected together through 'boundary-less networking' to respond efficiently to 'events', rather than being reliant on predetermined processes.

SUMMARY

1   As companies seek to be ever more agile and responsive to the fast-changing demands of the marketplace, the marriage of the old and new becomes paramount.

2   ERP and EAI have taken us much of the way there but only internally.

3   Now the challenge has stepped up a gear, becoming external. It requires organizations to become even more flexible and agile as they attempt to be prepared for any new opportunity the market may throw up.

4   The emphasis is on how back- and front-office systems are joined to a standards-dominated external marketplace, not only on how they need to be joined together.

5   Increasingly, the external requirement makes up the driver, definer and area of delivery for new IT projects.

6   The solution to bring the old and new worlds of IT together lies in a company's IT architecture. If organizations want to remain free of further legacy problems, the investment they need to make is in the platforms that bridge one system to another, both internally and externally, rather than in the systems themselves.

CHAPTER 10

THE IMPORTANCE
OF ARCHITECTURE

INTRODUCTION

Organizations today seek greater flexibility from their IT systems to enable them to respond more rapidly to new opportunities as they arise in the marketplace. They cannot afford to be held back by slow, rigid systems, which will not support new business processes as these are called for.

In IT terms, this translates to the need for maximum levels of connectivity and data sharing. This is changing the emphasis of IT investment and development from an application level, to an architectural level.

When the goal of IT systems or standards becomes the common good instead of the productivity of an individual user, it is no longer acceptable for everyone to have their own way of working. This is where the importance of architecture comes into play. If rules can be established at an architectural level, rather than at a system or application level, the way is paved for more collaboration to take place – that is, more interaction and, therefore, flexibility. Certainly, when companies begin to want to collaborate with other entities outside their own boundaries, having an open, flexible architecture becomes paramount.

There is a trade-off when moving to an architectural approach to IT development, particularly if building externalized capabilities at a front-office level. Organizations must sacrifice much of the customization they strived for with earlier IT systems, where applications were built or customized to suit the company's or department's individual requirements.

In an open connected world, where the objective is information sharing, bespoke development and proprietary ways of working can only stand in the way. While the use of methods such as EAI, can get a business so far in encouraging greater connectivity and collaboration internally, providing external connectivity with EAI is not a long-term, winning strategy. In the short term this works to provide a service to a limited number of external partners who all have to agree to adopt a common product from a particular vendor. This can then be connected on a back office to back office basis, but it soon becomes complicated.

The only prudent way to achieve long-term, flexible connectivity with a range of existing and future external partners is through innovation at an architectural level. Here, organizations can treat the back office, front office and internet dimensions separately and find optimum means to combine legacy systems with the new world.

DEFINING ARCHITECTURE

An architecture provides the ability to introduce widely accepted expectations concerning the functionality of processes. Applications, on the other hand, represent the delivery of unique capabilities to a limited number of dedicated users.

Think of the difference between a hotel, a house and a home. A hotel meets the general expectations of almost any occupant by following accepted rules about what is needed for overnight accommodation – a bed, a bath or shower, a telephone, a TV set, access to refreshments, and so on. It provides an agreed, basic, generic architecture. Anyone can go and stay there, knowing that their basic needs will be catered for. They may not like the décor, choice of food or the room service menu, but they will be able to sleep, wash and eat.

A house, by contrast, represents a more particular application of accommodation, with selected functionality to suit the particular lifestyle of a chosen group of users. A family house will have a minimum number of bedrooms, a garden and so on. A home, finally, is the customization of the house to provide very personalized functionality around the individual's specific use through the addition of specific features that only those users desire, such as a certain brand of music system, a particular taste in wallpaper, the addition of a conservatory, and so forth.

We can relate this analogy to the role of legacy systems, as discussed in Chapter 8, to view these within the greater scheme of an architecture. The internet is the hotel (a place for everyone to meet and use as a common environment), the front office is the house (for the general purpose of mixing a public and private life), whereas the personalization of individual users' needs is the home.

The separation of roles and use is an important point in the architectural approach to IT. The idea of having a direct entrance from a hotel into the bathroom of our homes is clearly a nonsense, yet in a very real sense that is what many enterprises have attempted to do by connecting their back-office systems directly to others via the internet. The public/private privacy issues are as apparent as the obvious mismatch in the roles of the two areas. Extending the analogy further, we should look to apply the application appropriately. The reception rooms of the house, for example, are where the public/private interfaces meet. You might invite a friend (who is staying in a hotel) to your house to enjoy a home-cooked meal (produced in a private manner in your own kitchen using your own creativity). This is the sort of model that we should be looking for when integrating public and private IT domains.

How does architecture help to achieve this? The answer lies in understanding how we have got to this point and then to recognize where we need to go next to support the current and future needs of the business.

WHERE DOES THE INTERNET FIT IN?

Before looking back, we should note that much of what is proposed today is made possible by internet technology – certainly at the level of communicating and sharing data with external parties. The internet provides an open infrastructure for process and services connectivity in the external marketplace, extending the original work that the International Standards Organization (ISO) introduced for back-office networking, on which system architectures are founded.

It is important at this stage to be clear that the internet and the worldwide web are not the same thing. It is the internet itself which represents the architecture. The worldwide web is a service for content distribution, built using open standards as part of the overall architecture of the internet. (Companies continue to discover that the internet architecture can also be exploited for specific internal services, such as intranet and extranet-based collaborations, which share knowledge and processes. These are definable as part of the front office, since their very nature is intrinsically based around sharing rapidly changing information and not on stable applications. It is rare that intranets do not contain at least some external links and, by definition, an extranet is an external/internal service.

TECHNOLOGY ARCHITECTURES: PAST AND FUTURE NEEDS

All enterprises use architectures today. Some are of a proprietary nature, comprising the software vendor's own architecture, which it uses to integrate its products together in a flexible, common manner. Others have been built in a more open manner as part of the legacy, especially in PC-based networking.

As the number and types of computers, applications, peripherals in an enterprise increased, and as the demands of both support and integration appeared as major issues, the concept of a technical architecture first emerged.

The immediate objective was to rationalize and standardize characteristics so that support staff could more readily understand similar key maintenance tasks. As the needs grew to move, at the least, data between systems (by means of tapes, discs or floppies), the need to standardize on formats and design databases around common architectural principles began to appear quietly in the corporate data centre.

A more zealous push came with the advent of networking. Initially, the architecture to support the integration of the systems was proprietary and belonged to the system manufacturer. These architectures were designed principally around the operating system and behaved accordingly, for example, IBM SNA hierarchical and synchronized, DEC peer-to-peer and opportunistic in its use of resources. The DEC model, incidentally, led to Ethernet being developed, allowing a whole generation of other systems and resources to connect.

These early beginnings showed the value of a technical architecture – to provide a consistent framework that could be used to increase the value of individual systems by allowing wider connectivity and integration around data. At this stage, the focus was around data and the resulting technical architectures were data-centric.

This trend was accelerated by the PC networking era, which introduced effective, 'open' standards, including the now universally accepted IP (Internet Protocol) initially known as TCP/IP (Transmission Control Protocol/Internet Protocol) covering the management of transport as well as Addressing Unix built on the same TCP/IP protocols and the pressure to use TCP/IP as a common architecture for networking slowly increased, with even the proprietary systems vendors such as IBM offering TCP/IP connectivity and functionality.

As the pressure for 'open' systems increased, so did the need for a widespread understanding of the interpretation of the standards to ensure that different products could be trusted to work together.

BEYOND APPLICATION-CENTRIC INTEGRATION

The ISO 7 layer model is concerned with 'application-centric' interchanges. This view has been the foundation of all technical architecture thinking until the advent of the internet, the worldwide web and the all-important browser interface.

The model is built around the transfer of data between machines, through a series of layers, to cross the network and then pass through an identical series of layers back to the application again. Crucially, the worldwide web, which is built around the browser, does not have the application at the seventh layer; its work is finished at the sixth layer of presentation. This allows any process to be presented and avoids the constraints and limitations of only being able to work through applications. This example demonstrates some of the fundamental technology changes that the internet introduces.

Technical architecture has become a vital ingredient to business adaptability as more and more integration is required to support the increasingly integrated business models. However, the integration has remained true to the data-centric or application-centric models.

Today, architecture faces new challenges. There are new technologies that have to be placed within the framework, such as mobile phones and interactive TV. Other significant changes have arrived with the technologies now available through innovation based on the conceptual capabilities of the internet and worldwide web. Finally, the definition of the role of IT within a business is changing as new business models are rapidly emerging. How should we move forward?

A NEW APPROACH

The internet calls for a different approach to architecture, since it adds an extra dimension to the connectivity most organizations now try to achieve. As discussed previously, we can think in terms of three basic conceptual levels – the back office, front office and the internet or external world. This basic structure is recognized by the major software vendors in so-called 'web services' offerings (web services is the name given to interactive process connectivity on the internet).

Organizations attempt to extend their IT systems outwards into their marketplace, to connect with those of suppliers, business partners and customers and so common rules of connectivity and process become paramount. The goal is to ensure that there is a common environment and some shared expectations about the IT transactions that will take place across these extended networks. This is where web services platforms aim to help, by providing a recognized, open way to share data and perform transactions between the diverse IT systems of multiple companies.

ARCHITECTURE VERSUS STANDARDS – WHAT IS THE RELATIONSHIP?

Where do standards fit into this picture? If we think of a standard as a collection of building blocks, the architecture defines how these will work together. Standards define the elements and formats themselves, but not how they will interact with each other in an extended process. This is where architecture comes in. This makes sense of the standards and defines how all the elements involved from systems to applications to data and processes will interact. Architecture defines the relationships and expectations around the transactions. In the case of a web service, this will apply to a transaction as it passes between one company's back-office system, front-office application and through the internet into another company's IT environment. The web services architecture must allow different software products to interact with each other, regardless of how these have been implemented by the respective companies. A tall order! However, it does work and many enterprises are already operating with processes that use a web services-based architecture.

For the IT industry and the IT departments exploiting the technology, this has been quite a cultural turn around. The top rewards were previously given for unique features which differentiated one product from another (that is, their differences rather than their support of common standards), all the major technology vendors have realized that openness is everything and now offer products that embrace this approach. Software choices are increasingly based on which products are the most 'open' around key standards. The term 'open' is a confusing one, applied both to the ability to allow interconnection and interaction around standards and to software that is supplied with source code under the terms of 'The Open Software Foundation'.

There are other advantages to tackling IT development at an architectural level. The pre-internet, application-centric approach was never intended to have to deal with external users not under an enterprise's general control. Organizations that try to adapt older technologies with the new world of the internet take risks. For instance, those that attempt to attach their back-end systems directly to the internet to improve customer service. It is no wonder that there can be substantial security breaches. What they really need to do is to employ front-office technology specifically designed for the purpose.

At an internet level, there also needs to be a shift in thinking. Organizations are ideally striving to connect people (e.g. customers, partners, suppliers and staff) to their business process and not to their website. Let them interact with your systems to get the information they need, but do not try to second-guess this and put everything on your website. Trying to make websites all-encompassing requires much extra work at your end, does not guarantee the user the experience he or she is seeking, and generally makes for a frustratingly slow site. Mixing information and interaction is more satisfying to users and delivers more value to the website operator about exactly what customers and the market are looking for.

BUSINESS VALUE LIES IN THE TRANSACTION

If we look at how the internet has developed, the premise of 'adaptive IT' for the desired new business and IT model begins to make good sense.

Although it started out as a data-centric research tool (developed primarily for the interchange of data in military-funded research and development), the potential of the internet was soon spotted by the commercial world, particularly following the advent of the concept of the worldwide web and its use of a standardized browser to display content.

There emerged a network-based intelligence, which allowed users to be connected to a universal network that handles many of the tasks previously thought of as part of an application in the ISO 7 layer architectural model.

The key was the service provided by the Universal Resource Locator (URL). The URL has taken over the location of the resources that would previously have been carried out within an application or possibly by an operating system. The ability of a URL to universally find resources, operating above the traditional network layer, together with the other features of a web server to provide content and a browser to display content in a standardized manner, changes the whole process. No longer does architecture depend solely on fixed relationships and the managed transactions of conventional 'middleware'.

The new architectural foundation for web services needs to be based on the new capability offered by internet/web/browser technology. This provides an intelligent network-based services model, allowing user-driven activities to both find information and to use processes for interaction leading to transactions.

This is happening already – the value of the first shared process, the worldwide web, has driven a global acceptance of a common set of standards. This represents a true revolution in the application of IT and one that drives new technology architectures to move beyond content, to the increased business value lying in the transaction (i.e. the interaction of the end user with the content, to create an ad hoc business process). The aim is to make this transaction the heart of the architecture, instead of holding actual content. This is crucial to the flexibility and responsiveness that today's organizations strive for. The Conclusion discusses how organizations are starting to do this.

THE ADAPTIVE ARCHITECTURE MODEL

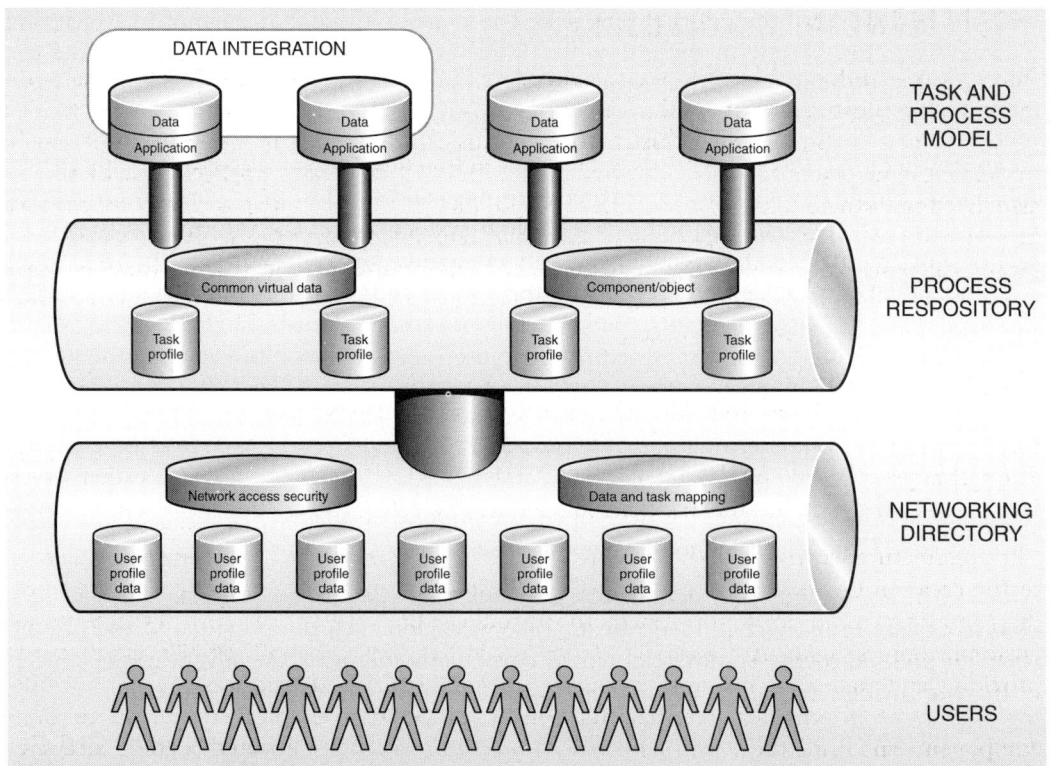

FIGURE 10.1: Adaptive architecture model

Cap Gemini Ernst & Young's 'adaptive architecture' model defines the use of web services for both external and internal transactions. It covers all aspects of back office to front office connectivity and data sharing, as well as front office to internet. It is user and process-centric, rather than application-centric, placing the emphasis on the data transaction, not the data itself.

The model focuses on the ability to identify users individually and to provide a unique management of the user to link to the required processes. Security is built into this by establishing that the tasks permitted are commensurate with the user's status and role – whether that role is a particular member of staff within the company, a customer, or a business partner. An important principle is that the user is never aware of or connected to a back-office system and, therefore, conventional security breaches of operating systems cannot be made.

This makes it possible to create value-added electronic supply chains, enhancing customer service and general business productivity, without compromising the integrity of your internal systems. The ability to interact with company data can be extended to include any user who will gain value from being part of the chain, whether a member of staff, a customer, or a supplier.

The extended network infrastructure provided by the internet uses many new technologies to achieve value-added supply chains, but all are open in the way that they integrate. This allows a choice of products and, most importantly, different enterprises are not required to use any particular product. This is the prime building block that extends the user/content model of today's worldwide web into the user/content/transaction model of web services and towards new, emerging business models.

INTELLIGENT INFRASTRUCTURES

This network infrastructure functions independently of any application or system; the infrastructure possesses a range of functions to be able to provide the necessary services. This is referred to as an 'intelligent infrastructure'. In this context, the term 'infrastructure' may be misleading and taken to be an expensive investment before any payback is achieved, as associated with the old networking infrastructure model. In an adaptive architecture context, however, infrastructure simply means 'common' technology and can be implemented on a piecemeal basis to address individual business projects, using project-based funding. Over time, these individual implementations should be linked to provide a common service capability of great value to the enterprise.

The prime capability of the intelligent infrastructure is to connect the user to the required task in a secure manner. Tasks are held in the next layer of the adaptive architecture in a way that is based on the growing use of components to provide a quick and flexible means to add capabilities. The technique is based essentially on a multiple tier architecture, able to use application servers for low-cost efficiency, but much extended in detail to create a real-time, custom task zone.

The architecture has to allow the insertion and removal of individual components in addition to the creation of processes, by joining the components together. This can be effected with drag-and-drop tools that do much to introduce the degree of both flexibility and customization sought. An adaptive architecture takes a different overall approach to providing and managing constantly changing, integrated tasks and processes in an architecture that could be internal or external. Its holistic proposition enables enterprises to build components and bring these into service in a style that guarantees repeated ongoing successful integration and reintegration of new processes as and when needed, and not only successful integration on a project level.

Finally, there is the need to connect to legacy or new applications in the current data-centric architectural manner. The data arising from a task or a process is considered an 'event' and is transferred according to best practice or established criteria within an enterprise by Enterprise Application Integration (EAI), to connect with existing legacy and ERP systems.

SUMMARY

1 An adaptive architecture seeks to combine new technologies, legacy systems and users, which have been individually applied in projects, in a complete and holistic single architecture able to use products from many different vendors as well as interconnecting with other enterprises in a secure manner.

2 Adopting this approach to architecture assists in addressing the cost factor by supporting the more rapidly changing business requirements and the challenges to budgets that this will create. Time to market is also improved, since flexibility of response will increase, you will not be locked into rewriting old applications or be hampered in your flexibility to respond to a rapidly changing market.

3 With the emphasis on standards to allow data sharing, architectural-based IT models encourage organizations to focus their talents on their core differentiation only, minimizing any reinvention of the wheel at a non-core-critical application level.

4 Concentrating development at an architectural level reduces the level of technology lock-in.

5 Do not think in terms of large one to two year systems integration programs. Focus on responsiveness and rapid paybacks for the business.

6 Aim to achieve an open, flexible IT architecture that allows you to reuse tools, resources and services developed elsewhere and that frees you from having to predict where the market is going next.

7 Think in terms of the intelligent infrastructure, define your architecture and adopt projects that move towards this goal.

8 Standards are everything. The technology challenge today is about openness, communication and interaction, not about complexity and cleverness.

9 Custom development jars with this approach, creating barriers for systems integration. If it is not critical to your competitive edge or in the back office, do not customize it.

10 Connecting with organizations that exist outside your business, such as partners, suppliers and customers, is the challenge now. The ability to pool knowledge and share resources has become more important than anything else.

11 A focus on architecture and business process, rather than function delivered through application, enables flexibility in the front office so that customer or market demands drive the business process – not the other way around.

12 Understand the difference in the business and technology requirements of the back office, front office and market ecosystems delivered via the internet. Beware of treating the internet dimension as an extension of your internal systems.

CHAPTER 11

APPROACHES TO INTEGRATION

INTRODUCTION

We have explored the value of legacy systems, examined the trends for external integration, and introduced the importance of architecture, especially with regards to adopting 'intelligent infrastructures' that enable business agility in today's challenging climate.

It is easy to paint a vision of how your systems might look in the future but it is recognized that the journey towards this vision may be fraught with practical problems. This chapter takes a more detailed look at some of the challenges involved in moving from a piecemeal, application-specific to a more integrated and adaptive approach.

KEEP THE GOAL IN MIND

When analyzing the challenges that lie ahead, it is essential to stay focused on the fundamental aims of what you are doing – that is, attempting to add value to the business by allowing processes to be supported across business functions and ultimately to provide high levels of flexibility in the way new business processes are supported.

Customer-facing systems need integration to access data related to the customer in order to fulfil a business process. The end-to-end technology infrastructure, which supports this, is now often thought of as an 'ecosystem' which may include ERP, supply chain and back-office systems. These systems may exist within or outside of the company. (See Fig. 9.1).

This all sounds desirable, but how easy is it to achieve? For many organizations, previous integration work has been approached on a piecemeal, application-to-application basis, leading to all sorts of potential hurdles. Certainly, to continue in this vein would be costly and counterproductive. Piecemeal integration does not provide the sort of flexibility that companies now need and it makes for an expensive to maintain IT environment.

Avoiding the challenge is not an option. Organizations that do not attempt to better integrate their customer-facing systems with back-end applications in a way that supports pan-enterprise business processes, risk poor execution of business processes and poor customer service. This, in a climate where the market leaders are automating everything to maximum competitive advantage.

As companies come under increasing pressure to coordinate their business in real time and to make them more responsive to their customer needs, they need to work towards a goal of end-to-end business process management. This is impossible unless processes are able to span functions and applications. Only by doing this can organizations create the necessary IT ecosystem. Indeed, the need for this integration of business processes across applications, business partners and customers was acknowledged as the top priority for CIOs (Chief Information Officer) during 2001, according to a Morgan Stanley survey.

Therefore, integration is now a key part of business strategy and not merely an item on the IT department's wish-list. Look at any major current initiative and you will see that this is true: supply chain automation; web commerce; business-to-business commerce and customer intelligence. All require new systems, which depend on data held in existing back-office systems. The result is that organizations need to consider new, flexible, future-proof integration strategies that link application and data architectures to business strategies, without the high cost of interfacing and supporting cross-application business processes.

THE NEED FOR PRAGMATISM

Nevertheless, although we advocate working towards the long-term aim of an adaptive architecture, politics, budgets or pressing business needs may not always allow you to adopt the desired approach. There may not be the time or money available to think about the future at this stage. Integration models need to relate to your own business whilst having the capability of 'integrating' to different integration models from outside the business in order to be adaptive.

Yet, this is where it becomes important to keep in mind the wider strategy of the organization. You may be under much pressure to produce short-term solutions for the business, but if these are likely to reduce future integration capability or incur higher costs in the long term, the organization should not compromise long-term strategy.

As always, it is a question of balance. Be realistic about what can be achieved and when. Even though you may try to attain an integrated, adaptive end game, there could be a good reason to take a more piecemeal, application-specific approach at some juncture. A marketing campaign may be needed to capture a sales opportunity, for example, requiring a system that cannot easily be integrated other than by tactical point-to-point interfaces. A piecemeal approach will take you further away from where you need to be as an agile organization.

LEVELS OF INTEGRATION

The goal for any organization should be to achieve an enterprise-wide view of its business. Specifically, stable and persistent data models and business processes which are generated as the customer interacts with the company, however and wherever these interactions take place.

Back-office, front-office systems and the external ecosystem need to be connected if you are to move towards an adaptive organization. In the back office, stable differentiation is required using internal systems that are relatively slow to change. This implies that technologies, such as Enterprise Application Integration (EAI), can be used to connect applications.

In the front office, rapid adaptation is needed, with systems able to change processes to provide business services in response to market opportunities. When connecting to the market ecosystem, network-based internet services are necessary.

Consider the issues of integrating applications, data and infrastructure in moving towards this future integration model. Achieving high levels of integration of business process across an enterprise will depend on high levels of integration at a data level. Indeed, the current difficulty experienced by many companies is that silos of data exist within current applications, whether back-office, supply-chain or customer systems. Application-level integration currently gives interoperability between departments and job functions, thereby providing support to an extended business process. Integration at the infrastructure level enables application integration.

Data integration

Business processes are changing and the complexity of handling business processes is increasing, particularly at the customer interface due to the types of interactions involved, the volumes of data these interactions represent and the increasing need for more information on the customer to increase the effectiveness of business processes.

For instance, channels for customer interaction have increased through the use of e-mail and the web in addition to more traditional telephone, fax and postal contact. Much of this data is captured electronically. This data, together with externally sourced data, is also accumulated into databases which can be subjected to analysis. For example, sales and customer services data can be turned into business intelligence, which can be used to drive marketing campaigns. If sales and marketing systems are well integrated, organizations can monitor the effectiveness of marketing campaigns by tracking their effects on sales.

Nonetheless, some customer systems are incapable of storing historical data, which means complex, bespoke data stores are required. These gather data for reporting purposes and can feed resulting analysis back into the sales systems. 'Upstream' data integration, through the use of data warehouses that are also used to create an aggregated view of the customer, have been used by large retailers for years. These create massive business benefits by enabling a detailed understanding of customer behaviour and preferences and thus increasing sales of products through the deployment of highly tailored marketing activities.

This approach can be costly, however, and in many cases the thirst for data volumes requires 'bleeding' edge technology and much bespoke work to achieve the levels of scalability and size required. This introduces cost and complexity into the picture – the very opposite of what today's organizations strive for. Moreover, achieving data integration through building special data analysis solutions creates a risk of reduced adaptability for the company, as singular applications are developed to manipulate the data and support business process. This can lead to new data silos, to add to those that already exist in other business areas (where systems may hold subsets and supersets of data on the same customer). If organizations want to attain any level of business agility, they must aim to reduce data silos and data replication in order to create a consistent view of customer and other data.

One way to accomplish this is through 'data bridging', an emerging capability originally offered by a few proprietary products, but now enshrined as a standard by the Open Management Group. Data bridging allows transactional and relational data to be recovered from multiple databases in response to a request, therefore allowing a task or process to have immediate access to the data required to complete the task. This data transformation, which allows real-time tasks to work with batch data produced by legacy, has profound implications for the user-centric value chain architecture and, in some cases, can negate the need for special applications, such as data warehousing.

Yet, there will be a trade-off in operational systems between achieving this connectivity and achieving the scalability and performance required where large amounts of data movement and manipulation are needed.

Application integration

Software development has evolved radically over the last 30 years. From building bespoke applications from scratch to meet specific business requirements, to using packaged applications from software vendors and relying on these to meet most core functional needs.

Nevertheless enterprise-wide application integration remains difficult since no software vendor offers a product range comprehensive enough to support the business process requirements of an entire organization.

Some vendors attempt to support the extended business process by rolling out greater functionality in their product suites, enabling organizations to better link their sales, marketing and customer services activities. In these circumstances, it could be argued that tight coupling between applications offers a better return on investment.

According to IT analyst firm Gartner, up to 40 per cent of IT budgets are spent on developing new interfaces or maintaining existing interfaces between applications and databases. Nevertheless, however extensive one vendor's product range becomes, it is unlikely it will ever satisfy all the business process needs of a whole enterprise, especially if the organization is large and multi-disciplined. Organizations will be unable to escape the need to address integration between applications from different suppliers and across organizational boundaries.

Generally speaking, in today's systems there are three main types of transactions required in any environment:

1 High-volume data manipulations carried out as overnight batch jobs to update data stores on dependent systems.

2 Workflow systems, where work items are posted from work queue to work queue.

3 Real-time transactions, such as a business query update or a deletion.

In any environment, the aim is to achieve synchronized, end-to-end business processes. Batch processes are typically high latency, costly and inflexible. Changing a batch process to a real-time process has to give some value; indeed many organizations have gone down this route to achieve faster and more expansive business processes. A business needs to achieve minimal latency. Changing the organization from mostly dependent on large batch processes to 'real time' means that data and information will become more transparent; data will be current rather than 24 hours out of date; business processes which were previously serial and often spanned operating days become more concurrent and lead to an organization possessing more actionable information that can be used immediately and in a collaborative manner.

Real standardization, allowing 'plug and play' within organizations, is only now becoming widespread. Still, some organizations do not bother, content to continue with point-to-point interfaces as a means of integration between applications – they may come unstuck, however, because sooner or later they may not be able to change quickly enough. Application networks or 'information bus architectures', commonly referred to in the marketplace as EAI make standardization possible.

EAI has emerged to give easier, standards-based integration between applications, and to enable the move towards real-time integration. The use of integration brokers to reduce the cost of developing interfaces has also reduced development costs by up to 40 per cent.[1] In addition, some companies have found that adopting an integration architecture has typically halved the effort required to develop and maintain new interfaces over point-to-point interfaces.

For example, one US retail company with 500 stores nationwide adopted an EAI architecture and went from a predominantly overnight batch architecture (for updating data throughout the company), to an integrated architecture across all its stores, pulling together all its essential business systems, including multiple legacy systems. This led to all the sales transactions nationwide being updated into the ERP systems within a fraction of the time and a Return on Investment (ROI) of over 350 per cent, due to faster and more accurate replenishment orders and reduced running costs.

EAI technology is valuable as a means of driving business process integration. Typical EAI tool-sets are able to map end-to-end processes, whether internal or shared with another organization, in isolation (or rather abstraction) from the technical integration effort. This allows the optimization – as far as is possible on the supporting technology, which of course may in part be quite old – and enables the configuration of the integration layer through technology adapters in order to bridge constituent systems such as ERP and financials.

The success of this approach depends upon sufficient adoption of integration standards. Indeed, dominant industry forces seek to adopt standards and interoperability to differentiate themselves. Yet, while innovations such as Extensible Markup Language (XML) are key to achieve standardization, the proliferation of XML schemas and the battles over which standard to adopt, for example, will ensure that complexity of integration remains high. A further complication is that integration technology needs to work in both application network environments and in point-to-point environments. It therefore needs to support a proliferation of standards, such as COM (Component Option Model), CORBA (Common Object Request Broker Architecture), J2EE (Java 2 Enterprise Edition) and XML.

Infrastructure integration

Central to the ability to create repeatable integration is the capacity to provide a range of 'services' that can be implemented repeatedly, minimizing wasteful repetition of effort through the reuse of existing components. 'Services' refer to the components or utilities commonly used by functional applications. Reusing them gives organizations faster speed to market, reduced development costs and, therefore, greater agility. Typical services that should be provided in each of these areas are:

☐ **Network services** – For example, the provision of local and wide area networks and the fulfilment of remote access requirements.

☐ **Presentation services** – For instance, HyperText Markup Language (HTML), portals, devices and desktop.

☐ **Security services** – Providing common identity, permission and isolation facilities, ensuring, for example, that organizations can enable users to log on only once to access all the applications and services they are entitled to use on the company network.

☐ **Storage services** – Enabling common support of transactions.

[1] Gartner, 'Integration Brokers: Market Vendors and Trends 2001'.

☐ **Integration services** – Providing standard transactions, for instance, a common facility for accessing various company database systems.

A number of these services can be provided by EAI products, which, as discussed, enable the transfer of data between applications in a standard way, using standard protocols and components and achieve a level of abstraction fundamental to the creation of a service. Applications written to use an EAI service do not need complex code to be built in for each interface. Instead, each application uses a standard definition and uses EAI-based services to locate the destination application, handle the transport of the data and carry out data transformations.

The more standard the services created, the greater the degree of commonality and extensibility of business process achieved. Therefore, an organization should frame its architectural requirements in terms of services, such as those outlined above, and build up a portfolio. When creating standard services, high value services should be implemented first and, if possible, should include EAI services. Implementing such a service will be more costly initially than implementing a simple interface; it will be important to frame the requirement in terms of implementing the service and not the interface.

The type of architecture that can be built up using these approaches is shown in Figure 11.1.

This architecture achieves a number of essential precursors to a fully adaptive architecture. It has an 'n'-tier architecture; it separates the architecture into a series of logical layers and

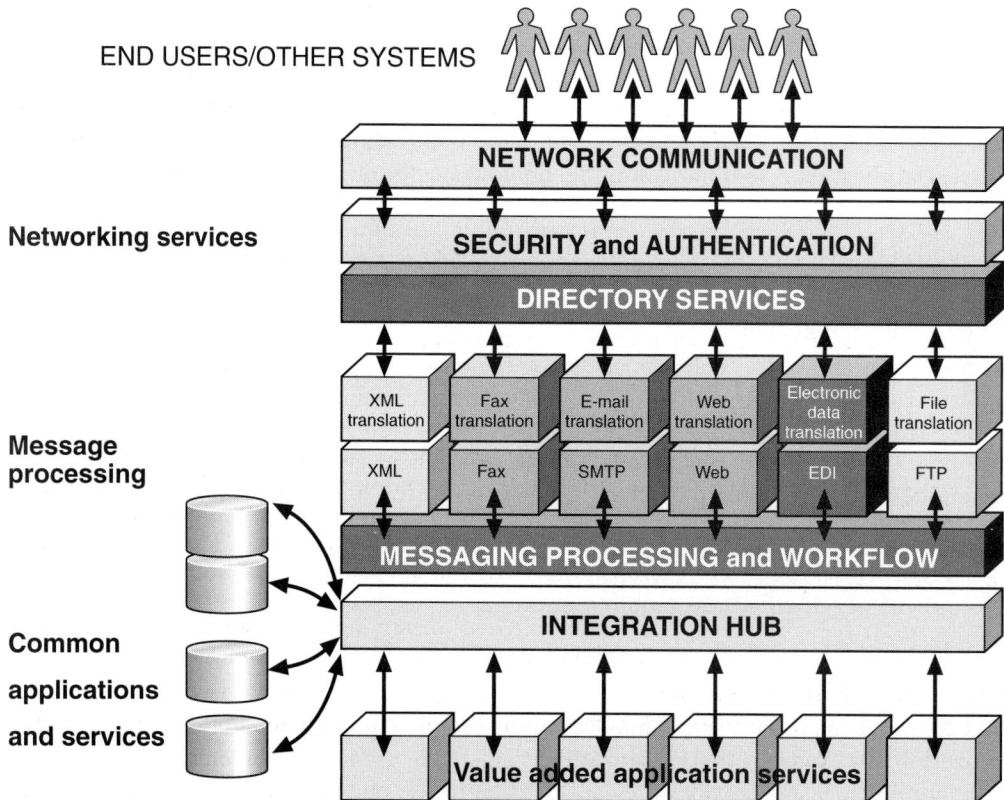

FIGURE 11.1: Integration architecture

components; it promotes reuse of components; it will assist in unifying the data model; and, if used correctly, it will feature a standards-based data exchange.

ACHIEVING REUSE

Widespread use and reuse of common services will help to bring the benefit of integrated business processes. Reuse also needs to occur at the component level and increasingly externalization of business is based on the use of components. What does this mean? In a scenario where packaged software is extensively deployed, the concept of what constitutes a component becomes blurred. The application package itself can be thought of as the component. To date it has proved difficult to achieve reuse at a functional application level; this was attempted prior to the widespread use of software packages.

Legacy applications can also be thought of as components and reuse is achieved through continued use. As we have discussed in Chapter 8, back-office 'components' should be treated as a business asset. Instead of developing a series of point-to-point interfaces to connect older systems to new applications, services such as legacy adapters should be used to create a wrapper around the legacy system. The adapter constitutes another layer of software, which can be understood by the more modern IT infrastructure and thus be subject to common services which the adapter understands.

Further, consider the extent to which components from outside the business can be bought in and reused. In a retail bank for example, 80 per cent of what it does may be the same as its competitors. The company's competitive edge is probably derived from no more than 20 per cent of its activities. So why waste time tailoring systems that perform non-differentiating context-based functions without adding value to your operations? This is expensive and time-consuming, the resulting systems will be complex and costly to maintain, and the whole process will have been highly wasteful. If you can reuse something that has been done before or even outsource the whole activity, it is probably a cheaper and better option.

To illustrate, in the early 1990s, the oil industry recognized the foolishness of repetitive programing. A group of competitors decided to pool resources to have a single application built to manage the accounting and tax requirements associated with extracting oil from the North Sea, thereby reducing the cost of complying with government requirements for each company. The resulting product, built as part of what came to be called 'Posix' – a cooperative agreement for sharing common software in the oil industry – was merely administrative software that each organization needed but offer the relative parties competitive edge.

Thus, the legacy system can form part of the overall 'ecosystem,' and the integration environment be engineered so that transactions are applied through all systems and data stores, as appropriate. This allows mainframe applications to be treated as components within the wider framework and avoids the cost and instability to both process and people of redeveloping the legacy systems.

Software package vendors, such as Peoplesoft, increasingly support extended business processes by providing common integration components of varying types in their architectures. These are essential elements for integrating packages, in which organizations have invested heavily to create business solutions. These components should be heavily reused and form critical infrastructure-based services.

Connecting with external business partners relies heavily on the existence of standard interfaces. Given the rapidity of change of many business relationships, organizations should not spend six months developing links with potential partners if there is a chance that the alliance will only endure for a short time. The more common the components are throughout the organizations, the more adaptive and agile the organizations can be, altering the configuration of their supply chains with less effort and less time consumed than previously.

WEB SERVICES

Web services will offer a further means of integration, and will play a critical role in extending business processes, particularly in the front office. Organizations looking to give access to information will make certain business processes available as web services – either internally or externally and both inside and outside the company's boundaries.

Web services are essentially applications that look for other web applications on the web and utilize other application services to carry out a business function. They do not require specific design to do this; rather, they invoke services that allow the fulfilment of a business function.

The sorts of services that may be carried out include procurement, billing and payment. In the near future, consumers will be able to use web services for activities such as making travel reservations. The Conclusion discusses the topic of web services more and considers how adaptive businesses are using new technology and integration to create new business models.

These services will, of course, require integration into the business and will demand integration of business process in order to fulfil their function. Web services will eventually provide the means to share information and business processes between parties, whether internal to a company or external between companies. Naturally, application integration services will be needed to provide services such as security, back-office integration and transactional integrity.

SUMMARY

1 Adopt a consistent, architectural approach to enterprise-wide systems integration, and keep in mind that visibility of data and the use of this data in extended business processes across the organization and beyond is what gives companies their edge today.

2 Use open standards throughout to ensure that you're not creating more legacy not capable of forming part of a joined-up business process.

3 Seek to maximize the re-use of infrastructure-based services – choosing how to implement these services will be among the more important decisions you make.

4 Use and reuse components in order to ease future maintenance, keep costs down and ensure maximum agility and speed to market.

5 Seek the ability to integrate multiple applications through common services.

6 Attempt, where appropriate, to convert high latency batch-based architectures to real-time applications. In time, this will enable your low latency business processes (upon which your business will depend) to react to external events.

7 Consider how web services will play a leading role in providing business process integration in front-office systems and into your business ecosystems.

PART 4

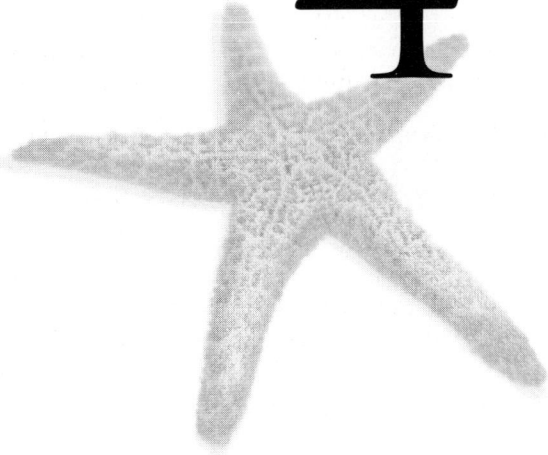

DELIVERING JOINED-UP
SYSTEMS

CHAPTER 12

CONTINUOUS THINKING FOR CONTINUOUS CHANGE

INTRODUCTION

This section of the book is not intended to be a definitive description of all the tools and techniques required to get from A to B when delivering complex systems integration. It should give a practical and reasonably comprehensive overview of some useful tools that can be employed at crucial points in the delivery and running of integrated systems. These take the form of approaches and frameworks that have been used over time.

For those who are new to working in an integration project, there should be enough information to understand how the tools work. For executives about to launch their company into an integration project, it should give you an indication of what to expect and enough information to distinguish good approaches from bad. For IT professionals, we hope it will jog some memories and perhaps be a useful check against your own good practices.

Large, one-off integration programs are becoming outmoded. Instead, organizations should aim for a process of continuous change – one which does not interrupt day-to-day business and which comprises a number of smaller, self-contained projects that will rapidly produce results for the business and can be adapted if market circumstances and business needs change along the way.

Almost without exception, the approaches described in the next six chapters were originally designed for projects with a finite beginning and end. Therefore, when they are applied today, they need to be adapted to fit into the sort of continuous, business-as-usual process advocated. In most cases, this is simply a question of taking the right cultural view of the frameworks and approaches and adapting them so that they can be used as part of a continuous process or to form a standard framework or set of principles.

CONTINUOUS CHANGE NEEDS CONTINUOUS THINKING

In Chapter 2, the hypothesis that it was no longer sufficient or economically viable to go through large, sporadic, single-step changes in a business was developed. Rather, it is necessary to build into every element of the organization the ability to continually reinvent itself.

To be able to do this without creating a totally dysfunctional organization, requires a new set of processes and approaches. These must be built on the foundation of current tools and knowledge. It is also vital that the appropriate management structures and cultures are put in place for the correct decisions to be made. It is not enough just to have the correct tools, you must be able to use them correctly. Even if the chosen objective is well understood, not having or using the correct tools and techniques can have disastrous consequences. So often today, organizations manage to arrive at their destination almost by good luck. This bears comparison with the eighteenth-century Age of Exploration:

> ❛ As more and more sailing vessels set out to conquer or explore new territories, to wage war or to ferry gold and commodities between foreign lands, the wealth of nations floated upon the oceans. Still no ship owned a reliable means for establishing her whereabouts. In consequence, untold numbers of sailors died when their destinations suddenly loomed out of the sea and took them by surprise. ❜
>
> Dava Sobel, *Longitude*, Fourth Estate, 1996.

You need a reliable means to establish your whereabouts.

The whole process of creating the joined-up company – of integrating systems in the three planes of business, technology and people within a dynamic world – leads to two important principles expressed by Tom Gilb.[1] These are the 'multi-dimensional tools principle' and the 'thinking tools principle'. The former states that: 'if your tools cannot operate in all critical dimensions then your problems will', while the 'thinking tools' principle is that 'dynamic environments require thinking tools instead of unthinking dogmas'.

The first is about ensuring the appropriateness and completeness of the approach's tools and techniques for the specific instance. The second is the area which, in the past, has probably led organizations into the most difficulty and has the potential to do so again.

During the mid 1980s and early 1990s, there was a rise of 'structured methods' to design software systems that were complete and consistent, such as Learmonth and Burchetts' Structured Method (LBSM) and its sequels, SSADM and then PRINCE. Now, approaches such as Rationale Unified Process (RUP) hold sway.

Like all methodologies, structured methods can be extremely useful if applied with intelligence. However, if used blindly or followed in a cook book way, they become an excuse to avoid the labour of thought. Although it was never the intention of their inventors that structured approaches should be followed doggedly, in many cases that is how they have been used.

This may have cured the problems of an incomplete solution versus requirements or lack of documentation, but it has lead to lengthy developments, which support a process of large-scale deliveries, rather than smaller, less risky and less costly implementation. More importantly, structured approaches have been used unthinkingly in so many cases that they have become ends in themselves and their initial usefulness has been eroded.

The current approaches are designed to overcome some of these problems. Rational Unified Process (RUP) is an example where rapid application development techniques of iterative

---

[1] Tom Gilb, *Principles of Software Engineering Management, op. cit.*

developments and deliveries have been merged with a structured method. All of these methods, however, have focused on software developments and left the development of business process and organization untouched. Consequently, they continue to have difficulties because they are a partial solution to the problem.

There is a good, solid argument for applying a standard approach if you are to be able to reuse core assets in an adaptive way, but any standards must be applied in a flexible way. Mandating that 'Everyone in the company will now use RUP on all projects' might have the advantage that everyone understands the same vocabulary and can work together but the downside is that it may not be appropriate or complete in any specific case.

Organizations that wish to promote continuous change must delegate and empower those delivering that change to use the most appropriate tools, not simply to deliver the immediate change but to enhance and ease possibility of future change. They must teach people to understand objectives and solve problems, not only how to use a process. Adaptation to rapid and unpredicted change will need to be delivered using standard sets of patterns, services and platforms that can be reconfigured rather than rebuilt. Promoting a level of required standardization, for assets to be reusable and adaptive, while allowing the necessary flexibility to enable problems to be solved in an imaginative way, dictates the use of 'frameworks', rather than prescriptive methodologies.

COMMON TEAM THINKING IS NEEDED TO KEEP THE ORGANIZATION TOGETHER

Promoting a level of common understanding across an organization requires team thinking. In the world of sports psychology, the objective is to develop general awareness of problems and situations. This enables each member of a team to interpret that event in the same way and move into the correct sequence of actions for each of them to play effectively as a team – without the need to communicate with each other.

Any 'play' is led by key team members, known as cultural architects. Their role is in understanding the executive vision, the organizational thinking and interpreting it in the dynamic way required on the field. In a business environment, which is as dynamic and unpredictable as a game of football, it is also the cultural architects who act as the glue, rather than the process.

Frameworks must be complete, yet flexible enough to be applied imaginatively. They must have some 'glue' – thinking that runs through them all and allows them to be used consistently, almost instinctively, in a way that integrates not only software engineering but business process and organizational development as well.

SIX ESSENTIAL AREAS OF FOCUS

The organizational thinking to join up the project and the organization must be based initially on a consistent understanding of six key areas. Each of these areas contributes to the overall management picture. It is an absolute requirement, though, that these areas of focus work together and do not become organizational tramlines or silos, where groups of functions or roles proceed in isolation. In detail, the six areas of focus are:

1 Leadership and communication

Establishing the clear leadership required to realize the vision, means being an effective communicator to all audiences. In addition to giving direction and setting strategies for achieving change, activities are about mobilization and encouraging participation.

Communication, which includes listening, is a vital tool for engaging the wider organization and ensuring that a consistent message reaches everyone concerned about the vision, its status, its achievements and the impact it will have on them. More than anything, this area helps to create the energy needed for change.

Leadership, meanwhile, must be able to authoritatively articulate the vision, to set direction to achieve it, and develop strategies that will produce the change. When you deal with an entire organization, this is more than individual effort can achieve. It requires alignment of groups of people who will make the vision their own and move it forward. The requirement is motivation and inspiration. The solving of most problems will be in the hands of the team, rather than the manager; he or she must ensure the teams retain the confidence and energy to keep moving forward, despite obstacles. In many cases, this requires dealing with people's basic needs and values, rather than technical problems, as discussed in Part 2.

Therefore, leadership must be complemented by effective communication, both with the organization and the delivery team. This has to extend throughout the whole of the organization and its suppliers. Although the program manager needs, individually, to be an effective communicator, again the scale of a continuous change requires a dedicated area of focus to support communication. Both aspects of leadership and communication necessarily have a strong influence on all other areas of focus.

2 Business benefits

This initially focuses on developing or refining the business vision and the benefits case, which initiates and justifies the activities taking place. Then this area of focus makes certain that the business remains in active control and that the expected benefits (both measurable and non-measurable) are delivered and remain responsive to business needs in terms of ongoing improvements. Business benefits centre on ensuring business gets what it expects and that risks to business are contained.

Business benefits is about confirming the business basis for the project or program, and monitoring this achievement. Within this area of focus, the business vision, which forms the aim of the program, is clearly defined and the business case elaborated. Relevant measurements and mechanisms are put in place to monitor this and to guarantee that it stays on track.

This process ensures that there is properly committed business sponsorship of the project or program, which, particularly through the leadership and communication activities, is translated into willingness to achieve the objectives at all levels in the organization.

3 Relationships

The relationships area of focus makes certain that all stakeholders are able to work in partnership. That expectations are correctly set and managed and that satisfaction remains high as a result.

Practical issues, such as the commercial relationship, the contract, financial arrangements and the ongoing relationship with suppliers, are handled in this area of focus. It is important to all parties to have targeted control from the outset to ensure that commercial risk is contained.

The fundamentals of the partnership necessary for a project or program to succeed are established. This includes mapping individual relationships, managing expectations and dealing with transitions or set backs.

Ultimately, this area of focus guarantees that the commercial and contractual relationship between the supplier and the client is successful. Also that relationships between the project and the rest of the organization are successful. If the program is large, it will be a significant business undertaking for suppliers as well as the client; the engagement must ensure that suppliers' goals are achieved, as well as the client's. This will typically include knowledge transfer and a successful future business relationship, in addition to regular margin and revenue goals.

4 Resourcing

The implementation of complex systems integration presents challenges in terms of finding enough of the right kind of people and recruiting, training, motivating and retaining them. The changes brought about may have profound effects on staffing, career management, capability requirements and people development.

If a major knowledge transfer (e.g. from suppliers to the client) is to take place, this needs to be planned and managed effectively. Equally, the project or program may instigate a new approach to resourcing (e.g. outsourcing or subcontracting) and the effects on people and the organization must be sensitively managed.

Here we put together the activities required, not only to ensure effective staffing of the project or program itself but also the general issue of resourcing of services within the organization, which may be affected by the project. These two areas are closely related in several respects:

☐ Recruiting supplier's and client personnel will form a significant activity.

☐ Suppliers are likely to become owners of many of the ongoing services and will need to address optimally any transition or outsourcing.

☐ In all areas there is a need to deal with personnel issues, such as career change and personal development.

☐ There is a contractual element, either with regards to subcontracting services to third parties, or defining service level agreements.

The issue of service delivery and coordinating third-party suppliers is closely related to the next area of focus, integration.

5 Integration

The aim is to deliver integrated end products, whether new IT systems, other physical systems or new business processes. Identifying and if necessary, creating business, application and technical architectures are a vital part of this.

It is equally important that the planning of deliverable development, deployment and the accompanying changes to business processes and organization are integrated. This requires careful management of interdependencies, integrated testing and a common approach to acceptance. Integrating planning and control mechanisms, particularly where no common culture existed previously, is a major challenge. The integration area of focus covers two different, but closely related, aspects of integration:

Firstly, producing deliverables that are integrated – they work seamlessly with each other and their design reflects all aspects of the business need, including deployment and operational considerations. The deliverables may be business processes as well as systems. Secondly, integration of the program delivery mechanism itself, the coordination of engagement activities, to ensure productivity and predictability. The organization structure to achieve this and the knowledge for developing it, are also deliverables. All the areas of focus holistically support this objective; this area of focus includes activities central to achieving it.

Management may expect and require the project or program to deliver the benefits from either or both aspects. The relationship between the two springs from the fact that it is highly unlikely that integrated deliverables can be produced without an integrated organization being built. Thus, this area of focus has a number of areas in common with governance (the next area of focus), for example, in planning. The main difference is that governance is concerned with creation, administration and auditing of coordinated planning and control processes, whereas integration is concerned with the functional content of planning as a tool to promote integration.

6 Governance

Projects or programs must be under control. Within such a complex and diverse undertaking, measuring process, monitoring risks and assessing the impact of issues needs to operate at a level above that of the individual project. This area of focus puts in place and manages such processes, ensuring that the management organization is itself integrated. Quality management is fundamental to achieving integration of the organization and its deliverables, through adoption of consistent terminology, standards, procedures, techniques and tools.

Governance will also make sure that the approaches are subjected to review, through a coaching and counselling approach to quality. Governance is about the formal structures and processes that will guarantee coordinated management and consistent and predictable delivery. Giving a total view of interdependencies at any one time. Many of the processes, such as planning, administration or risk management, derive their content from other areas of focus. The key is to define a common terminology and way of doing things, backed by an audit and review process, to both explain and enforce the chosen approaches. The support activities of the program office, which provides governance, are central to this.

SUMMARY

1 You will need tools that operate in all critical dimensions. In a dynamic environment, you cannot afford to deploy tools and techniques in an unthinking way.

2 Current structured methods and project approaches are inapplicable for the world of reuse, without adaptation.

3 You will need standard approaches, applied in flexible ways. To make any sense of this dynamic environment, you need some 'glue', generic enough to be applicable in all cases.

4 There are six essential areas of management focus, which serve as a common thread through every stage.

5 When choosing the right management approach, remember that projects have well-defined scope, while programs achieve strategic goals by delivering business benefits.

CHAPTER 13

DELIVERY APPROACHES

INTRODUCTION

Most of the tools for integration have been born out of the major programs of work created from system and business transformation. They have led to the rise of three very different approaches to delivering change: the project, the program and the factory.

The argument for their use, where they are appropriate, is founded on two principles: understanding the size and shape of the task and the one-off major change view. Before going further, let us look at a comparison of these three delivery approaches.

THE DELIVERY APPROACH MAKES THE DIFFERENCE

Understanding the size and shape of the required outcomes is critical if you are to avoid being surprised by its complexity. In Chapter 18, the case study describes what can happen if the complexity of the objective is sorely underestimated.

Equally, overkill in terms of organization can not only create an unnecessary cost, but can be a major cause of lost opportunity. Throughout this book, 'projects' and 'programs' have been referred to frequently. It is important to understand the key differences between the two and, when the opportunity is right, to use one or the other management approach.

Typically, projects will satisfy business requirements by focusing on the deliverables. The management will manage tasks and activities as the primary objective in order to deliver to a fixed time-scale and within a pre-defined budget. Projects deliver products and services.

The scope of project management can be easily and clearly defined (see Figure 13.1). A project manager has four variables with which he or she can respond to events that affect the project. These are: time, cost (resource), functional scope and quality. Usually one, if not two, of these variables will be fixed in advance of the project start date. These are cost and time, leaving only quality and functional scope with which to respond to the vagaries that will beset the project. The events that may influence the project can be classified into four areas: issues, risks, problems and changes.

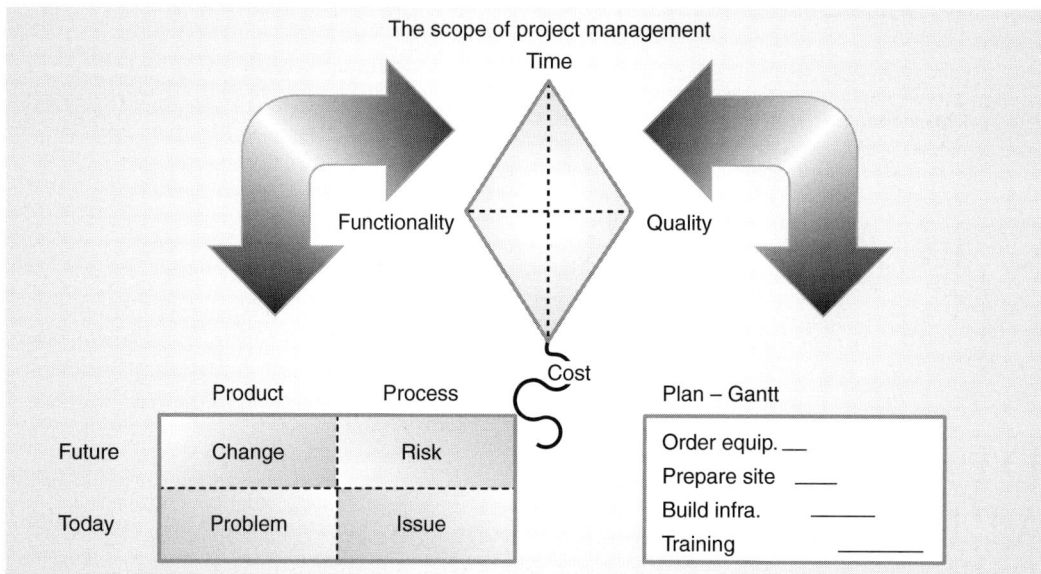

FIGURE 13.1: The scope of project management

Such events affect two elements of the project: the deliverables or product and the processes used to create the deliverables. If the events dealt with alter the product and happen in the future, they will be defined as 'changes'. If they happen now, they are 'problems'. Similarly, if the events act on process and are forecast to happen in the future, they are 'risks' and, if hitting the project today, they are issues. The critical tool for expressing all of this is the project plan and the tracking processes associated with it.

Programs, on the other hand, are set up to manage large-scale complex change. Programs achieve strategic goals. They deliver business benefits and manage integrated portfolios of projects. Generally they have less well-defined time and budget horizons than projects. Usually, to date, they are set up to deliver a one-off step change.

If one accepts, however, that programs deliver business vision through a managed change process, the results of which are measured in tangible business benefits, then the program approach provides an ideal framework for the continuous change process. A program is the vehicle for communication between executive management and the myriad portfolios of projects, which will be active in the new, dynamic, business-as-usual world.

THE TOTAL CHANGE CYCLE

In the total change cycle explained in Chapter 2, the need to speed up the process of feeding strategic design into pragmatic, practical process to effect continuous reinvention as part of the normal business-as-usual process was discussed. An operational program management structure will facilitate the transition from designing and establishing, through to everyday management. Therefore, the position of program management is to ensure continuous alignment of projects in the three dimensions of business process, people and technology. It is through this level of management that an organization can guarantee that business value is delivered in a prioritized way, while minimizing risks and controlling costs. Program

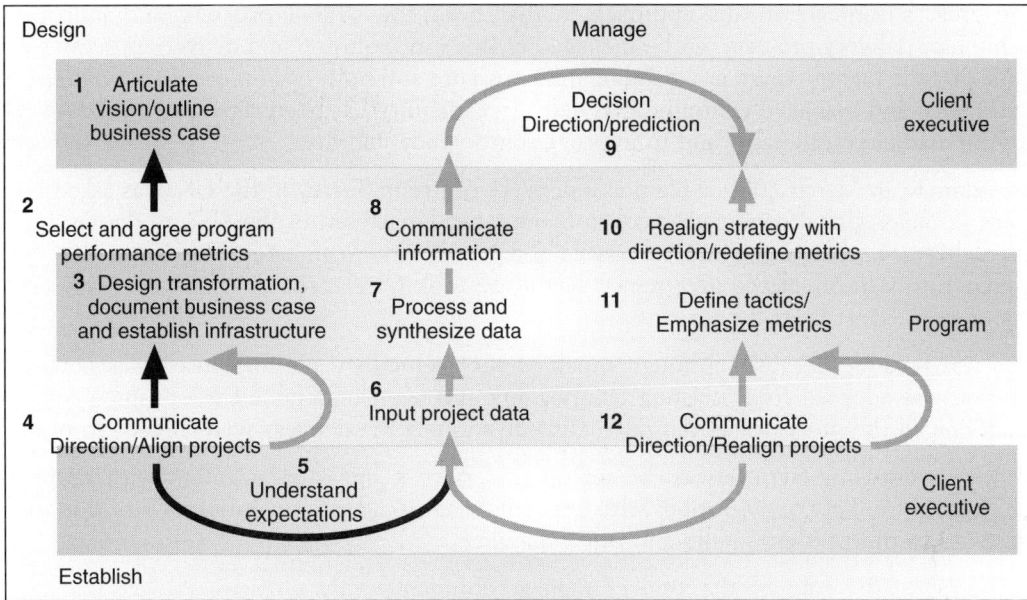

FIGURE 13.2: Operational program

management owns the big picture and can present a comprehensive view on corporate initiatives (see Figure 13.2). As Bill Gates once said, 'If you cut a job into too many pieces and involve too many people, no one can see the big picture'.

Within the context of a project or program, a number of decisions must be taken on how to deliver and on what sort of relationship is required with individual or teams of suppliers. Does the organization have all the capacity and expertise in-house? Are some specific skills required? Should the project or program be delivered with the aid of off-shore resources? What role should outsourcing play?

Key questions frequently overlooked are: 'To what degree will we continually mobilize the organization?' and 'How will we be able to easily facilitate the transition of the new state to the ongoing processes?'

The norm, at the conception of a new project, is for a project manager to be appointed and given the task of putting some plans and estimates together. Once the go ahead is given, people are allocated to the plan. From that point on, the majority of the team will work full-time on the specific project. The project will build and establish its own unique processes and culture.

THE 'FACTORY' APPROACH

There is an alternative – a 'factory' or 'delivery centre' approach. With a delivery centre approach, all the infrastructure required to manage project or program delivery can be set up once and used for multi-client delivery. Each new project becomes another work package to process through the factory. Each skill set group within the factory works on a number of work packages simultaneously. This improves individual utilization because peaks and troughs caused by delays and difficulties on one work package can be smoothed by managing the workflow from alternative work packages, which require that particular skill set.

The great advantage of this approach is that both the overall program and individual technology delivery projects can be managed in this way. Solution and delivery processes are owned by the factory, there is a standing infrastructure and both resource and knowledge can be retained and managed centrally. This delivery capability has been shown to cut down the time to market considerably and to improve solution adaptability.

For example, in March 2000, a team at a delivery centre in Surrey in the UK, was asked by a client (a major global engineering conglomerate, headquartered in the US), to design, build and deliver an integration hub to service the North American operation. From that first approach to sign-off of the acceptance certificate took 65 elapsed days and involved 1200 man-days of effort from the team.

This was possible because, although much of the technology platform used was new, the solution was adopted from existing components, the team understood the business and its needs and all the processes and infrastructure to support the delivery were already in place.

Delivery centres or factories can be set up to service a single organization with multiple solutions, or multiple organizations with a specific range of adaptive solutions. Critical to their success is complete 'think, build and run' capability.

Furthermore, the role of the project manager fundamentally changes. Project managers become product managers. They are now responsible for the specific work package deliverables to the client. The client may be an internal user department or an external customer. Project managers are not, however, responsible for the people carrying out the work. The 'factory manager' is responsible for the workforce and for allocating and managing time and productivity. This is done through a front-office interface, which is the liaison with the business and handles demand or capacity management.

Each of the work packages goes through an appropriate life cycle. They can be compared to different models of car on the production line – some will share a production line, while

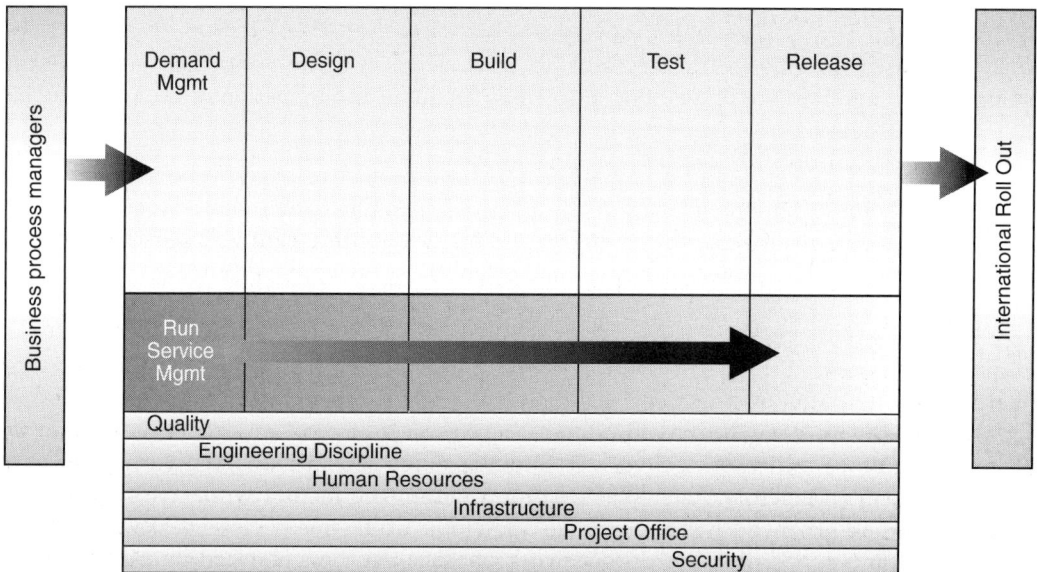

FIGURE 13.3: Scope of factory delivery

others will have a separate line set up for them. All will be supported by a set of standard functions, such as infrastructure management and quality management. Capacity of the factory can be flexed depending on demand but these support functions will remain as a fairly stable and consistent base.

From this description, it becomes clear that projects, programs and factories are not mutually exclusive and can and should be used together. In a business world that is rapidly developing and where time is of the essence, program management tools and approaches can be used to supply the management framework for the 'total change cycle'. The factories will be the owners and enhancers of services, standards and principles, while projects will manage and deliver specific packages of work.

CHOOSING THE RIGHT METHOD

We have discussed the strategic level of delivery approach: project, program and factory. Within each of these, a decision about which method to use to deliver any one or multiple projects has to be made. Do you need to use Rapid Application Development (RAD), for example? Do you have the correct environment to take advantage of collaborative working? Must you go through the old standard waterfall approach of defining requirements, building, testing and implementing? Can you accelerate the development processes by overlapping phases and deliveries?

To make these decisions, it is necessary to understand the key benefits and risks involved. Often the approach is not selected until budgets have been defined and contracts signed. Frequently, opportunities are lost or difficulties created for delivery teams when contractual terms and conditions do not match the delivery approach.

Let's examine the common root problems that arise, which program teams try to address, often without success and go on to consider what criteria you should use to assess how appropriate a particular approach may be in a given set of circumstances. One thing is certain – none of the individual methods, approaches and frameworks described in this book are guaranteed. Moreover, they must always be used with a healthy dose of common sense, frequent tuning and constant development.

Before you start:

☐ Ensure that your objectives are clearly and unambiguously stated – even those that might appear obvious.

☐ Try to achieve a balance of minimizing risk and cost with achieving the objectives.

☐ Build in early and frequent feedback loops to make sure that you can implement improvements early enough to affect the eventual outcome as well as learning.

It is rare to see objectives clearly stated. Without a clear statement of goals by management at the outset, it is not surprising that few projects clearly achieve their goals. When there is added confusion between objectives, requirements and solutions, solutions often become expressed as requirements or even as the ultimate objective. This frequently happens when senior management – who should focus on detailing the objectives, why they are required and how they know when they have been achieved – become involved at a detailed level in solving the problem. There obviously needs to be clear separation between objectives and solutions.

Once the objectives are clear, the second critical question, concerning balancing risk and cost to achieve objectives, can be addressed. You will need an effective means of prioritizing your steps towards the ultimate goal – a way to measure the relative merits of each potential solution. This is more than a question of phasing your plans. As Gilb notes:

> ❛ Phased planning asks a dangerous question: how much can we accomplish within some critical time constraint (budget, deadline, storage space)? Evolutionary delivery planning asks a very different question: how little development resource can we expend, and still accomplish something useful in the direction of our ultimate objectives?

> More formally, in evolutionary planning today, we use the concept of selecting the potential steps with the highest user value to development cost ratio for earliest implementation. This is really like skimming the cream off the top of the milk. Such 'user value' may be financial. It may be of other kinds. ❜ [1]

THE ADAPTIVE WORLD IS ASSET-LED, NOT REQUIREMENTS-DRIVEN

In the past, decisions about how to prioritize and select have been exclusively requirements-driven. We are trained to look at the needs of the business and determine the solutions we should build or buy to address these.

Yet, this has often introduced further complexity into an already jumbled IT environment, creating new legacies and data silos. If organizations want to be more efficient and integrated in their IT development plans, a better approach is to take the business need, examine the assets the company already has (e.g. software components), which could help to address the problem and take any development plans from there.

Think of the design process like building a house. Instead of starting from scratch each time, adding time to the building process and using customized materials, a far more efficient process would take appropriate combinations of pre-fabricated building blocks and use these as the basis for the main construction. Any customization can happen after this stage.

Being asset-led, rather than requirements-driven, is the only way program managers stand any chance of managing the volatility they find themselves working within.

This means that not only the problem solvers, the analysts and the infrastructure technologists, but the whole organization must approach program design by asking which existing components they can use and how, to reduce development costs and achieve rapid implementation.

We can examine this proposal in more detail because it affects new system development. Firstly, there is a need to see where components can fit. This means that there is a need for an open and flexible architecture.

Secondly, where components are developed from the start, these can no longer be built as one-off, bespoke pieces of engineering for later patching and enhancing. Each component must be built in such a way that it can be configured for new situations.

Technology applications, which are now the fundamental core of most business processes, need to be constructed with pre-programed capabilities, which can be selected for the future, replaced or extended in order to adapt to new survival needs. Each component will have its own characteristics, a credit and authorization service, a piece of business logic or a

114

---

[1] Further reading on this subject can be found in Tom Gilb's, *Principles of Software Engineering Management, Op. Cit.*

distribution channel. The proposition must be made available to re-combine and reinvent easily, using only the required elements.

As the project manager's role must change, so the analyst and technologist must change their cultural outlook. It should no longer only be regarded as career-enhancing and exciting to create the new but instead to use the new to adapt the existing – in a way which provides a total solution of organization, technology and ongoing service.

HOW DEVELOPERS MUST ADAPT

What difficulties does using traditional approaches present to developers? We can look at some specific problems in relation to Rationale Unified Processes (RUP) – not that these issues are specific to RUP, but they demonstrate the thinking and the adaptation, which must be made to current practice, if reuse is to be paramount.

RUP and the 'Rational tool-set' are a combination of six best practices in software engineering:

1   Develop iteratively.

2   Manage requirements.

3   Use component architectures.

4   Model systems visually.

5   Verify quality.

6   Control change.

RUP is a process definition. It prescribes the phases to be followed, the activities to be carried out, the deliverables to be produced (artefacts) and the roles and responsibilities for their production. The so-called Rational tools are based around database-driven requirements management, Unified Modelling Language (UML) modelling and automated test tools. To use these tools involves the creation of a database of requirements, which can then be decomposed to different levels of detail. At each level, the requirements can be related to various deliverables, such as functional definitions (use cases or specifications). These provide details of the functionality that will satisfy the requirement or interaction diagrams that elaborate how the required behaviour will be implemented.

The added dimension over other structured methods is that RUP supports an iterative, risk-based development approach, where 'architecturally significant' use cases are developed first. Design is based on the object-orientated paradigm, with the production of business objects represented as classes. These class definitions and behaviours are then exported to be developed in the selected programing language.

For the reuse model, a distinction needs to be made between the development of what one might call 'core assets', and the configuration of these assets. A further element needs to be in place – the framework that will enable core assets to be configured in a standard way.

While developing the assets and framework, RUP is applicable. In 'configuration' mode, the six principles still apply and use can be made of the automated testing tools, particularly during regressing testing. Unless there is heavy investment in reverse-engineering the existing assets to populate the requirements database, there is little to be gained from RUP in its present form in the configuration process.

SPEEDING UP THE DEVELOPMENT PROCESS

Before moving on to look at particular hotspot areas in program delivery in Chapters 14 and 15, consider how developments need to move forward in future.

Since the realization that program managers can no longer take nine months to deliver business benefit, there have been numerous attempts to improve time-scales, such as rapid application development, accelerated development and time-boxing. All of these endeavours at collaborative working have been designed by technologists or IT practioners in response to the valid criticisms made by the business.

Collaborative working approaches are highly successful when the area to be tackled is well defined, the teams or skill sets are not too varied and therefore small and all team members are empowered. This means that each has to have both current and comprehensive knowledge and the trust of both peers and management. Interdependencies also have to be well understood and planned for.

This book is about collaborative working but on a much grander scale. No longer can you afford to hand problems from one specialism to another. Rather, there is a need to accept joint responsibility and multiple discipline teams as your starting point.

SUMMARY

1   With the pressures facing program managers when it comes to strategic systems integration in the current business climate, the key to achieving the flexibility that so many companies are searching for from their business processes and supporting IT systems, is structure. There are so many variables to be aligned and under such time pressures that program managers need to have a carefully formulated plan to ensure that objectives are met and nothing is left to chance.

2   While rigid templates can be too prescriptive, it is important to follow some guidelines to make certain that you define a path and stick to it.

3   Program management frameworks, factory delivery and project management need to be considered to deliver continuous change.

4   There is a new role for project managers, focusing more on the management of the product than the process of development.

5   The demands of faster, cheaper, better delivery mean that you must be asset-led, not just requirements-driven.

6   The focus of successful delivery is to guarantee collaborative working at all levels. How people work effectively across disciplines and cultures can make the biggest single difference.

CHAPTER 14

PUTTING THE ARCHITECTURE TOGETHER

INTRODUCTION

We have returned repeatedly to the business drivers that create the need for integration projects and programs. This is because the secret of success is never to lose sight of the real reason the project or program was initiated. The drivers will be as diverse as competition, velocity of change, cost pressures, industry consolidation, resource pressure, a need to focus on core businesses or customer service demands.

Once the work has been initiated, these drivers will often be obscured from the problem solvers by the issues that they are confronted with, such as the fact that the organization is fragmented; the organization's slow response to market demands; its vulnerability to competition; its current low leverage of corporate assets; its slow time to market; the fact that IT values are not synchronized with the business; the shortcomings in customer satisfaction and general operational inefficiencies.

The focus of the frameworks described below is to create an environment for change that rapidly aligns, then keeps aligned, both IT and business. The frameworks cover three aspects:

1 **How to transform** – in terms of strategy and direction across marketing and sales, core activities and products, business and operational process. The scope can be as wide as required, covering the whole supply chain or just looking at specific issues, for instance, productivity, investment or profitability.

2 **Architecture** – that is business driven and integrates architectures for business data, infrastructure, application, security and governance. The steps described in this chapter will enable you to take strategies through to an operational plan. The construction of the strategies is driven by the constant referral to the desired outcomes. What difference will they make? The results are realized through the collective deliverables of interlocked projects. Success is achieved through structured management of governance, benefits, people and resources, risks, expectations, integration and communication.

3 **Deliverables that are required** – to make sure that the delivery team at least starts with the best chance of providing the enterprise with what is really required in the appropriate time frame.

The basis of design should begin with a process that makes certain, by the end of the design phase, that there is a good understanding of those dimensions that define complexity (Chapter 2). Secondly, four key risk areas must be kept in mind and designed for:

1 Non-realization of benefits.

2 Lack of control.

3 Conflicts of interest.

4 Unsolicited change.

Non-realization of benefits

Process must be designed for expectation management and for frequent reference back to stakeholders, including the business and operational management, about the acceptability and continual applicability of benefits. Thought must be given to how quality will be built in at all levels and managed. Also, right from the beginning, any design must pay critical attention to how project deliverables are going to be transferred into the day-to-day business.

Lack of control

Critical to addressing this risk area is a clear definition of the program or project. A well-documented charter that clearly and unambiguously states the objectives, scope, approach and benefits to be realized, is a vital deliverable from the design process. Strategies need to be defined concerning how third parties are to be managed and projects coordinated. Finally, a view must be taken on which standards, processes and methods will be most suitable.

Conflicts of interest

It is inevitable that during the lifetime of all but the shortest projects, there will be conflicts of interest. In order to mitigate and manage these, it is best to expose them as early as possible and define how conflicts will be managed going forward. This is usually a good vehicle to ensure that there is complete stakeholder commitment to the project.

Typical areas from which conflicts may arise include:

☐ Existing projects and programs.

☐ Commitment of resource, particularly where business and operational skills are required to run the day-to-day business and to define the new.

☐ Internal politics.

These issues need to be eradicated if the continuous change organization is successful. 'Eradicating' is not a euphemism for ignoring. Most projects and programs are set off course, completely diverted or sunk by poor management or changing requirements.

During design, all the stakeholders and the core management team charged with delivery responsibility must be aware of where change is likely to come from and define a management strategy to handle these changes. Part of that strategy must be to decide if the approach to change will be a 'change control process' or a 'work reception process'. Much will depend on the clarity of objectives, the planning horizon and overall complexity of the venture on which of these approaches is taken.

Change control

A change control process is typically put in place in all circumstances. The process is usually designed with elaborate bureaucracy to defend the defined scope and budgets.

For any individual change, the gatekeeper's default answer will equal 'No'. For well-defined projects, with targeted goals and short planning horizons, this is probably acceptable. For programs at the other end of the scale, the assessment process for any change must be linked back into this initial design process and the questions asked: 'Do we want to do this?', 'How far does this move towards our strategic goals?' and 'What impact will it have on the realization of benefits?'. Then look at the impact on the delivery engine.

Typically, both change control and work reception processes fail to assess the impact of the totality of change on any project or program. The natural tendency is to look at each request in isolation, until arriving at the one that breaks the budget or the capacity of the delivery team to absorb. In designing the change strategy, there must be iterative interaction with budget definition and overall financial management processes. Referring back to the list of six key areas of focus for program delivery outlined in Chapter 12, it becomes clear that this must be a crucial business benefits deliverable, rather than a governance issue.

Unsolicited changes

Unsolicited changes could be defined as a risk to the planning horizon, introducing delay. The danger is that the longer delivery and implementation takes, the more likely the project or program will be open to changes in legislation and regulation, market forces, the impact of new technology and changing objectives and new initiatives driven by the business.

In some cases, the project or program will have to be designed and driven during a time of great flux. Those who managed Euro implementation programs during 1997 and 1998, developed an understanding of the complexities in terms of management organization and the governance processes required.

Financial organizations required a long period to change their systems, but the European Union member states took the same time period to make some vital decisions affecting the way in which systems and processes would need to work. Those companies with global or pan-European reach had the most problems.

There were three key issues. No one knew which countries were going to meet the criteria to be in the first wave of Monetary Union until very late in 1998. In addition, each country was developing its own plan and legislation for the change over to Economic and Monetary Union (EMU), with which any organization would have to comply. Finally, there was huge conflict of interest, particularly in non-European companies, with the well-publicised need to prepare for the Year 2000.

Those companies that were successful, like Citibank Corporation, recognized the issues early on and designed their whole programs to meet the seemingly insurmountable barriers to achieve clarity of vision and objectives. They were able to absorb a trickle feed of requirements definitions and yet still meet the fixed end date.

ARCHITECTURE

Clarity of both vision and objectives is aided by development of architecture. A market-leading architecture discipline integrates the full scope of business and technology issues.

We defined architecture in Chapter 2 and stressed why it is important in Chapter 10. Architecture bridges the development of both strategies and design by creating a reference model that can be drilled down from concept to physical reality.

Architecture creates the reference mould and serves as the key commitment vehicle during the design phase. Architectures are built in layers and contain, at the highest level, the strategy definition, the technology strategy, the business strategy and how these are aligned with the technology and business vision.

It allows you, then, to define the implementation of these strategies in terms of IT capabilities and competencies, technology principles and business principles. It also includes at the next 'Logical Level' not only competency definitions but functional requirements and new business processes. At the lowest level, it physically defines the projects to be run and the technical infrastructure to be purchased.

THE INTEGRATED ARCHITECTURE FRAMEWORK

The Integrated Architecture Framework (IAF) allows business process, technology and organization to be aligned at all levels in an ordered way (see Figure 14.1).

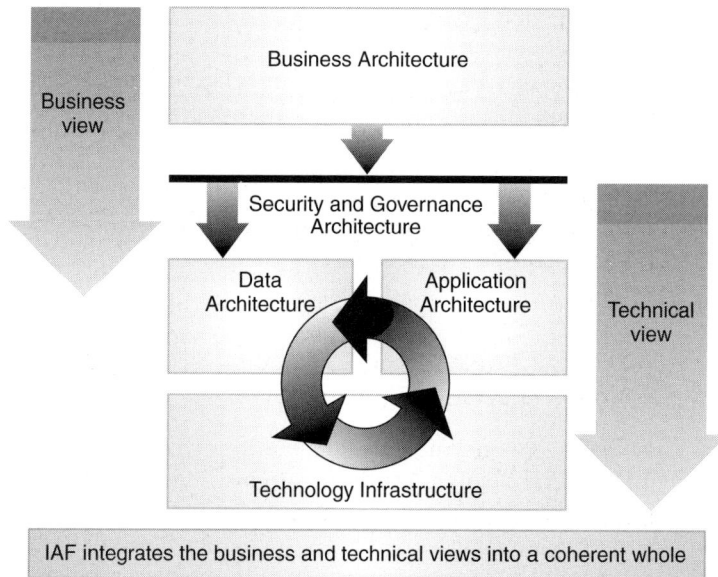

FIGURE 14.1: Architecture concepts

Architectures and architects will be used to resolve many different problems and business issues. In an era of continuous change, it is essential that architectures are open and flexible. To ensure this, any architecture framework must separate the approach to problem resolution from the capabilities deployed to resolve the problem.

An architectural framework needs to contain:

☐ An area for positioning and defining the business drivers and issues.

☐ A definition of core asset services and processes – what the required capabilities and capacities are.

☐ A definition of some standard or proven approaches – the roadmaps.

At the lowest level, you must be able to define within the framework the different elements you wish to use, such as the business process model and service component and the tools and techniques you may use. A good framework should focus on reducing complexity by separating issues and addressing them at the highest level. It needs to be able to encompass business processes, information components, delivery channels, plant maintenance, people and organization, security and hardware. (See Fig. 14.2).

With constant change, there is a high potential to create a dysfunctional organization. The framework has to allow you to distinguish between different aspects, while being able to understand the interdependencies, impacts and integratability of each aspect on the other and on the whole.

A typical aspect will group business issues, business patterns and business/organization structures, while another will focus on technology issues, patterns and structures. The design process must deal with five questions: 'Why?', 'What?', 'How?', 'With what?' and 'When and where?'. The architectural framework needs to be built to cover the first four of these, with the planning processes dealing with the 'When and where?'. By layering the framework, you can address each level of question as you dig deeper.

Why?	Layer 0	Contextual
What?	Layer 1	Conceptual
How?	Layer 2	Logical
With what?	Layer 3	Physical

At the very highest level, the Contextual Layer, the drivers to the business and the external forces that affect it are dealt with. This layer will not be divided into different 'aspects'. Below this layer each aspect will be considered in conceptual, logical and physical layers. This enables each individual aspect, business, technology, or information to be addressed in the same way but with specific focus in each case.

What you are building, therefore, is a matrix – the beginning of understanding the spaghetti world and defining it as modular, self-contained layers. In reality, in the physical layer things usually get into a mess because there is incomplete understanding of the three layers above it.

With a comprehensive framework, it is not necessary to complete all steps in all layers. This is the advantage of separating the approach from the content of the framework. An approach can be selected, depending upon the business issue, the context or indeed the architectural objectives. Any individual approach will link content tools and techniques, as appropriate, to solve the specific problem.

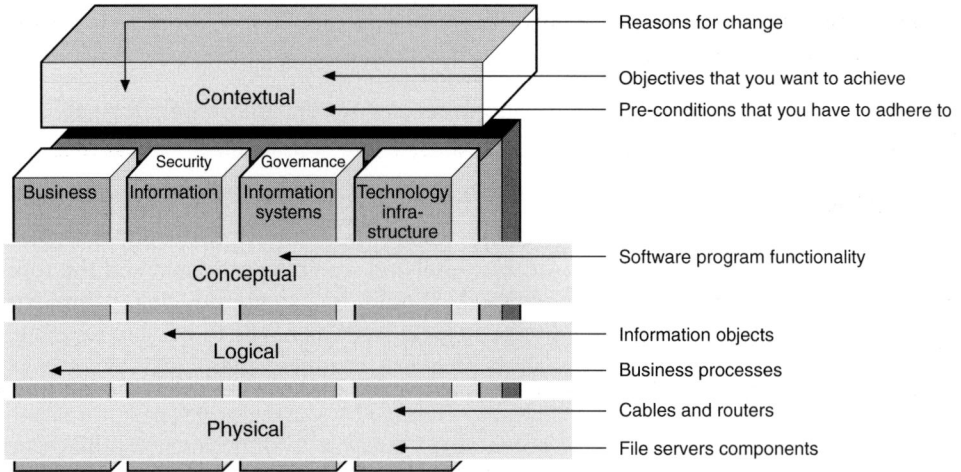

FIGURE 14.2: Integrated architecture framework with some examples

THE IMPORTANCE OF PRINCIPLES

Any architecture must be founded on a set of principles, which must perform certain functions and are essential to the overall design process. They give direction, make implicit conditions explicit, define boundaries of scope, set priorities and check for completeness.

Points made earlier (in Part 1, Chapter 4), such as that cost/value thinking is fundamental to all work, is a good example. A principle could concern flexibility of the work environment, in terms of providing 24-hour services. Perhaps these principles will consist of design constraints such as providing the required services with proven technology or having levels of security which do not interfere with the working design of primary processes.

Some principles are common to all architecture design as a matter of good practice.

Simplicity

☐ The simplest solution is usually the correct one.

☐ Extreme requirements should remain under scrutiny.

Sanity

☐ The earlier that contextual constraints and severity checks are made on assumptions and requirements, the better.

☐ Do not assume that the original statement of the problem is necessarily the best or even the correct one.

Keep looking around

☐ During the design phase refine, add or change principles.

☐ Remember that the most serious mistakes are made on the first day.

Completeness

☐ No complex solution can be optimized for all stakeholders.

☐ Performance, cost, time and quality cannot be specified independently. At least one of the four must depend on the others.

Quality

☐ You will not achieve quality unless you specify it.

Future-proofing

☐ Predicting the future may be impossible, but ignoring it is irresponsible.

There will be a number of different types of principles:

☐ **Business principles** – 'Choices must be justified in terms of return on investment'.

☐ **Context principles** – 'The administration data must be archived for a minimum of seven years'.

☐ **Scoping principles** – 'We will investigate the sales and production processes but not the financial process'.

☐ **Architecture process principles** – 'The architecture must really be implemented within two months'.

☐ **Modelling principles** – 'Components must be reusable'.

Some of the principles may conflict and be taken out. Many principles will make the creation of the architecture either too complex and lengthy or create paralysis by analysis. Therefore, you need to prioritize the principles. This process should create consensus.

This list of principles needs continuous updating. It will change over time, as will the priorities. Principles need extending and refining and, provided that you keep looking, you will find some that are ignored initially or have been forgotten. They are the essential tool against which conceptual, logical and physical architectures need to be validated. The list of principles will be your compass during your stormy voyage.

FROM ARCHITECTURE TO TANGIBLE SERVICES

Essentially, the purpose of the architecture is to allow you to understand complexity by defining 'boxes' and their inter-relationship. The architecture will then have to detail 'things' that can be built and delivered. Let's call them services. Different services will need to be defined and built to support the different aspects you have described (business, information, information systems, technology, security and governance).

These services will directly relate to the principles that have been determined. They are both derived from the same business mission and vision. Principles explain how the services will perform. These services are the lowest level of your architecture and will be combined and reused to provide the functional components, which will operationally drive the business.

Figures 14.3 and 14.4 show examples of a business service and a security service.

To recap, some basic principles are shown in Figure 14.5. A business requirement creates a change to IT systems in support of business processes. This results in a change from current architecture to future architecture 'as is' to 'to be' – the 'to be' architecture should be an adaptive architecture.

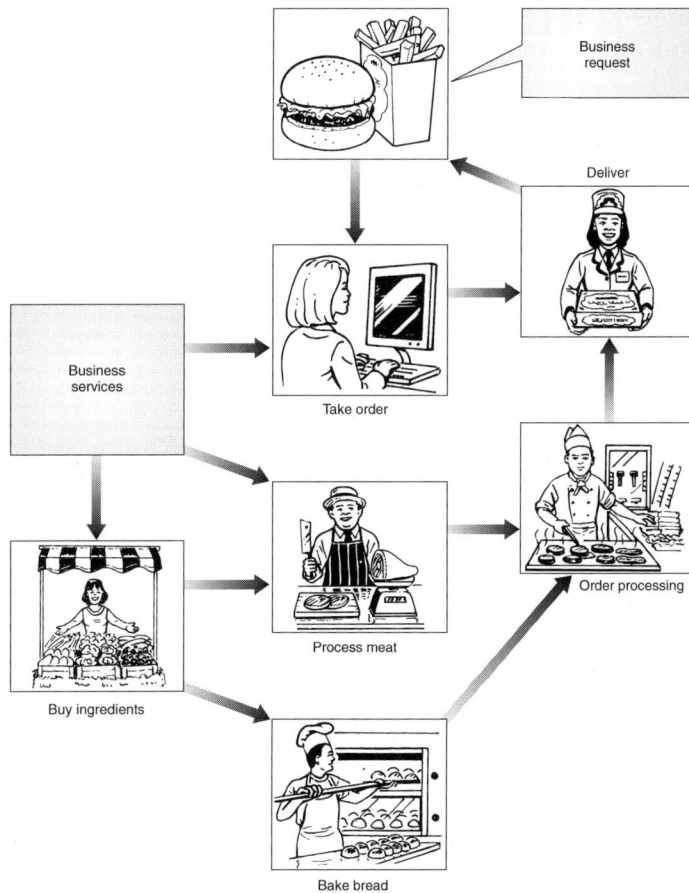

FIGURE 14.3: Examples of business services

PROJECTS PROVIDE THE ROUTE TO CHANGE

The vehicles for making this change to an adaptive architecture are projects, each of which should create some benefit and move the organization closer to being adaptive. All projects must use a framework of principles, patterns, guidelines and standards as its environment for delivering business benefit.

A project must not be allowed to decide its own role in creating the future and must always follow the principles set out. For example, a principle might be to use open standards always. A standard may be to use web services or Enterprise Application Integration (EAI) tools always. Patterns are logical designs applied to standards. Patterns can then be applied in the design of the architecture, which the project(s) seeks to create.

Creating an adaptive architecture depends entirely upon projects applying this framework of principles, patterns, guidelines and standards consistently, in order to move from one state to another. In the past, a particular set of architectural frameworks may have been applied in the creation of current systems. Now, a set of adaptive frameworks is required in order to build adaptive systems. It is the definition of this framework that plays a critical role in achieving adaptability.

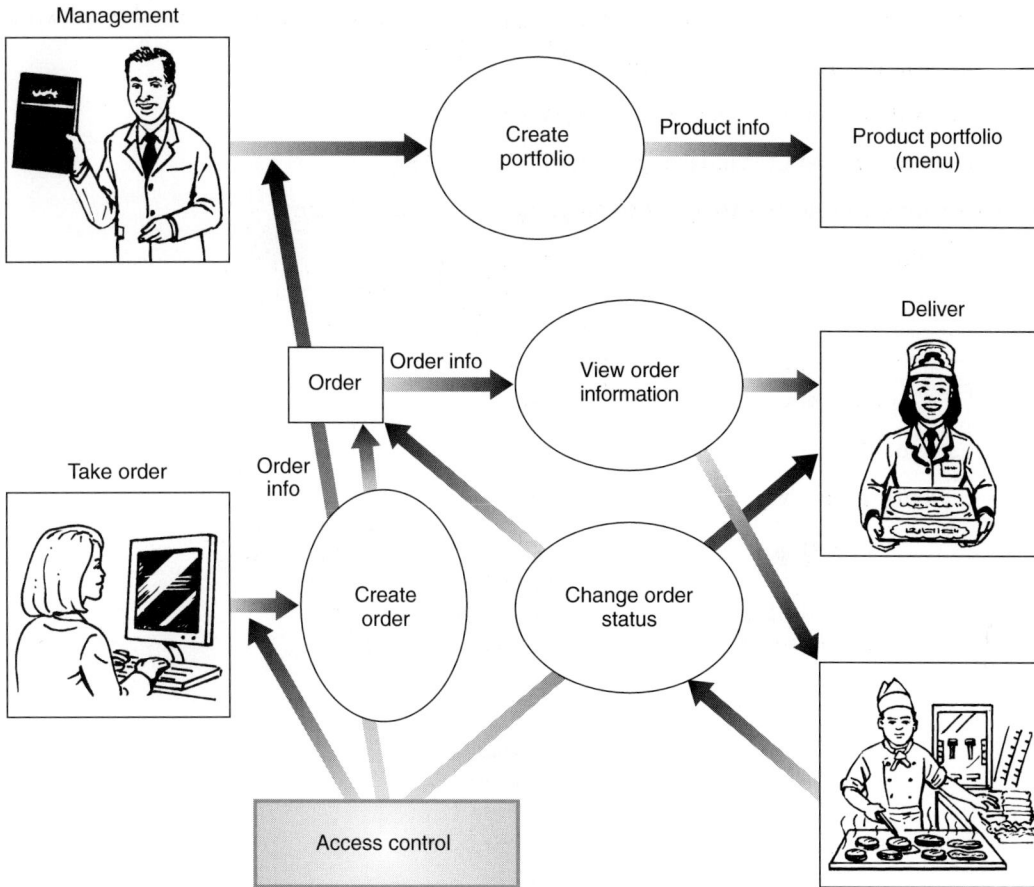

FIGURE 14.4: Examples of security services

PLUG AND PLAY, NOT EAI

Currently architectures are using technologies, such as EAI, to achieve levels of integration. However, this does not necessarily mean that a company has an adaptive architecture. It may have standardized interfaces and data structures for data movement between components and this may have taken huge amounts of investment to achieve. Nevertheless, adaptability comes with achieving true 'plug-and-play' capability among components, in support of rapidly changing business process. This gives adaptability and long-term life.

SUMMARY

1 To take strategies through to an integrated delivery plan requires an integrated architecture, which will provide the key reference models.

2 The deployment of an Integrated Architecture Framework (IAF) allows business process, technology and organization to be aligned at all levels in an ordered way.

3 There are some essential elements which must be continued in any architectural framework:

- ☐ An area for business drivers.
- ☐ A definition of core assets and services.
- ☐ A definition of standard, proven approaches.

4 There are six principles to apply to all good architecture design:

- ☐ Simplicity.
- ☐ Sanity.
- ☐ Keep looking.
- ☐ Completeness.
- ☐ Quality.
- ☐ Future-proofing.

CHAPTER 15

DESIGNING THE DELIVERY

INTRODUCTION

Planning is necessary to make the architecture work. Just as a building project begins with architectural designs, drawings and plans, then moves to calculating the quantities and the logistics of managing the site, so you need to understand how you can deliver the business vision, the new IT infrastructure or the modified product. The steps and process described here take the widest possible view but, with common sense, can be applied at any level from a major transformation program to delivery of a simple one-off project. A three-step process is presented, which links the planning process with the architectural development and articulation of the business case (Figure 15.1).

TACTICAL VISION

The first step is to take the tactical vision and identify preferred benefit scenarios to drive the definition of the overall program of work required. Commence the definition of the conceptual architectural model and initiate work on the business case.

We'll focus here only on the planning steps required during the first phase. It is important to note that there needs to be constant iteration between the three areas of business case, architecture and planning, and between the three phases – developing the approach, defining the projects to be performed, and integrating the management approach, plans, physical architecture and business case. This does not have to be a lengthy process. With the right information available and a small but dedicated team, even a major program of work can be planned in as little as two weeks.

The purpose of this tactical vision step is to ensure both integration with and understanding of the drivers. It is an essential step to ensure clarity and base decision making. The three planning deliverables are:

1 Benefit scenarios.

2 Program or project charter.

3 Program or project strategy.

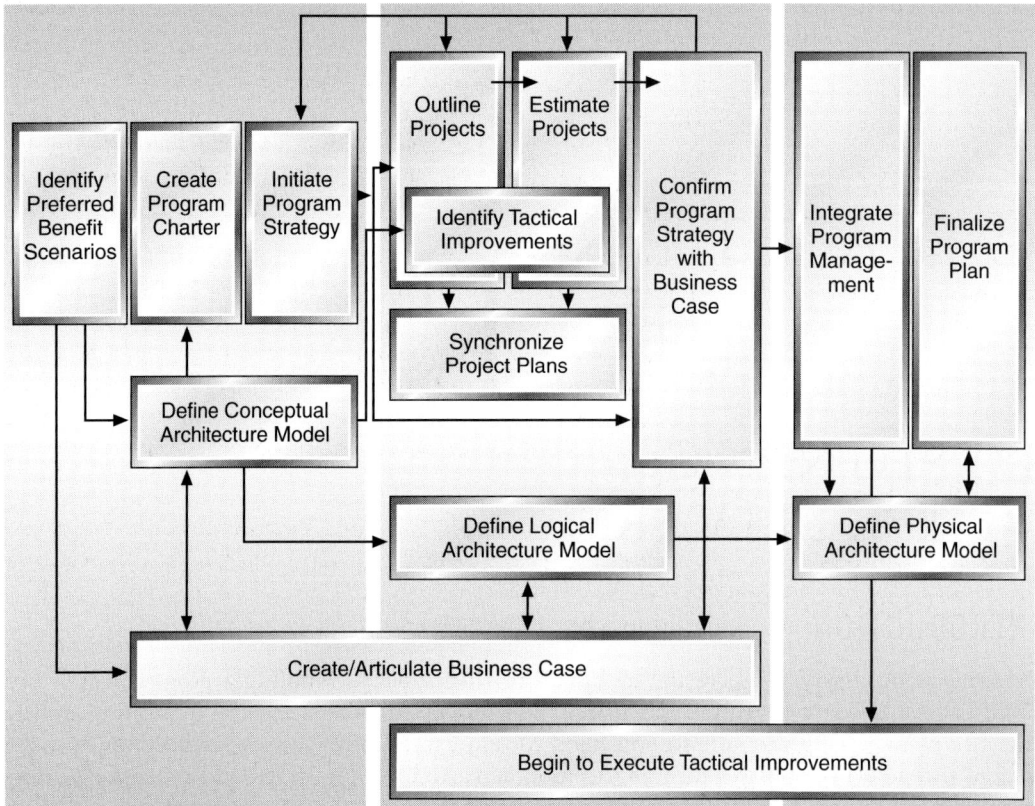

FIGURE 15.1: Design process

1 **The benefit scenarios** – The benefits scenarios are developed by identifying the key business requirement benefit areas with relative priorities. These can be assessed against the business drivers and the vision of what the 'final' preferred scenario or vision is. The time frame for the business to achieve the preferred state also needs to be considered, along with any critical business milestones and specific windows of opportunity.

In order to understand the constraints to the planning process there should be, even at this early stage, an assessment of ongoing initiatives and their impact from both a business and an IT perspective. In addition, a list of organization constraints and cultural dependencies has to be compiled. It is no good attempting to plan a series of quick-hit, three-month deliveries as part of the delivery approach if the organization's decision culture involves large numbers of people and the convening of many committees.

2 **The charter** – Different organizations have different names for this deliverable, such as terms of reference, quality plan and charter. It is a formal definition of both the scope of the project and the principles that govern how it will be run. It should be kept brief and readable. The formal definition of a charter is a legal document usually written on a single sheet, which embodies principles and confirms contracts and other transactions. It therefore seems an appropriate vehicle to describe your deliverable, which will detail assumptions, objectives and scope, and will note any constraints along with preferred solutions if there are any. It will be the initial reference point to define the capabilities of

the stakeholders and to say how this venture is aligned with the business and IT strategies. It should also contain an initial view of any risks.

3 **Program or project strategy** – The strategy takes the previous two documents and uses them to develop the management view. What should the delivery fundamentals be? In developing the rationale, you need to explore closely the fundamental logic of why you need to take a chosen delivery approach. You need to examine some alternative planning scenarios and begin to map out the areas of focus for work that needs to be planned.

This is the point when you should assess what size of steps need to be taken towards your goal. In the earlier discussion on evolutionary delivery, being able to deliver significant business benefit was mentioned. At the time of delivery you also require space to assess what has been achieved, to learn and implement lessons and to reorganize if necessary. Within your strategy development, you must identify what these 'islands of stability' will be and take a view of what associated projects are necessary to take you to each of these islands or stepping stones. These can be represented as a map, which will also show how each project is inter-dependent.

The process of arriving at the completed deliverable is more important than the deliverable itself. To provide the three deliverables described here, the correct thinking has to be carried out. Documenting the process provides a firm anchor to understand why actions should be taken going forward and returned to when things get rough. As they will!

PROJECT PORTFOLIO ANALYSIS

Most project managers find it easy to take a set of requirements and plan a project. Very few, however, have had experience of planning how to create a portfolio of coordinated projects or of how to answer questions, such as 'How many projects?', 'When should they run?' and 'Which requirements should be part of the scope of each project?'

This second planning phase outlines the projects to be run, defines the scope of each project, creates effort and cost estimates at a project level and synchronizes all the project plans. It is essential that a logical and practical approach is taken to define what projects should be run and their individual scope. The difficulty is not in describing the project plans, but in deciding the phasing, the areas of focus, strategy and the organization.

By this time, you will have a good command of your business goals, the business scope and the required business strategy to pursue. A vital element needed to complete the input to your process will be what information is required. An example may be:

- ☐ Goal.
  - ☐ To achieve competitive advantage by providing better service than X within a faster time-scale of Y and at a cheaper price than Z.
  - ☐ We will achieve a lower cost base by reducing erosion of revenue per shipment.
- ☐ Strategy – consistency meet/beat promised competition.
  - ☐ Transit time.
  - ☐ Quality.
  - ☐ Status information.

☐ Cost.

With a 98 per cent target rate.

☐ Information required to achieve the strategy.

☐ To know where order is at all times on demand.

☐ To be aware of relevant incidents.

☐ To be able to provide proactive information.

☐ Functions/areas impacted.

☐ Order acceptance.

☐ Materials ordering.

☐ Production plant.

☐ Quality control.

☐ Order shipment.

At this stage in the process, the area of focus on architecture should create a logical architecture, of which these elements are also components. From this work, you can derive the logical systems architecture to help you define which business function and information is going to be affected. Then you can produce a system map and identify candidate 'application areas' for each information area touched by your project(s).

MAPPING BUSINESS PROCESSES TO APPLICATIONS

The next step is to map all the business processes to the candidate application, confirm that all the business events are covered and identify all the main information flows. You can then classify each of the applications by type. There will be some applications where calculation will take place, such as applying pricing discounts or calculating duty and taxes, and others where information will be registered, such as posting to ledgers.

This classification allows grouping of similar types within an application area, so that they can be combined if appropriate. The final step is to map the application to the current systems that support them. You now have a comprehensive view of what needs to be done and where and how you might perform individual projects.

A real example of this view of the program design is shown in Figure 15.2. Here, the defined areas of focus were client interfaces, group interfaces, transaction processing, administration and technology environment. This was a project that touched all parts of the organization because it was to enable a major financial organization to prepare for economic and monetary union. Within the 'transaction processing' area, a number of systems areas were identified, including customer position and cash management, trade payment integrated processing, and clearing management. Within customer position and cash management, three 'application areas' were identified: customer position management; cash management and risk management and treasury.

This structural view cut across the way the bank was organized by divisions and functions within division. For example, the retail banking and investment banking divisions both had sales and marketing departments. They were able to work together in an integrated way for the first time as part of the customer interface area.

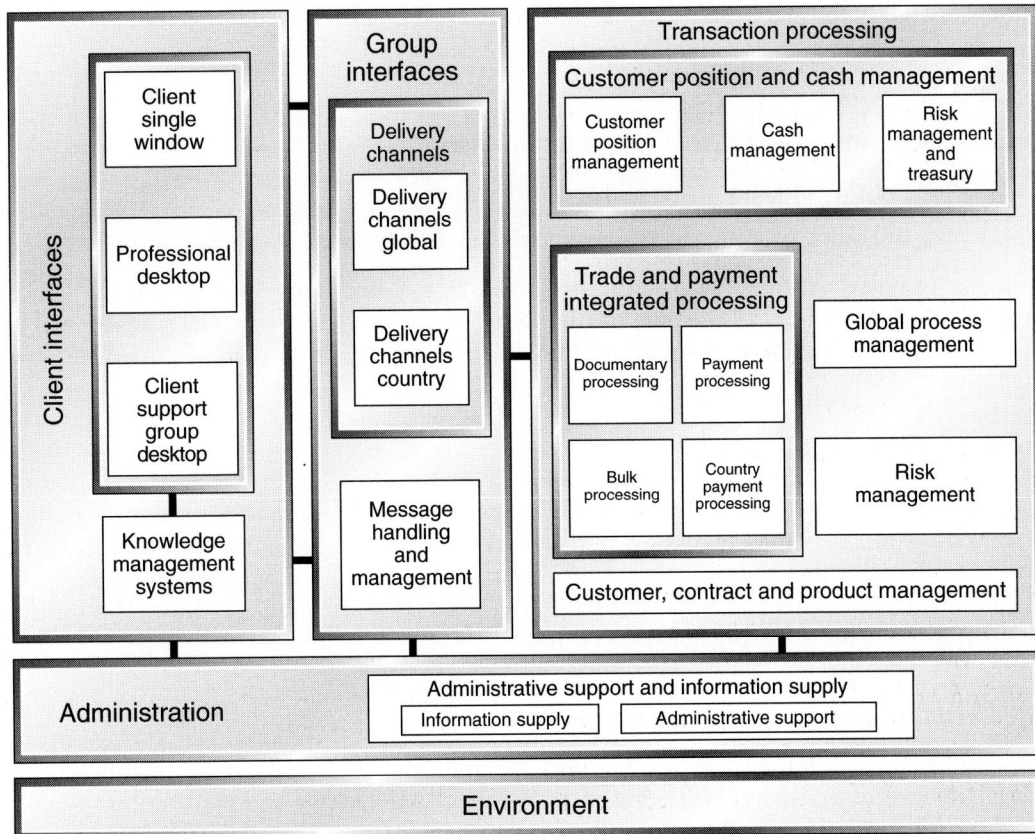

FIGURE 15.2: A working program design

Although this view was, in this case, put together for a major one-off program, it demonstrates how a single standing organization 'logical view' could be set up to cope with a world of continuous change. It provides a more flexible approach to change issues and yet promotes a degree of specialization and integration across the whole organization. The work to identify the systems supporting specific application areas also creates models that can be maintained and eases the path to faster and more effective change.

PLANNING AND ESTIMATING

Once this level of rationalization is reached, work can begin on planning and estimating each individual project that has been scoped and on looking at how each project fits or is dependent upon another within its system area of focus. Questions need to be raised about whether and how these projects fit with the initial requirements list and how well they support the timing required by the organization. A certain amount of re-profiling may need to take place at this stage.

An iterative planning process should be undertaken now, developing estimates per project by whatever is the chosen method(s), but also looking to factor your common functions within the project. Seeking common functions across all projects and raising these to be performed at a macro or program level not only reduces individual project times, it lowers costs, improves quality through consistency and helps to ensure delivery. An integrated plan, firstly by area of focus, then across areas of focus can be developed, which will show:

- ☐ Areas of focus.
- ☐ Projects and project timelines within the area of focus.
- ☐ Phase of the program across all areas of focus.
- ☐ Size and scope of 'program management' functions.

This has to be reconfirmed against the program strategy, the business case and the logical architecture. Determined by the planning horizons involved, some plans and estimates will be more detailed than others. It is important that all planning assumptions are recorded and then managed.

INTEGRATED STRATEGY

It is not until this third step that you should be making your decision about the management organization. It is only now that you will have finalized the size and number of projects to be run concurrently, the time frames, the common functions to be performed and the management constraints and risks. You know the what, the when and the how. The missing element is the 'who' – the organization structure.

ORGANIZATION

Organizing for continuous change requires personnel at all levels to be adaptable. For consultancies this is a prerequisite, but in many organizations, role and relationships remain fixed for years at a time. The culture, which prevails in organizations like consultancies with a project ethic, where teams of people come together for a short period to focus on a specific set of goals and then reorganize and are reassigned for the next assignment must become the norm for everyone.

The criteria for putting a successful team together was dealt with in Chapter 7. Now, you need to address how to create a structure that can engineer the correct environment for the team to be able to deliver. There are six 'musts' for a project organization structure:

1 Appropriate for the project in hand.

2 Flexible enough to adapt to changes in direction.

3 Able to promote clear and speedy communication.

4 Empowering for all team members.

5 Capable of addressing the need to manage both content and functions/roles.

6 Integrated.

FLEXIBILITY TO ADAPT

The appropriateness of the structure will be defined by the design work just detailed. This will have described not only the scope, but how you wish to deliver in terms of leadership approach and methods. Use of the integrated architecture approach allows you to determine

FOCUS AREA	TACTICAL VISION	PROJECT PORTFOLIO ANALYSIS	INTEGRATED STRATEGY
Leadership communication	Benefit area analysis ☐ List of benefit areas ☐ Benefit priorities ☐ Benefit scenarios ☐ Business time frame ☐ Key milestones ☐ Window of opportunity ☐ Ongoing initiatives list Program charter ☐ Assumptions ☐ Objectives ☐ Scope ☐ Constraints ☐ Stakeholders' preferred solutions ☐ Stakeholder of business, people technology alignment ☐ Program risk assessment	Change profile ☐ Change area analysis ☐ Migration steps ☐ Interdependency map Migration strategy ☐ Rationale ☐ Islands of stability definitions with associated synchronized projects ☐ Planning scenarios	Program management justification ☐ Effort estimates (man days) ☐ Resource profiles ☐ Role description ☐ Organization chart ☐ Risk assessment ☐ Areas of focus/system areas outline ☐ Integration issues ☐ Stakeholder capability ☐ Statement of benefits
Business benefit	Benefit area analysis	Migration strategy	Program plan
Relationships	Program charter	Migration strategy	Program plan
Resources	Program charter	Change profile Migration strategy	Program plan
Integration	Program charter	Change profile Projects overview ☐ List of key projects ☐ List of 'quick-fit projects' ☐ Other work areas Migration strategy Draft project charters ☐ Objectives ☐ Scope ☐ Constraints ☐ Man day estimating ☐ Release profiles ☐ Draft staffing plan ☐ Interdependency ☐ Risks	Program plan
Governance	Program charter	Projects overview Draft project charters	Program management justification Program plan

TABLE 15.1: Design phase planning deliverables

your plans not only by application area, but also by application type and so you should have a good view of the skill sets and numbers of people required at this stage. That other vital ingredient to success, getting the team balance right, will also be helped by decisions on the leadership/management principles. These will help to address the personal competencies needed by team members as well as by managers.

The plans and business case will have shown the size and complexity of the team needed – how many concurrent pieces of work, in what time-scale, and affecting which areas of the business? We can then make an initial assessment of the breadth and depth of the organization. Consideration should be given to which groups or skill sets need the most contact and what would be the best lines of communication for decision making.

In the Citibank EMU example used in the previous chapter, the EU and individual countries defined business requirements so late that a group of 12 'super users' had to be created to rapidly hot-house the impact on the bank. Processes for them to work within and a way of managing not just the group, but their inputs and outputs, had to be defined. Having the right people available at the right time and in the right numbers is also key. It is important, therefore, to look at the build up and run down of teams and levels of management or grades and experience required. In other words, profile the resource and management structure in order to maintain the right forms throughout the life cycle.

THE IMPORTANCE OF CONTINUAL REVIEW

On major integration projects, it is useful to spend 20–30 minutes of 'quiet time' each day assessing whether the organization structure is still correct and if the people fulfilling the roles are still performing as required. On longer projects it is also a good idea to be aware of 'burn out' – question whether the everyday stresses have reduced the effectiveness of individuals.

The structure put in place must be appropriate not only at the beginning, but throughout the project's life and must itself be subject to continuous change. This would indicate that in order to address personnel requirements and the need to come together, deliver, reorganize and deliver again, a matrix management approach offers the greatest flexibility. Thus, an organization where the 'continuous processes' of salary, promotion and personal development are dealt with through one line, while day-to-day operational management is dealt with through another.

Operational management can be further subdivided by function or role and content. For example, in a multiple project environment it would make sense to have quality management grouped as a common function. A quality manager would, however, have responsibility to both an overall quality manager and a project manager for the quality of the scope of a specific deliverable within a specific project. At the same time he or she could have a separate staff manager who has no involvement with the specific assignment.

INTEGRATION AND EMPOWERMENT

Matrix management organizations can be very successful. Nevertheless, they can only succeed where roles and responsibilities are clearly defined, ownership of issues readily assumed and lines of communication put in place that are direct and well understood. It is also essential that escalation paths are established that allow concerns to be addressed at the lowest possible levels.

In the management organization in Figure 15.3, project management is the responsibility of the business areas and the provision of common functions, such as integration, business modelling and risk management, the responsibility of a program directorate. In the event of a dispute over risk between a project manager and the risk manager, this can only be resolved at the program sponsor level.

This raises the issue of ensuring that the big picture – what you are trying to achieve and how – is owned at the lowest possible level and that responsibility and authority to resolve issues across content and across functions is vested at the lowest levels. If quality is to be built in at the lowest levels, there has to be empowerment of individuals to resolve matters that affect

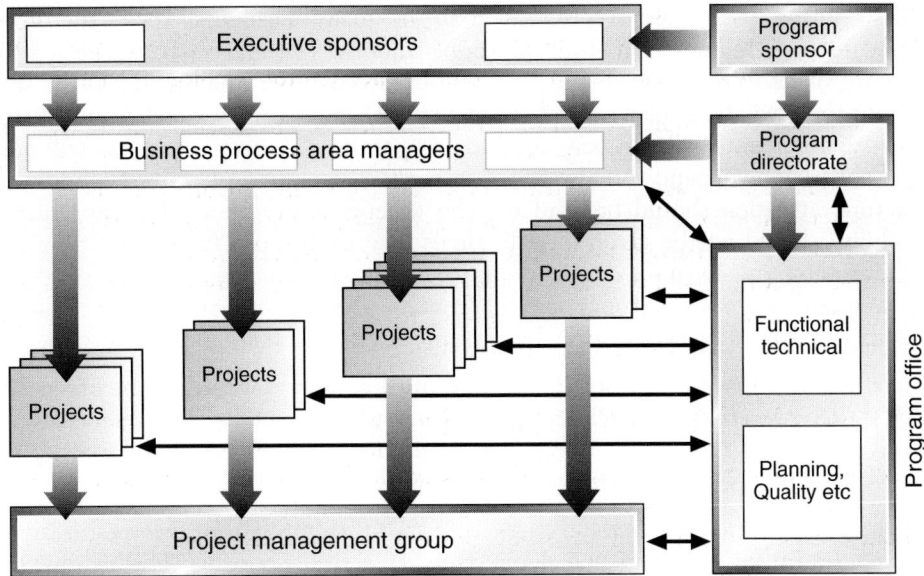

FIGURE 15.3: The management organization

interdependencies and integratability. This demands that everyone knows and understands the context within which decisions should be made and do not act and think as mere ciphers.

CLEAR AND SPEEDY COMMUNICATION

Communication of the big picture and key messages from managers to all team members as the context for making decisions, changes or simply to restate and sustain current approaches is vital. In addition, communication from team members across and through the organization is crucial when decisions that have cross-functional or cross-content impact are made.

In Chapter 12, the sports psychology approach, where decisions are made and movements produced almost instinctively by a well-drilled team, was referred to. In business, where you deal with much larger teams of cross-discipline and cross-cultural make-up, you cannot rely on instinct.

Communication will be dealt with more fully later in Chapter 16 but it should be noted here that clear lines of communication, which are well understood, frequent and two-way, can be a great positive influence on delivery productivity.

MANAGING CONTENT DELIVERY AND COMMON FUNCTIONS

Figure 15.3, showing the matrix organizations, could easily be modified to address the responsibility and escalation issues. It could have both business area and common function reporting or responsible to a 'Program directorate' or the change management role proposed in Chapter 2.

Business areas and common functions will vary from one organization and project to the next. The example Figure 15.2 had the business areas as client interfaces, transaction processing, group interfaces, administration and technology environment. They could, however, have been sales, order fulfilment, production and support services.

There also needs to be an acceptance that, in many instances, the structure must accommodate participation from multiple organizations. This has to be addressed at two levels. Firstly, in terms of management participation. Recognition that in all but the simplest of situations there will be important and complex problems to resolve quickly, means that key suppliers or participants will add benefit by taking part at executive level. This will have the benefit of ensuring ownership and also focus on the fast resolution of issues. Secondly, within the structure, attention should be paid to who accepts responsibility for particular areas. Responsibility should not be given to individuals or organizations to be politically correct, although it is tempting. Even if a decision is made to appoint a manager from one organization to lead a team delivering a functional or content scope from another or many other organizations, it should be done on the basis of merit first and team balance second.

In the final analysis, the organizational structure must be one that can win hearts and minds by quickly demonstrating that it aids the ability to deliver, rather than pandering to any preconceived ideas of how to do things. The structure, after all, is simply another tool to facilitate delivery. Thus, the 'thinking tool' principle (Chapter 12) should apply.

The easiest way to demonstrate effectiveness is to shift the emphasis of the organization from process and set up into delivery and deployment as early as possible. Throughout the life cycle, there should always be a challenge on the structural composition to test whether the ability to continue to lead change still remains. If it does not, then it is the fault of the structure, the way it is implemented or the personnel involved. If a decision is made to change an organization and to restructure, it is imperative that old excuses are not built into new organizations.

SUMMARY

MANAGEMENT DELIVERABLES AND THE DESIGN PHASE

1 Building the organization model requires synchronization of a number of key factors, influenced by:

- ☐ Scope of empowerment.
- ☐ Objectives and measures.
- ☐ Skills required.
- ☐ Stakeholder needs.
- ☐ Roles and responsibilities.
- ☐ Geography and cultural needs.

2 An accurate assessment of the organizational maturity of the major participating partners is crucial to successful operation. How good are the partners at delivering this sort of scope? How quickly do they make decisions? How many people or management layers have to be involved in making decisions? How good is the day-to-day business team at absorbing change?

3 Designing delivery does not have to be a lengthy process if the objectives are clear.

4   Each deliverable can be mapped to the six areas of management focus discussed in Chapter 12.

5   The organization of a project needs to be appropriate for the job in hand and feasible in terms of the working practice of the overall organization.

6   The 'right' organization is in need of change every day.

7   Integration projects and programs have to be organized to manage both content delivery and common role and functions.

8   Move the emphasis from the development process and set up into delivery and deployment, as early as you possibly can.

FOCUS AREA	MANAGEMENT DELIVERABLES	COULD/SHOULD PRODUCE DESIGN
Leadership and communication	Leadership principles and communication plan Communication material	Organizational and cultural knowledge
Business benefits	Business vision	☐ IAF compliant process vision ☐ IAF compliant IT vision
	Business case	Business case
Relationships	Stakeholder management plan Contracts	Stakeholder and escalation maps ☐ Transition and strategic agreements ☐ Draft contract and budget
	Contracts management plan	☐ Transition and strategic agreements ☐ Draft contract and budget
	Program price budget	☐ Transition and strategic agreements ☐ Draft contract and budget
People and resources	Program organization model	Outline program staffing, organization and infrastructure requirements
	Staff management plan	Outline program staffing, organization and infrastructure requirements
	Training plan	Outline program staffing, organization and infrastructure requirements
	Knowledge transfer plan	Draft knowledge transfer plan
	Staff objectives and career plans	Identified key change agents
Integration	Project plans	Identified projects/initiatives
	Program plan	Management structure, migration strategy, project phasing, key interdependent and milestones
	Program quality plan	Identify quality requirements (e.g. legal, certification)
Governance	Risk management file	Risk assessment
	Program office file	Knowledge of issue/risk/project/change/ configuration etc. management statement of principles (SOPs)
	Program infrastructure file	Knowledge of existing project management tools, hardware/software environment etc.
	Program status report	Outline reporting structure

TABLE 15.2: Management deliverables in the design stage

CHAPTER 16

FUNDAMENTALS TO GET RIGHT

INTRODUCTION

A number of delivery activities or projects can be underway before the design process is complete (see Figure 15.1). Some of these might be prerequisites to begin major pieces of work, such as infrastructure changes or re-engineering of business processes.

The activities or projects will usually fall into two categories. Either work packages to remove obstacles or constraints, or areas where the benefits are so high, risks so low and time-scales relatively short and they can deliver early wins, moving the project rapidly towards defined goals, building team motivation and engendering stakeholder commitment to the overall project or program.

There are also some specific topics, which are not part of the mainstream design process or which need a radical approach. These include contracting, mobilizing and communication and testing. These are all fundamental to getting things right.

CONTRACTING

To achieve the real benefits from your delivery approaches, the correct relationship has to be set up. Chapter 2 argued strongly that the client-supplier relationships, which are the current norm, fall short in the era of continuous change when, although risk can be minimized, it needs to be shared by customer and suppliers. In the case study in Chapter 18 you will see some of the consequences of both poor working relationships and contractual conditions, which do not map to the scope of work, and the leadership principles that should be applied for a successful outcome. The timing of drawing up contracts will vary, but it is pertinent to address the topic at this point.

In order to deliver complex integration projects, intimate knowledge of the context and the environment in which the project is to be performed is essential if suppliers are to be totally committed and expected in some way to share the risks. They need to participate in the design of the project. An ideal approach is to have a number of strategic partners with an over-arching contract for each one.

An 'umbrella' agreement should clearly set out elements such as the basic principles of the working arrangements. It will also need to cover a description of the scope of services to be supplied and any specific commercial terms. In fact, it needs to cover everything that will be consistent, regardless of the scope of any particular piece of work (see Figure 16.1).

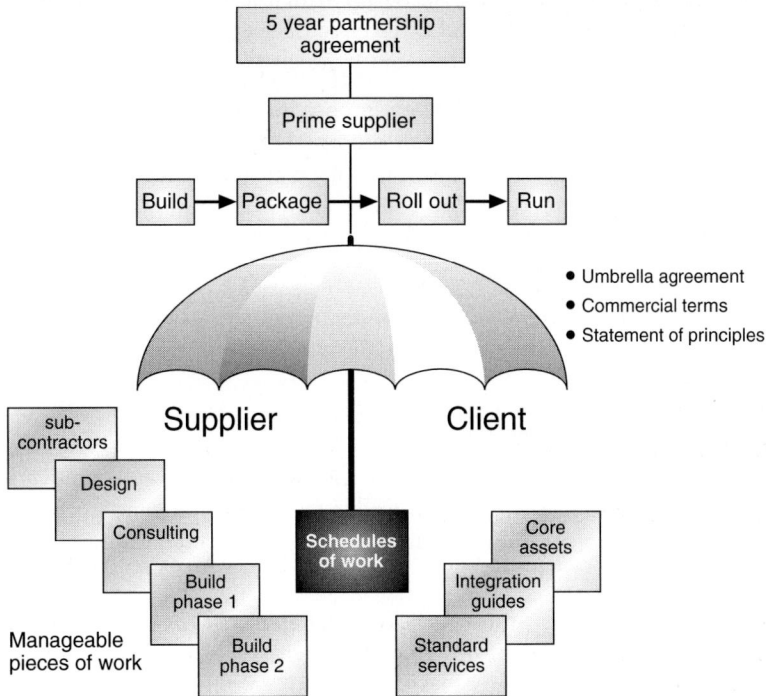

FIGURE 16.1: Partnership

The benefits of this approach are that better commercial terms will be available for longer term agreements covering a broad potential scope, than would normally be negotiated for individual packages of services or projects. Moreover, the amount of effort and time-scale to derive contracts for individual packages of work is radically reduced. Thus, cost is reduced and productivity enhanced in the same stroke.

Contract management becomes less confrontational and relationships are improved, both for the procurement and the delivery teams. This will induce behaviours that are adaptive, not adversarial. It is worthwhile noting here that there will be cultural differences in attitudes to the importance of contracts and the contracting process. Some comments have been made on this subject in Chapter 6. It is essential, before going too far, that there is a mutual understanding of the different cultural attitudes. It should not be forgotten that these differences in attitudes can also exist between companies of the same national background.

In addition to the teams responsible for negotiating and procuring, the team with the job of delivering needs to be aware of this. The delivery team also need to be fully cognizant of the implications of the delivery contract. Good practice will link elements of the project or program charter with the contract. Cross-checking, not just legal detail but also adherence to the stated leadership principles, should take place before contracts are finally signed.

MOBILIZATION AND COMMUNICATION

Although we are discussing approaches to mobilization and communication in relation to starting a project, there are of course activities which are ongoing and, like leadership, need constant focus and reinforcement. The difference between mobilization and communication needs to be explained and also why they can be dealt with together.

Mobilization covers activities required when intense involvement and commitment are needed. They usually involve a wider audience than the immediate team. Mobilization always happens at the beginning of a project but will also take place at major stages, such as achievement of a major phase or changes in direction. The vehicle for mobilization tends to be focused on large-scale events, half-day workshops and seminars or vast meetings and exhibitions.

Communication is the ongoing, daily process, which uses a number of different media to send messages – meetings, newsletters and regular technical forms are all good examples. They all have one thing in common – they occur regularly and there is a consistent pattern or system to them.

An interlacing fabric of tools and techniques

Both mobilization and communication have the same objective: to engender commitment and achieve involvement. They improve understanding of, engender commitments to, and canvas support for the project in hand. They need to be targeted at improving knowledge and changing behaviours and attitude.

There is a whole fabric of tools and techniques available. These can be grouped into 'hard' and 'soft'. By hard, we mean, for example, regular progress meetings and reports. The soft tools are more likely to be those usually associated with marketing or public relations, such as branding and positioning. All of these have a common thread and a degree of iteration. The essential skill is to be able to match the message to the media and to the audience.

Although there is a greater acceptance of change and technological advance than ever before, there is still a need to recognize the emotional rather than logical response to change and decision making of any type. Kurt Lewin, a noted guru in the field of change management, spoke of the need to unfreeze, move and re-freeze opinion. Meanwhile, Kubler-Ross, an American psychologist, talks about the emotions involved and the passive and creative reactions to change, passing through the stages of denial, anger, bargaining, depression and acceptance.

If we understand and can identify the emotional roller-coaster, which takes both delivery team and stakeholders from certainty at the beginning, through doubt and hope to confidence in a satisfactory outcome, we can use communication skills to overcome many of the seemingly impenetrable barriers to success. Emotional resistance to change is almost certainly driven by the 'FUD factor' (fear, uncertainty and doubt). Fear is created by lack of knowledge, uncertainty is about whether the new will mean more or less work and doubt is about whether the new will be an improvement over the existing.

Building shared vision, setting clear goals, involving participants, encouraging cultural awareness and timely recognition of issues are all activities that are equally critical success

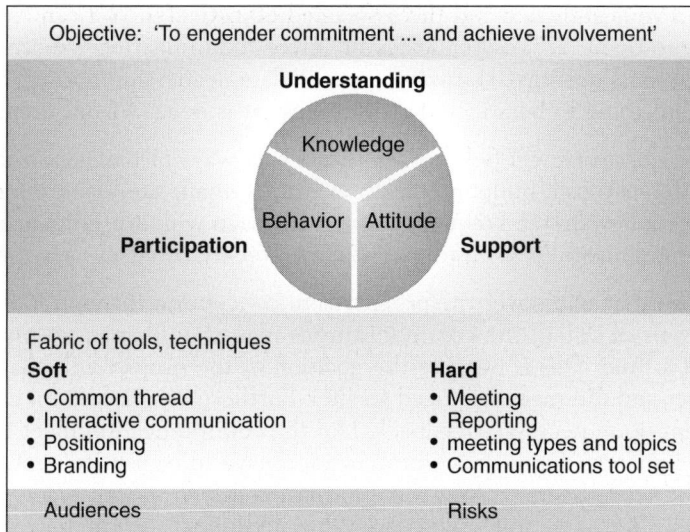

FIGURE 16.2: Communication

factors for a small integration project or for producing a joined-up business. They all depend on effective communication. How this is achieved depends on the complexity of the scope of the project and the cultures of the organization involved.

Mobilizing requires action on a number of different levels, for instance, identifying and using 'change agents' – influencers who are demonstrably supportive of the objectives – and 'action learning teams'. Action learning teams are groups from across disciplines, put together to own and resolve tough issues or obstacles to progress. Their other function is to disseminate solutions and how these are achieved.

Cascading information about the process and results by using developers and actively involved participants from the business is vital. The vision is to move to a state where there is no distinction between development of the new and the operational business or service. Even when this is achieved, there will be some groups who are more remote from the new state than others. These will need to feel involved and thus it is important that feedback is continually obtained.

The communication cycle begins with planning Who? and Why?

The end deliverable is a 'communication plan'. This must be produced, regardless of the size and scope of the project. It will encourage the project manager to focus on what needs to be done, to ensure that communication is planned for and that sufficient time and effort is allocated in the overall schedule.

Begin the communication cycle by understanding who you wish to communicate with and why. Typically you need to know: who will be impacted, who will have to change their behaviour, who will have to change their way of working, who can be a barrier and who will be key to making the change happen. For each of the audiences, groups or individuals identified, you should know why you have to communicate with them. Is it to create buy-in, keep them informed of process, educate them about new processes, minimize rumours or measure barriers to progress?

Having identified your audience and the associated objective(s), you can choose the type of things to convey to them. What would they be interested in hearing – success stories, lessons learned, practical hints and tips, status/progress to date, leadership/coordination issues, how their daily lives are going to be affected or simply what is needed from them?

Answers to these questions will help to define the best ways of passing on the messages. For example, by conference call, bulletin boards, website, e-mail, site visits, interactive meetings and workshops or a newsletter. Frequency of the message will also influence the medium of delivery – do communications need to go out daily, weekly, monthly or as needed?

Unlike other plans that will cover the project from conception through to completion, even if at different levels of detail, the communications plan should span no more than a three-month period at a time. This is because the position of the project will change in that time, and the audiences and messages will need to alter. Furthermore, successful communication is heavily dependent upon necessary feedback. Did the communication meet the requirements of the intended audience? Does the communication have to be sent to another audience and if so how might it need changing? Was the information in a form that made it easy to use and share? Was it delivered in a timely fashion? What additional information should have been added or should anything have been deleted?

The cycle can then begin again with problem solving, feedback and planning what needs to happen next, before designing further communications. In this way, you can continually monitor and troubleshoot most of the typical communications breakdowns.

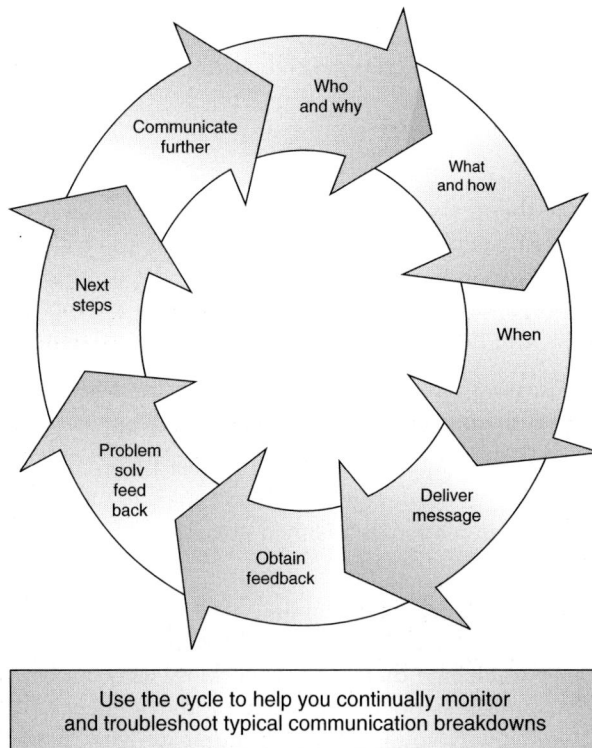

FIGURE 16.3: The communication cycle

In all communications, there needs to be a thorough and consistent message. A complete understanding by the management team of the key messages will help to reinforce communications about where the project is heading. Particular emphasis should be paid to communicating results delivery.

It is particularly important in complex integration projects for the project or program manager to understand the critical part they must play in the communication process. It is vital that they are proactive. To demonstrate their leadership, they should take every opportunity to send out messages on the necessity of the changes taking place. They should also demonstrate that they know where they are heading and have a viable plan to get to the destination. This will demonstrate stability. There is, however, more to be done. Managers have to be seen to actively support the team, involving them in decisions and changes and regularly recognizing and rewarding actions that are consistent with moving forward. This will greatly enhance team motivation.

TESTING

It might seem strange to deal with testing at the very start of planning. Often, this is done just before delivering, which means testing is given only cursory attention. Frequently, things do not go to plan and, by the time you get around to testing, all the contingency time and effort has been used up and the poor old testing teams have to get on and do the best they can.

On the other hand, testing teams tend to be proud of their particular skills and may rightly insist on doing the job thoroughly. They only have to point at all those past disasters, when new systems failed to integrate on going live, to send shudders down the spine of business and project managers alike. Nevertheless, it does not have to be like this. By making some key changes to the way you work and to the development process, you can ensure that the pressures are relieved, contention is removed, quality is guaranteed first time and deliveries are made to dates that business operations can rely on.

Planning the testing first

The first step is to start some 'right to left' planning or 'back-scheduling' (planning from the end of the process backwards). The usual planning approach is to decide what the business needs and by when, and then to plan the development process – starting with requirements gathering and functional specification, regardless of the method, structured waterfall or rapid application you have chosen.

To get things right, at the earliest stage address what testing will be carried out and how. Only then can decisions be taken on how long this will take, how complex it will be and what logistics will be required. Taking this view can often radically alter what is thought to be the critical path through the whole project and, therefore, the order of priorities for when and how components are built and changes made.

Repeatedly, teams forget to test anything but the software. What about the business processes and any organizational changes? These may look acceptable in theory, but will they actually work? The most successful programs sometimes come when the new business process and organization are implemented ahead of the supporting technology becoming available. This can have two benefits – creating some early wins for the business and proving that the heavy investment in supporting software is worthwhile. This can lower risk, boost morale and gain commitment from executive sponsors.

Clarity about the goals of testing

With a set of measurable testable objectives, clearly defined from the beginning, no one should claim that insufficient information is known at the beginning to plan testing. If you are making full use of reusable components, there should be a good basis to make some judgements about how complex the task is likely to be. This will naturally lead you to exactly what you need to test, and what you are testing for. Over the last ten years, there has been a tendency to increase the time and effort spent on testing, often without any real knowledge of how or if this is effective.

In his book, *Effective methods for testing software*[1], William Perry noted

> ❛Testing is an unnecessary and unproductive activity if its sole purpose is to validate that the specifications were implemented as written. If the developmental processes for software work correctly, they would implement these specifications as written. Thus testing, as performed in most organizations, is a process designed to compensate for an ineffective "software development plan".❜

Yet, many teams leave the testing until the development process is largely complete, and rarely examine the results of testing beyond the need to rectify the immediate defects. If you wish to address one of the main reasons for project failure (not building quality in at the lowest work unit or component), you need to make testing part of everyone's everyday job.

Early investment in testing gives payback

There are a number of ways in which this can be done. In the early 1970s, Mike Fagan and some colleagues at IBM developed an inspection method that goes some way towards addressing the issue of developmental processes failure as the key cause of defects.

Fagan's inspection method looks at failures in understanding, by rigorously checking documentation at all critical points for clarity, ambiguity and consistency. Inspection is carried out at all stages and levels and involves everyone in the team. It has strict, even prescriptive rules, which may at first seem bureaucratic. However, because the ground rules are laid out very clearly, the process is inclusive and covers all types of defects, not just software, logic or functional errors. There is proven payback for the time and effort expended. This comes in the form of early delivery and fewer faults. The ability to deliver on time and above end user expectation has to be a prize worth fighting for because it begins to reduce business risk.

You should not forget to look at the delivery process, and try to deliver 'completed components' into testing as early and frequently as possible. You should aim to make sure that the testing team does not become a separate unit formed at the end of the process, but is a standing team working for the duration of the project. As a common function, there is a strong inclination to create a totally separate unit to carry out testing.

Certainly there are some very specific sets of skills, knowledge and personal competencies required for 'career testers'. If testing and thinking about testing is to be part of everyone's daily life on the project, it cannot be outsourced to a separate team. A 'centre of excellence' approach can be a highly effective compromise. The 'build' teams retain responsibility for all stages of testing up to final 'integration testing', when all components come together. The experts in the centre of excellence provide strategy, help and guidance and act as a 'hit team' if particular problems start to threaten plans. They then carry out and manage the final stages of testing up to operational running.

[1] William Perry, *Effective methods for testing software*, John Wiley, 1995.

Strategy is needed to give overall guidance

Whatever shape of testing – daily, multiple drops or a big bang end phase – there needs to be a guiding strategy. That strategy must define what testing stages are to be carried out. For each stage, the strategy needs to clearly lay out the rationale.

For example, a technical integration testing phase may have, as a testing objective, 'To ensure that all components required for the business to implement X are technically reliable (service availability of 96 per cent), integrate (expected through messages received 100 per cent of the time) and perform in a robust enough way (error entry rejected without crashing the system) to allow full functional testing by users to take place.'

In order to fully understand what each testing phase will contribute, and to ensure that there are no overlaps or gaps created, both the focus of the phase and the scope have to be determined. This should be done in terms of data, for example, to guarantee the system detects only accurate and up-to-date data, and functionality. Performance will need to be tested to a certain level to prove robustness and to give an indication that performance, size and capacity requirements will be met.

All the statements made here refer to software tests, but could be applied equally to testing business process and organization. Dependencies also have to be understood and defined within the strategy. For example, this phase is dependent on the successful completion of a previous set of testing. There must also be a location allocated and installation of hardware. Of course, there must be resources available to carry out the tests.

In Chapter 3 a proposal was made about how to decompose initiatives in order to make sure they were complete and that their upstream and downstream impacts could be understood. The testing strategy needs to break down the final deliverable into its component parts to achieve a thorough understanding of what needs to come together at what point for testing to make a useful contribution.

Keeping your head while all about you...

Once testing is underway, everyone appreciates that this is a very dynamic time, subject to changes almost by the hour. Consequently, it is important that well in advance there is absolute clarity about roles and responsibilities and about the management processes that will be used. What reporting will take place? When will it be produced and what will it cover? How will defects be prioritized? How will you classify defect types? You should also clearly lay out the required steps to produce an acceptable test and guidelines on how to plan testing, what sort of test data is acceptable and how to define expected results. It should be an 'engineering guide' for anyone wanting to put tests together, decide what to test, or decide when testing is complete.

Determining when testing is complete requires statistics. Choosing what to test requires some careful thought. With previous bad experiences of failures in live systems, the natural temptation is to test everything to destruction every time you make a modification. In our current world of spaghetti systems, this is probably wise.

However, in an adaptive environment, where you are simply reconfiguring standard, reusable components, all you should test is those elements that are new or modified, where and when they interact. This should be the standard set of testing from unit testing through to end-to-end business flow testing. Check the handshake and check the flow. Only test to destruction the new. Testing then becomes the third area for major reduction in time-scale, after you have radically improved mobilization and hand-over to operations.

Shortening the time-scale by using statistics

In many cases effort and time are estimated by looking in detail at a specific development phase like Functional Specification, and then applying a percentage of total effort to other stages. This type of 'rule of thumb' approach is based on data gathered from numerous similar projects over a long period. However, the rules of the game are changing rapidly. Improvements in the areas of mobilization, testing and handover to Operations mean that the balance between development phases changes. When developing for reuse the build profile is different. When reusing core assets the amount of build and test effort is radically altered. The use of statistics to give reliable and immediate feedback of your particular real world is essential.

You should look at defect reports raised and closed against numbers of tests and functions tested to date, and you also need to trace back where the faults have arisen, to obtain vital feedback into development process failure. In one recent experience, 50 per cent of all defects were traceable to two use cases (specifications). These use cases were found to be overly long and complex. A guideline was published to inhibit the size of any single use case. In the next phase, defect rates dropped by nearly 40 per cent.

Use of statistics and intelligent examination of their messages can have a beneficial impact on the testing phases and also on estimating overall time-scales, definition of individual training needs and amendment to management direction, all of which will improve productivity and quality.

Nevertheless, making wrong assumptions about the amount of help that automated processes can give, and particularly the use of test harnesses, can have an adverse effect on testing plans. In many one-off integration projects, the savings made are a close call when valuable time and effort is spent building test harnesses to allow earlier testing of individual components. A decision needs to be made in each case. Firstly whether the specific component is or is likely to be defined as a core asset, and secondly how much reuse is anticipated of any test harness in the future. Test harness decisions and probably the building of them should be the domain of the centre of excellence.

The ideas proposed here are that testing should be more interactive and cut across all aspects of the development or change and that there is a need for testing responsibility to be left with the builder or creator as part of the quality process, but supported by a centre of excellence staffed by highly skilled resources. If these ideas are developed, a scenario arises where you can create 'construction control' (a control function across all suppliers to the integration project responsible for oversight and management of software and processes quality).

This would cover all phases and all teams. It could also encompass management of any release process because acceptance and also delivery criteria would have to be proven against construction control guidelines and methods. Such a function would also be responsible for improving the development and delivery organization against any capability maturity model.

SUMMARY

1 Contracting needs to be at the strategic level – once and very early. Subsequent pieces of work should not need a confrontational negotiation.

2 The delivery teams have to be involved to ensure that contractual commitments facilitate rather than constrain the delivery approach.

3 Mobilization is always essential and should be done at all key milestones, not just at the start.

4 Communication needs to match the message to the media and to the audience.

5 Failure to communicate can lead to rumours and put you on the defensive.

6 Testing has to be planned at the design phase. It is not a 'big bang' process to be saved for the end of the project, but should be part of everyday life.

7 Testing experts will be required to assist, but these should not take away responsibility for the quality of the end product.

8 While you do not have to test everything, everything you do needs to be testable.

9 Improvement in testing time-scales and efficiencies can be gained by using statistics. This can lead to major improvements in the overall delivery time-scale.

10 In a 'reuse' world, the what, how and when of testing needs to be thought about differently.

CHAPTER 17

MAINTAINING THE INTEGRATION VISION

INTRODUCTION

There are many aspects to integration. Fundamentally, integration is about ensuring that people work together first, and then that systems and processes work together.

Part 2 discussed and described practical ways to ensure that people work together. Part 3 has also shown an approach to creating change agendas and plans – governance processes for change and issue and risk management contribute to integrating people. In addition, the focus on structuring the organization shown in Chapter 15 was to guarantee integration.

These are the vital links, which, if not in place or not worked at, will cause breakdown. You still need to address the issue of how you integrate application and business processes, how you think about designing interfaces so that both sides are always kept in step, and how you think about both data and functionality to avoid duplication and identify commonality. You have to look hard at the infrastructure, middleware, development tools and approaches to facilitate integration and, finally, how you test to prove that everything fits together.

It is worth considering once more, why integration is important. In the past, it has simply been a matter of making sure that systems were not divergent or that when delivered there were no gaps. The risks were that resources could be wasted or business needs not fully satisfied. Today, however, integration provides the path to the future for systems and for the organization as a whole. Without an integrated and flexible approach that can be adopted dynamically to meeting changing needs, companies are at a major trading disadvantage to their more forward thinking and agile competitors.

HOW CAN YOU MAINTAIN INTEGRATION?

In the ideal world, starting with zero, you could take the integration approach that everything is fixed and you do not want anyone to go and break it. You could build a model of what you want to end up with and go and build it, keeping people on track through organization, plans, fine-tuning or enhancing your tools and models.

Nonetheless, in reality and as described in Chapter 2, for most organizations things are already broken. They need to fix them before they get any worse. In this scenario, you have to be in reactive mode. Systems have evolved and are still evolving with no consistent tools. There is no grand plan and never was. There are only fragments of architecture, business models and overall design. For most organizations in this situation, the starting point has to be with the business processes. You must look for significant, if not quantum, leaps forward as things progress.

The initial step must always be the creation of an architecture or set of models, which bring together technologists and business experts and provide a common platform and vocabulary for all professionals to understand the implications of a change.

Chapter 14 described in some depth an integrated architecture framework. A world standard architecture has, for many years, been John Zachman's Framework for Enterprise Architecture and Information Systems Architecture.[1]

In Zachman's framework, there are six layers, the highest is 'Enterprise', then 'Operational' and 'Engineering'. These top three layers can be viewed as 'above the line', dealing with the creation of a view of the business. The engineering layer begins to define the logical systems and forms the interface between business and technology. Below the line, the bottom three layers, are the 'Construction', 'Sub-contractors' and 'Maintenance' layers. Every layer deals with How? (function), What? (data), Where? (network), Who? (people), Why? (motivation), and When? (timing).

In straightforward terms, the framework helps to define the business you do (or want to do), and the set of tools you need to do it. The layers above the 'line' give projects a context to work in. The three layers above the line will give the total view of the requirement. Below the line, you create your logical systems and define the projects needed to build the tools – the 'design phase'. The projects you run can provide the lower level models.

Therefore, it is possible to create an architectural big picture over time, by using the work of delivery projects. An initial piece of work needs to provide the enterprise model layer. However, once specific areas below this have been worked down to the engineering layer, and guidelines for modelling produced so that standard formats are available, the building of the overall model begins in parallel with delivering products.

THE INTEGRATION LIFE CYCLE

In the same way that there is a development life cycle, there is also an integration life cycle. The two life cycles must be properly balanced and prioritized. Figure 17.1 shows the typical activities carried out during the life cycle to guarantee an integrated project or program. The balance has to be achieved by weighing the business drivers against the real world constraints.

Good planning, standards setting and all the other proposed elements should be carried out early to facilitate integrated delivery. It is inevitable, though, that not everything will be in place in time to make the first deliveries to a new integrated model. Integrators must, accordingly, learn to accept that while they hold sway during initiation and design as building and deployment takes place, the operational delivery team and their needs take precedence – even if this means compromising in some areas.

[1] www.zifa.com.

INITIATION	ENGINEERING	CONSTRUCTION	INTEGRATION TEST, DEPLOY and SUPPORT
Confirm current architecture and baseline	Initial high level analysis	Coordinate detailed analysis	Test shared elements and systems
Confirm business drivers and requirements	Formal scope confirmation	Coordinate detailed physical design	Test integration of systems
Develop first cut view of scope	define partitioned release model	Coordinate shared elements development	Test integration of business flows
Prioritize and align	Confirm shared elements and systems	Coordinate physical systems development	Coordinate deployment and support

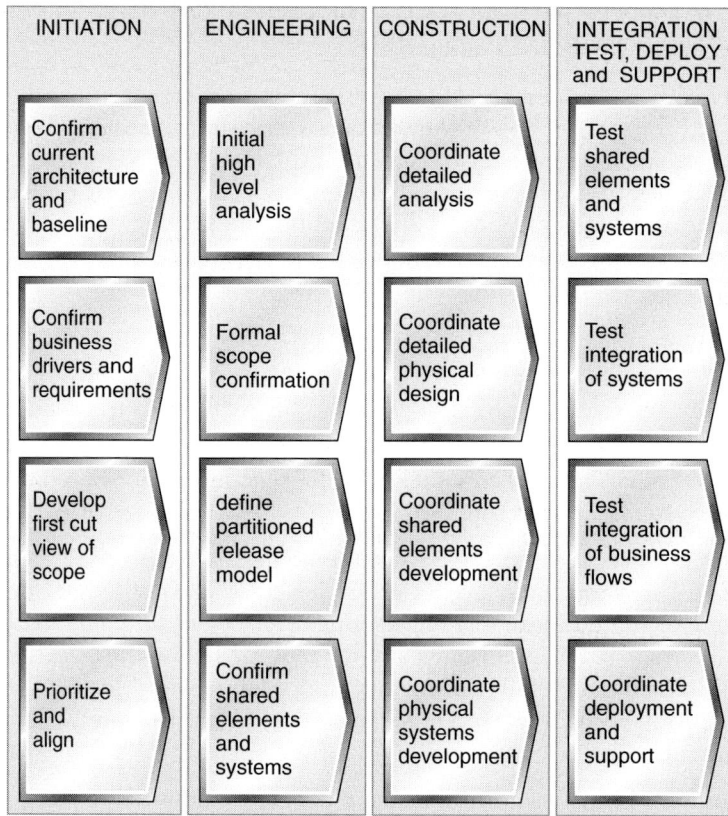

FIGURE 17.1: Integration life cycle

A key element in that compromise, which sets up many difficult choices, is the integration of technology capability with current and future business need. Integration is the way to prevent overreach, provision of unnecessary capacity and technical function for today, or shortfall. Integration establishes a technology platform that is current and proven, supporting current business needs with promised future technology and aimed at stated future business needs.

MANAGING THE ADDITIONAL STRAIN OF ITERATIVE DESIGN AND DELIVERY

Keeping things joined up while multiple levels of design and delivery are taking place and multiple project phases are in progress, requires well-documented guidelines and added layers of management around the build process. This management role is required to achieve the correct balance. We can call them integration engineers.

During the design and build stages, integration engineers become the conduit for project teams, to make certain that high-level outline and low-level detail stay joined up and that changes in physical and technical design documentation are reflected back into logical and functional design, and continue to help to build and enhance the architecture. At the build phases, they will work closely with all suppliers to ensure adherence to guidelines and to check that component deliveries can integrate. Even earlier, integration engineers can provide support to the procurement process by briefing suppliers on the integration requirements and contributing to the production of any invitations to tender.

DEPLOYING THE END PRODUCT

Deployment can be more complex than the development process itself, even in an era of continuous change. When multiple branches or a global roll-out is required, it needs to be planned as a program within a program. Moreover, it has to be thought through at the design stage and not left as an add-on at some later date, or your destination may loom out of the mist and surprise you.

The four key areas when starting any deployment planning will be to look at data, information systems, people and organization, and technology. Initially this can be done in a series of separate workshops for each topic, and then by combining outputs to produce an integrated plan and complete understanding. The objectives, at first, should focus on key areas and establish a common understanding of possible issues. All of this can come together in a series of management and planning workshops. For example, a deployment workshop for the roll-out of a capacity planning application might cover the following topics:

- [ ] Supplier data.
    - [ ] Requirements and checklists.
    - [ ] Source, collection and storage.
    - [ ] Content and quality.
- [ ] Interfaces.
    - [ ] Systems, data content and ownership.
    - [ ] Data quality.
- [ ] Data conversion/migration.

The information systems workshop, meanwhile, would have the following objectives:

- [ ] Identifying the extent of changes to local processes.
- [ ] Identifying the extent of local customization.
- [ ] Exploring options for overall control during support/service phase.
- [ ] Identifying and pursuing system issues.

Most importantly, the 'site' for the deployment needs to be surveyed. The site has to be defined along with any prerequisites and a site checklist produced. The current infrastructure status can be ascertained and any necessary changes defined well in advance. At this point, local staff involvement should be planned and some training needs analysis may have to be initiated. As with the other workshops, any issues will need to be clearly identified and an action plan put in place to pursue and resolve them.

Once again, this approach needs to be carried out as an intensive, short, sharp exercise. Each workshop needs to be time-boxed, limited to a maximum of two days, but taking place in one day if at all possible. There needs to be continuity across the workshops and these should be planned so that some attendees can participate in more than one, but they should not be spread over more than two weeks' elapsed time. In this way, a quick-start approach to deployment can be generated, common understanding established and any assumptions quickly validated.

In planning multiple roll-outs, particularly a transnational deployment, the deployment phase or roll-out should not take longer than the time taken to develop the next phase. This seems a fairly obvious statement to make. However, it is not unusual to see that when 70 or 80 country organizations are involved, with perhaps as little as a week to deploy new processes each time, it can be 18 months before everyone has a system deployed, if only one team is doing the roll-out. This begins to severely restrict progress. In such circumstances, training local staff, but with central support, to deploy seems the only viable approach. Web-based deployment and remote training can greatly facilitate and shorten such deployments.

SUSTAINING THE VISION

In any change process, whether one-off or continuous, it is vital that impetus is maintained. This can only be done by sustaining the vision and ensuring that operational activities remain aligned with that vision. We return now to the six areas of management focus outlined in Chapter 12.

The role of the program or project manager is pivotal to ensure that the executive management view of the vision and the operational program view stay aligned. It is inevitable that, from time to time, they will drift apart. Only the program manager is in a position, acting as the prime interface between the executive and the projects, to recognize when this drift requires adjustment. The following points may help to make that judgement:

☐ Programs and complex integration projects may be described as a sequential process but everything happens in parallel.

☐ Time required in the market is the key factor to determine time required to develop and deliver.

☐ Reality always changes.

☐ Different people have different expectations.

☐ Expectations are manageable.

☐ It is critical to success and personal salvation to understand what benefits are expected.

MANAGING THE BENEFIT DELIVERY

Upholding the vision requires constant refocus on business benefits. Benefit areas, benefit priorities, benefit time-scales and new opportunities are always subject to rapid and constant change. Therefore, it is vital to understand who the benefit owners are. A benefit owner is more inclined to be the operational manager charged with delivering the benefit, than the executive who described what it should be. During the annual budget cycle, the financial controller is liable to be a benefit owner using benefits to adjust company-wide budgets. It is extremely useful to manage his or her expectations correctly in unison with the operational management.

To do this, comprehension of a whole network of relationships is necessary. A Dutch colleague always has a whiteboard in his office, in plain view of everyone. On it he keeps a record, using notes, for each stakeholder and sponsor of the benefits they own, any relationship changes and any issues. By being open and honest about what he is doing and why, he always gets a positive and interested reaction.

One of the things that being open will help you to do is to make sure that you are managing relationships and communicating at all levels, from chief executive, and the executive board to departmental managers and the shop floor. It is useful to keep a view of 'customer satisfaction ratings'. Accepting that this rating will vary over time, the 'how' and 'when' of communicating can be crucial in timing important announcements and deliveries. Timing is often severely underestimated in terms of its worth in combating resistance to change.

Key stakeholders for any program manager are the resources – the people who form the team that will deliver the integrated system. While keeping focused on the big picture and overall trends, do not forget that people need individual attention.

Finally, returning to integration, the touchstones are the architecture and the road map provided by migration plans, the integration strategy and the program plan. These all need to be constantly updated, reinforced and their linkage with the vision constantly communicated.

SUMMARY

Leadership and communication	Define / know target audiences, know what are their expectations, different interests, personal agendas Match the media to the message and to the audience
Business benefits	Benefit owner maps
Relationships	Stakeholder map Ownership map
Resources	Competency maps Induction programs Education Plan Knowledge transfer plan
Integration	Update / maintain currency of: ☐ Program plan ☐ Migration plan ☐ Integration strategy ☐ Architectures
Governance	☐ Reactions to changes / updates ☐ Organizational charts ☐ Feedback ☐ Processes / guidelines / standards / templates etc. ☐ Organizational process

TABLE 17.1 Relating maintaining the vision deliverables to areas of management focus

1 Integration needs management process and roles to ensure alignment throughout the delivery life cycle.

2 A pragmatic view has to be taken of the priority and importance of delivery over integration.

3 Iterative design and delivery requires a radically different governance process and much more sophisticated management.

4 Planning for and deploying the end product should be treated as a program within a program. The development and the deployment cycles must be attuned.

5 To sustain vision requires constant work.

6 Benefit delivery is the sole purpose of the program. Make sure that it is continually managed, tracked and that expectations are correctly set.

PART 5

CHAPTER 18

THINGS GO WRONG

INTRODUCTION

There are many (too many) instances, where integration projects and programs go wrong and the success rate does not appear to be improving. Chapter 2 provided some insight into why.

The projects that fail are entered into with nothing but good intent by all of the parties involved. Yet, in every case, the fundamentals of failure are the same. In the vast majority of cases, programs that go wrong do so within the first two months of starting, even if the symptoms of failure do not present themselves until much later. Here are the main, recurring reasons that contribute to program failure:

- ☐ Unrealistic project plans.
- ☐ Deadlines set without reference to logistics or work content.
- ☐ Deferring issues rather than addressing them at the right stage.
- ☐ Inadequate scope control procedures.
- ☐ Non-recognition of joint goals and responsibilities.
- ☐ Poor relationships.
- ☐ Lack of planning regarding resource take on.
- ☐ Lack of project control at the lowest work unit to ensure that quality is built in.
- ☐ Lack of commitment.
- ☐ Lack of shared, clear, measurable, testable objectives.

What follows is the story of a major integration program. The case study considers the background and start up of the program, the recognition of problems and corrective action, and finishes 12 months on, with an update of where things stood at this point.

You can assess whether the key causes of failure were correctly identified and rectified. You may want to consider the chances of success for this particular program in the light of the measures that were taken. What might you have done? What would you do now?

SETTING THE SCENE

The organization concerned, which will remain nameless, is a consumer-facing business with many thousands of customers. In common with businesses across the world, the primary objective for the planned integration program was to introduce flexibility into the delivery of its products. The company had carried out a wide-ranging review of its business and decided that, to stay in the sector, it needed to grow its business. In order to do that, it would have to automate and integrate its various customer-facing activities, using technology to simplify selling through multiple delivery channels and speed up bringing products to market. The program would have to greatly enhance the company's services to customers and the range of products on offer. It would have to maximize cross-selling opportunities and reduce internal overheads.

The company, referred to here as Hoogstraat B.V., decided on Program X as its solution, an integration plan that would radically change the way it operated, by outsourcing all of its business processes, except for its sales and marketing functions. The board was convinced that, by outsourcing its existing business processes to other companies, it would be able to offer better choice and value to its customers much more quickly.

Meanwhile, out in the marketplace, some of the suppliers had thought about how the sector should be moving in the days of mass customization (where products are designed to a base configuration, but then tailored to a range of differing customer needs on a large scale), and what that would mean to them. Suppliers of back-office services, such as call centres, were realizing that they would have to offer more functionally rich services at a lower cost per unit. One of them (referred to here as Outsourcer) knew that this would mean offering end-to-end processing services, but it had no way of integrating all of its services in an automated, yet flexible way. Thus, it sought a systems integration technology solution.

A third company, a major systems integrator (referred to here as Integration Company), had been thinking about the problems of its clients across all sectors – how the clients must now manage multiple delivery and supply channels; bring on new channels and products quickly; draw on third-party services; and yet plug easily into legacy systems whether these were built by the client or existed as packages. Integration Company had come up with a prototype that took a single, holistic view to solve all of these problems, which could be easily customized for individual clients. Recognizing their synergy, it did not take long for Outsourcer and Integration Company to join forces, so when Outsourcer was approached by Hoogstraat B.V. to provide a back-office outsourcing solution, it had a ready response.

HOW THINGS BEGAN TO UNRAVEL

Although Outsourcer and Integration Company had agreed to cooperate, they had frequently been in competition in the past. Therefore, there was a certain anxiety on the part of Outsourcer that Integration Company might try to muscle in on its client. Outsourcer also felt that it did not have the resources to cover all the 'side issues' that Integration Company seemed to want to constantly discuss, such as how this new approach offered to Hoogstraat B.V. could be enhanced and sold to multiple clients. Outsourcer made very sure that it owned the client relationship and kept Integration Company away from as many direct discussions with the client as possible.

Hoogstraat B.V. was very concerned that it should get value for money. It put one of its senior, and most trusted purchasing people in charge of the negotiations. Sheila and her assistant Fred had no experience of what was involved in delivering a program of this size and complexity but they knew their industry sector well and had risen through the ranks of Hoogstraat B.V., so they were well aware of what the company wanted. They were very good at driving a hard bargain in terms of price and making sure that contracts with suppliers were set up, which severely punished late or non-delivery. In short, they were the ideal people to make sure that the board's deadlines were hit. Sheila was very happy to deal with Outsourcer as the prime contractor, while ensuring, diligently, that what Integration Company was delivering would fit the bill.

Initial discussions were thorough and tough but began to take some time to complete. Hoogstraat B.V. had a problem; indeed this was part of the reason it was embarking on Program X anyway. It took a long time to make decisions in the company because ownership of the business flows was so fragmented. As a result, each meeting became an all-star epic with a cast of thousands.

Things dragged on and meanwhile commercial pressures mounted. As its year-end approached, Outsourcer needed a big deal to make its balance sheet look good. For its part, Integration Company had sunk millions of Euros into developing its product and needed to get this into the marketplace to start getting a return on the investment. Meanwhile, Hoogstraat B.V. knew that, with every day that passed, it was potentially losing competitive advantage.

All of these factors conspired to create a sudden urgency to get contracts signed and the program underway. It was agreed that some pre-contract activities, such as due diligence investigations and mapping the business requirements to the supplier's view of what they were being contracted to supply, should be done in parallel with starting work.

The initial estimates for the supply of the new, integrated systems did not meet the allocated budget, nor the deadlines demanded by the board. Even though Outsourcer and Integration Company had done further work on the prototype, while negotiating with Hoogstraat B.V., there was still much work required to plug in both Outsourcer's systems and to integrate with Hoogstraat B.V.

Outsourcer and Integration Company agreed reluctantly to Hoogstraat B.V.'s timetable. This was on the understanding that the business would make decisions rapidly and mobilize its people to meet the company's commitments – to put more detail around the business requirements in time to meet its suppliers now very aggressive time-scales. Sheila and Fred readily agreed to this and made some changes in the scope to give their new suppliers a fighting chance. They even volunteered to provide overall program management.

Outsourcer and Integration Company put their respective teams together and began work against the plans submitted to win the business. The team also began to support the unplanned due diligence and requirements mapping exercise. Hoogstraat B.V. found an up-and-coming project manager (Herman) who had done well on a number of small projects and put him in charge.

Herman began by defining his Hoogstraat B.V. team, planning its effort based on the high-level plan in the contract and producing a project charter for Hoogstraat B.V. Outsourcer, as prime contractor, appointed a manager (Olivia) seasoned in taking on outsourcing business, but not in developing new software and systems integration. He asked Integration Company to take management responsibility for the integration of the IT effort. Olivia, Outsourcer's project director, created a project definition document for her area of responsibility and set up a series of regular meetings with Herman.

As this was such a strategic change for Hoogstraat B.V., the company appointed one of the members of the board to have overall responsibility (Harry). Harry arranged to 'face off' on a more or less regular basis with Herman, his project manager, and Olivia from Outsourcer, but also less frequently with directors of both Outsourcer and Integration Company.

Within a month of starting the program, Herman was concerned that business users were raising issues about the contracted functionality being different to their stated requirement and Olivia was delivering messages about Hoogstraat B.V. not meeting the dates in Outsourcer's plans. The outsourcing of the back-office staff, the first step to reducing costs, was going well and, despite a few problems, was on schedule.

Harry was very pleased about this and Herman found it very difficult to explain that all was not as well as it looked, that everything had started to be delayed by two or three days and that people exhibited little sign of urgency. He had two problems. This was his big chance and he did not want to look weak or, worse, be shot as the messenger. Also, he was not quite sure what was wrong – just that people took a little while longer here and there to make decisions. Each week they kept saying they would deliver next week, so the delay would not be much anyway.

He was probably worrying unnecessarily. He discussed it with Sheila who suggested that the reason Olivia (not the world's best diplomat) was stressing about missed deadlines was probably because Outsourcer and Integration Company could not meet theirs and were trying to put the blame on Hoogstraat B.V. to avoid the punitive damages. Sheila told Herman not to worry since, when the suppliers failed, she would 'enforce the contract and sort them out'.

As each milestone slipped, the going got tougher. There was less and less time to talk to people in the other teams, even if you knew who to talk to. It did not help that the teams were hundreds of miles apart and could not take time out to travel all over the country to see each other. That was not estimated in the cut-down plan! All anyone was interested in was that failure would not be their fault, even though everyone within the teams with any common sense could see that the plans were unachievable.

The project managers in the three companies were busy building relationships with each other and trying to make things work – trying to find ways around delays, to replan, alter workloads and to bring forward pieces of work to keep things rolling. They were assured by their respective directors that this was a long-term relationship, which had to be made to work.

Olivia and her IT development manager from Integration Company (Alex) were becoming increasingly frustrated by what they saw as Hoogstraat B.V.'s inaction and worried about the contractual implications of failure. Herman did not seem to be passing the messages that there were problems up the line, and none of the meeting minutes ever gave an accurate picture of the problems.

Olivia decided that she would have a big showdown at the next steering meeting. She announced without preamble that, after running for three months, the three-year program was already three months behind schedule and that Hoogstraat B.V. would have to stand the cost of the overrun which was looking like some 4 million Euros, as far as she could tell. That certainly grabbed everyone's attention for once.

TAKING STOCK

The directors of the three companies were shocked. No one had told them how bad things were, even though they were very approachable people (when they were available). They agreed to sponsor a full review of proceedings to date, to gain an understanding of why things were going so wrong. To this end, they brought in two independent program directors, with a brief to quickly identify issues and recommend a way forward. This team spent two weeks talking to members of the teams at all levels and concluded the following:

'To date, the scale and complexity of the tasks involved in Program X have been underestimated. The rush to contracts left pre-program work unfinished, and strained relationships. There has been no program-wide management in place, and a lack of leadership has resulted. This has been compounded by poor communication and governance structures that are slow, complex and enforce a silo mentality.

'The above are the root causes of the lack of any real or viable plans, in spite of tremendous efforts put in by the whole team to achieve an integrated plan. Additionally, the current contract constrains the delivery team, leaving little of the required flexibility needed to deliver. There has been both a lack of real program management skills, in what is a large complex program, and distance between the program management and their executive management. This has meant that the program was allowed to drift for two of the three months of its life. This occurred in spite of warnings of issues that were given as early as the end of the first month.'

There were numerous things that had gone wrong but the following were stressed as key causes of the problem:

☐ Long, protracted contract negotiations, which strained relationships rather than creating a mutual trust.

☐ A final rush to sign contracts leaving loose ends to be pulled together during the start-up phase.

☐ Underestimation of the scale and complexity of the undertaking.

☐ Changes to the content of the final contract in terms of systems, processes and delivery schedules, which were not fed back to the business teams.

☐ Agreement by the suppliers to the clients time-scales, which were felt to be over-ambitious given the complexity of decision making.

☐ Failure by Hoogstraat B.V. to provide the promised program management.

☐ Failure of the Outsourcer and Integration Company managers to effectively escalate the issue of non-program management.

☐ Non-engagement of executive management group during the first two months of the program.

☐ The absence of any mobilization phase during the first two months, which would have largely mitigated the above issues.

☐ Appointment of a management team that did not have the correct experience.

☐ Absence of a shared objective common to all three organizations.

FURTHER OBSERVATIONS

'The contract included a detailed plan, but there is doubt that it had ever been communicated to the Hoogstraat B.V. team at large. In fact, the contract has constrained the delivery team from doing the right thing and flexing the plans to accommodate reality – e.g. "We can't change the plan because that will change the cost profile which is in the contract". There was initially no recognition of the need to mobilize and align the respective organizations – only the need to deliver to time, cost and quality that part of the contract that each manager felt responsible for.

'There had been a singular lack of recognition of different cultures or of the difficulties presented when one team, Outsourcer and Integration Company, largely dedicated to delivering their services and related products and familiar with project disciplines, had to work closely with another, Hoogstraat B.V., whose involvement is part-time and who had many day-to-day business demands to satisfy.

'The lack of integration across the program, lack of leadership and lack of ownership appears to have gone unnoticed or unrecognized. The operational management team has been left to its own inexperienced devices. The executive management's duties at set up are particularly onerous in terms of providing continuity and business direction at a time of rapid enlargement of the team and these were ignored.

'Communication across the organizational silos was non-existent at the program level. Any information, which floats to the top of each company team's silo, is reinterpreted and re-keyed before being passed on. The whole program is dependent on contact at the management area level. The project managers have acted as buffers, rather than facilitators in the communication process. This has created further loss of productivity, increased frustration and misunderstanding.

'From the time of the contractual negotiations, there has been an assumption that the different governance processes in place in the three participating companies could be overlaid and made to work effectively in conjunction with each other. With no manager taking responsibility for the whole program, the management team have been "flying blind" with slow, over-complex, and incompatible governance processes, which did not join up.

'Managers and teams were unaware of the critical path and cannot prioritize work or the allocation of resource. There are, in short, no effective means of controlling progress, expenditure or allocation of resources. Unless the planning process is fundamentally changed, there is little hope of the current team ever achieving an integrated plan that can be used as a management tool.'

THE RECOMMENDATIONS

Over 50 recommendations were made as a result of the review process. The key ones are given below. The reviewers also made it very clear that the changes had to be carried out quickly and the contracts had to be changed. The contracts had forced the teams into wrong behaviours. Changes needed to be put in place so quickly that they could not wait for contract renegotiation. These changes had to have the effect of creating a true partnership for people from all three organizations, such that they put the well-being of Program X first and the parochial interests of their own company second.

The main recommendations were as follows:

☐ All parties should examine the contract and seek to make changes that will create a partnership framework.

☐ A management strategy document should be produced as an early program deliverable. This document should set out how the style and process, in terms of management control, is to be exercised. This will include details such as authorities, empowerment and escalation processes.

☐ A program management structure must be implemented with the correct responsibility and authorities throughout the program. This organizational structure and management team must be created from across the partners, to be effective and empowered.

☐ A communications manager needs to be appointed as quickly as possible. The role will manage all internal communications. Two immediate priorities for the communications manager are to lead the management team in developing a 're-launch' event and an induction pack. These need to clearly demonstrate the 'three partners, one team' approach that is required to drive this program forward.

☐ Set up a single program office with the specific responsibility to establish a common work breakdown structure and a set of 'shared services' – planning, risk, change control, identification of dependencies, audit, etc.

WHAT HAPPENED NEXT

The sponsors, not surprisingly, accepted the recommendations in full and Hoogstraat B.V. immediately replaced Herman with a more experienced project manager (Hans). The program reviewers worked closely with the teams from the three companies to architect a new management structure. This structure was based on a matrix management approach. Teams from the three companies, with common roles such as IT and business development, would come together under one manager for that role regardless of company. This was the new vertical responsibility, taking charge of liability across the whole program. Focusing on managing by release provided the horizontal part of the matrix.

The new team put together a new plan. Firstly, they decided to micro-manage current deliverables so that they were brought in as early as possible and to the time-scale set by them – an early win. Secondly, they created a plan for a further release of functionality, which was owned by a new program office and the Release 2 manager. It was very detailed, with over 4000 tasks on it. They also began working to develop a new planning process and tools and a new change control process.

The commercial teams from the three companies sat down together and renegotiated prices and time-scales to fit the new plan and structure. Sheila was insistent, though, that it would be a huge task to rewrite her beautiful contract (look at how long it had taken before). It was agreed then, to only vary the existing contract with the new numbers and dates and to ease some of the punitive damages.

By the end of three months, the new management structure was populated. Each company had made sure that it was politically well represented in the new management team, even if they had struggled to find the right person. Hoogstraat B.V., faced with increasing costs and lengthening time-scales, made sure that most new roles within the team were filled by Hoogstraat B.V. staff. It would be a good learning ground for them now. Sheila was also asked to take a much higher profile role in running the program on a day-to-day basis, with Hans, the new project manager.

Hans had successfully managed big projects with aggressive time-scales before. He knew that, when you have so many people moving in different directions, you need to give them clear instructions and make sure they deliver. If they do not deliver, or say they cannot, you usually get a result if you give them a bit of a hard time. He has, of course, not written this down anywhere.

Olivia was disappointed with the review and felt that she took some unfair criticism. She is unsure about her current position but feels that she can reclaim control. Her main concern is that Integration Company now has a seat on the new operations management group, and she will have to watch out that, as sub-contractors, they do not try to undermine Outsourcer's position.

Integration Company has appointed one of its most senior program managers to represent the firm on the new operations management group.

ONE YEAR ON FROM THE REVIEW

The first release of software was delivered on time and implemented flawlessly. The second system release has just been implemented – only one month later than planned originally, but with many additions to the scope defined 12 months previously.

Meanwhile, only half of the review recommendations have been implemented, either partially or in full. The team has been unable to stem the tide of late changes flowing through from the business. This is in spite of the fact that Sheila and Fred take ages on each change to ensure that their suppliers are not cheating on the estimates for changes and clawing back some of the profit lost in the renegotiations.

It is a little early to tell for sure, but it does look as though this second release is beginning to deliver some of the flexibility that Hoogstraat B.V. first envisioned. The service levels across the board are vastly improved and those salespeople already using the new approach are delighted.

The downsides are that Hoogstraat B.V. delayed the whole program for a further six months while it struggled to put together detailed requirements for future phases. The macro-economic factors have changed for Hoogstraat B.V., however, and the company now needs to change some of its stated business priorities.

Relations are becoming strained between all parties and each company is beginning to look hard at the contracts to see what redress or protection they have. In the program, however, the company silos have broken down and each management area is working hard to make sure it is not responsible for any delays.

LESSONS TO TAKE AWAY

At the beginning of this chapter, it was said that you could draw your own conclusions from this case study. This particular example has been included not only because it is interesting in itself, but because it reveals cycles of events that many readers will relate to in their own environments. Nevertheless, there is a fundamental observation to make – the program failure had little to do with technology, but was a failure to get the right people with the right experience into the right roles.

The following questions will help you to diagnose your own circumstances. Consider what action should be taken.

- ☐ Is Program X under clear and consistent leadership?
- ☐ Are there clear common objectives in place?
- ☐ Is the management team the right one in terms of experience, skills, culture?
- ☐ Are the management principles documented and agreed?
- ☐ Is the management style the right one for this program?
- ☐ Is there a coordinated communications strategy in place?
- ☐ Have the complexities of the multiple delivery sites been addressed?
- ☐ Do the management team, executive sponsors, operations management group and program management understand the complexity of what they are dealing with?
- ☐ Should a mobilization phase have been planned even at this late stage of the review?
- ☐ Is there a clear view of the overall business benefits for all of the parties, which sets out the financial case for working together?
- ☐ Is there any mechanism in place that allows all parties to share their financial view of the program? Should there be one? What would it need to make it successful and meaningful?
- ☐ Are the correct relationships in place to make this work?
- ☐ Are the correct people in place to manage the relationship?
- ☐ Was the decision to leave the current contract in place a good one?
- ☐ What sort of contract would effectively help to deliver this program?
- ☐ Is it too late to make any changes to the cultures involved?
- ☐ How could Outsourcer and Integration Company be encouraged to work together more effectively?
- ☐ Are resources being effectively managed?
- ☐ How do the management team know in advance if and when they will have any resource constraints?
- ☐ Is this integration program 'integrated'?
- ☐ Who has overall responsibility for integration?
- ☐ Are all common functions grouped at a program level?
- ☐ Where is the 'big picture' of the program owned?
- ☐ How far down in the organization is the big picture understood?

☐ What activities, functions and people are in place to ensure integration?

☐ Is the management team in day-to-day control of this program?

☐ How do they know where they are and how to make decisions on where they are going next and in the longer term?

☐ Do they understand competently and factually the impact of changes and delays?

☐ Can they make effective decisions?

☐ Is Hans in control? Is anybody in control?

CHAPTER 19

RISK MANAGEMENT
IN PRACTICE

INTRODUCTION

As illustrated by Chapter 18, few integration programs run as smoothly as their teams would like. Goalposts may change, there may be unforeseen technical problems or budgets may be exceeded. These are potential risks to the success of the program.

This chapter explores the different guises that risk can take, with the aim of helping you to recognize, quantify and manage risk. To improve the probability of your project being delivered on time and to budget, and of achieving its targets.

While other books on the subject have focused on the theory of risk management, the intention here is to explore how that theory is applied. The concern is with the practice of risk management, rather than the science.

DEFINING RISK

Risks are associated with any events that may occur in the future and which will adversely affect any of the program aims, benefits, time-scales, costs and performance. Since it occurs in the future, a risk inevitably has a measure of uncertainty associated with it and, by definition, a degree of loss. A risk also has a third element – the choice to do something about it.

Once the risk has been identified, a process of risk management offers the program management team the opportunity to implement appropriate mitigation strategies that prevent or reduce the probability of occurrence of the risk and/or the reduction of its impact. If mitigation activities are unable to completely remove the impact, you will be left with what is referred to as a 'residual risk'.

Choosing to do nothing but accept the risk is a valid option and, in some instances, this may be the most cost-effective strategy to adopt. Risks may or may not occur, thus it is uncertain whether there will be an adverse impact on the program if no action is taken.

Many people intellectualize about risk. An important distinction is between risks and issues (see Chapter 13) without following practical measures for avoiding or addressing risks in their own projects. Although there are useful formulas, which can be applied practically on a daily basis, the theory of risk management is not important. The main thing is that your project team agrees what the risks are and how to manage them.

WHOSE JOB IS THIS?

Apportioning responsibility for potential risk is a key part of managing it. It is wrong to assume that the IT department must be the one to take on the burden. If a project has been ill defined or ill managed by the business, then the business will suffer and the business is to blame. Yet, at the same time, if the IT component of the project falls short of its obligations, with a resulting negative impact on the business, this too becomes the business's problem. It may not be the business's fault, but it is the business's risk.

An important first stage is to ensure that any discussions about risk and risk management have the full involvement of all parties. At a very early stage in the project's life cycle – preferably when the program is being defined – all program managers, technology managers, delivery managers and business sponsors should sit down together to contemplate the issue of risk.

Topics for discussion should include:

☐ What are the various potential risks and which are the most dangerous ones?

☐ How are the risks interrelated?

☐ Whose risks are they (i.e. who will be affected if they are borne out)?

☐ Who will own these risks and ensure that they are managed?

☐ What impact could these risks have, financially and otherwise? How can they be quantified?

☐ What is the probability of the risk coming into play?

☐ What mitigation measures could be put in place?

☐ What cost does mitigation have? Is it justified?

Successful risk management is heavily dependent upon joint assessment of business process, people and organization and technology risk. Also on formulation of a joint strategy and continual team work in managing both risks and mitigation actions.

EXAMPLES OF RISKS

There are literally hundreds of potential risks that could apply in a systems integration scenario. Some of the more common ones are:

☐ The project overruns.

☐ The new processes do not deliver the expected efficiency gains, for example, processing more work with less resource.

☐ There is a mismatch between the goals of the business and the goals of the IT department. Worse, a business process has not been defined at all.

☐ The IT infrastructure does not have sufficient capacity to do the job it was designed for.

☐ Future scalability needs have been underestimated.

☐ Contracted service level agreements are not relevant or achievable when new releases of the system are implemented.

☐ Any new, unproven technology involved does not live up to expectations.

☐ A third-party supplier goes out of business.

☐ Key personnel in the project are lost.

SEPARATING OUT THE SERIOUS RISKS

Of course, not every risk will come into play. Even if this eventuality were likely, making provisions for everything would not be economically viable. Consequently, it is important to identify the most pressing risks – ones that could bring the business to a standstill or cost the company dearly.

Table 19.1 can be used to assess the likely impact of risks and issues:

AFFECTED PROJECT ATTRIBUTES	NIL	LOW	MEDIUM	HIGH
Business benefits	<2% decrease in revenue <2% increase in operational costs	3–5% decrease in revenue 3–5%increase in operational costs	6–10% decrease in business benefits 6–10%increase in operational costs	>11% decrease in business benefits >11% increase in operational costs
Performance/Quality	Negligible impact on business function/ service performance	Degradation of an essential business function/loss of non-essential business function or degradation in service performance	Severe degradation of an essential business function or degradation in service performance to cause complaint	Loss of an essential business function or severe degradation in service performance to cause complaint
Project cost	<2% increase in project costs	3–5% increase in project costs	6–10% increase in project costs	>11% increase in project costs
Project schedule	Additional activities required to meet key milestones	Key milestones will slip, but the release can be implemented on time	The release will be implemented behind schedule, but will not cause high level political awareness	The system will be implemented more than four months late and/or will cause high level political awareness

TABLE 19.1: Impact evaluation

Meanwhile, Table 19.2 can be used to assess the probability of a risk occurring:

	LOW	MEDIUM	HIGHLY
Probability of occurrence	<20%	21–70%	> 70%

TABLE 19.2: Probability assessment risks

DO NOT JUST OBSERVE THE RISKS, MANAGE THEM

Successful risk containment is an ongoing, interactive process. It is as important in the middle of project delivery as at the beginning. It is all very well recognizing a risk and writing it down in the project logbook, but if it is then forgotten, the process has been a waste of time. Many organizations are guilty of this. Risk management needs a certain degree of formality. This means regular meetings whose sole purpose is to review the risk log and assess where the project is in terms of the main identified risks.

If a project is deemed to have 20–30 risks, including a hit list of some five to ten, which could really hurt the company or its objectives, the meetings should be used to review each of these, establish whether they have come into play and whether mitigation has or should be started.

At the beginning of a project, meetings should take place every two weeks; these can drop down to once a month once the program delivery is underway. The important point is to continually re-evaluate where you are in relation to any risks. This may also include the identification and management of new risks that creep into the project along the way.

DOING THE MATHS

Assessing risk can involve some complex maths. Formulas can be applied to establish which risks are serious and when it is prudent to make financial provision. Risks must be assigned financial values so that mitigation measures can be planned sensibly – there is no sense making $400,000 worth of provisions for a risk that, if borne out, would only cost the company $20,000.

These sorts of calculations must be recorded in the risk register, which should include the following:

☐ Valuation of the total risk and how this is apportioned, for example, among the various parties involved, including any external consultancies that are working on the program.

☐ Descriptions of the various risks and how their effects could be felt and by whom. The value of the risk, the probability of it occurring, the mitigation measures that have been suggested and the ownership of it should be clearly set out for each.

☐ Any financial provisions that have been made by the various parties to protect the company against the effects of those risks if they come into play.

☐ A record of all review meetings and what happens at these. This should include a record of any changes that are made to the risk management process, for instance, noting risks that have been escalated, downgraded, merged or revalued or which have changed ownership, as well as a record of any mitigation measures that have been invoked or that have been additionally requested for consideration.

By going through each risk systematically and regularly, companies are less likely to lose sight of the lurking dangers that could upset the program. Instead, they will be forced to acknowledge and deal with them at an early stage.

FINANCIAL PROVISIONS

Preparing for risks means allowing a financial resource to cover contingency plans where these are practical. Risks and budgets should, therefore, be identified at the same time. Risk management needs its own, dedicated budget, which should be reviewed regularly as part of any risk meetings.

If one risk appears to be running higher than the others, parts of the risk budget can be reallocated, if there is agreement between the various risk owners. Keep an eye on the gap between reality (the available risk budget) and the financial demands of any contingency plans. If several risks are looking dangerously close to coming into effect, it may be necessary to make a plea for an extension to the overall risk budget. Far better to recognize this in plenty of time, than to bury your heads and ignore the problem until it is upon you.

MITIGATION

A key challenge in risk management is realizing when a risk starts to come into play and taking steps to keep it under control by a process of acknowledgement, planning and action. If reviews take place regularly and frankly, proactive, preventative measures can be taken more easily.

If a project is running late, one solution may be to bring in extra resources in the way of more technical staff – provided, of course, that these are available. Accordingly, mitigation plans must be realistic – there is no point planning the impossible. A good mitigation plan is one that has been properly thought through – it should look like a mini action plan.

For example, having people with the right skills for a program will always be critical to ensure delivery. If three key people are due to finish their contracts in three months' time, it is important to spot this in advance and establish an appropriate course of action. It may be that one contractor intends to leave no matter what, while another is wavering and the third plans to stay. Someone who is proactively managing this situation will ensure that a replacement is lined up for the first and that the second is monitored, with a contingency plan lined up if he or she should decide to leave at the end of their contract. The difference between proactive risk management and ignoring the problem is that in the first scenario, the possible problem (of losing up to two members of the team at a potentially crucial stage in the program's delivery) is anticipated in advance and hopefully averted. The alternative is to wait until the three months are up and hope for the best.

A DAY IN THE LIFE OF A RISK MANAGER

Here is a typical day for a program manager concerned with risk management.

☐ Had the initial risk meeting between program and business. They want a joint risk register, covering both the program and the business. I argued against this, noting that the IT delivery program will have risks that it will not want to share with the business and vice versa (if we have only one risk register rather than three, this would mean that some risks would not be included). Not sure if I won my argument – some people interpreted it as 'not joined up'. In any case, the IT delivery program will have two risk registers – a shared one and a private one.

☐ Stressed to the program management office (PMO) that I want the risk register distributed to all attendees of the joint risk management meeting 24 hours before the meeting. This deadline was missed (as usual) – the register will now be distributed just before the meeting. The PMO offered the excuses of late updates from the risk owners. We agreed to change the process so that in future the register is updated and distributed 24 hours before the scheduled meetings and, if the updates have not come in from the owners in time, the guilty parties will be exposed at the meeting.

☐ The risk meeting started with the usual five-minute debate about the definition of a 'risk' and an 'issue'. I urged that this should be the last time we have this debate! (The definition we are using is clearly stated in our process.) The meeting went well, generally, though the business is very eager to get involved in discussing the IT technical and development risks. I had to stop the discussion on a number of occasions, noting that we are not redesigning the solution here, just assessing the potential risk and associated mitigation plans.

I have some concerns that the business did not come into this understanding their risks – they offered some mitigation plans but I'm not sure whether they believe they can deliver on them (e.g. we have a risk that the business will not have sufficient skilled resources to support the IT development of the next program release. They're saying all the right words, but I'm not convinced that they mean them). I pulled the business manager aside after the meeting and asked him to come to the next review with a detailed mitigation plan, which contains the escalation points, rather than wait until a month before he needs the resource. He agreed.

☐ Following the joint risk meeting, I kept the IT development management team behind to look at the IT delivery risks we don't want to discuss with the business. I am concerned that the IT architecture and design might not be capable of supporting the volumes that it will need to. We spent some focused time examining this risk, questioning whether it is in fact a risk and whether the design team fully understands it. The conclusion was that we might have a significant exposure on some parts of the solution. The technical people are to put a plan together and schedule some testing of the design to see if we have a problem or not.

I was also concerned that we have not yet engaged the service organization, but have started the development – what if they need changes to the solution from an operational perspective? After the meeting, we discussed the fact that we are not yet ahead of the game on risk management and that I now want to start to hold two meetings specifically focused on risk management. One will be a review of the register as it is at that particular point in time; the other will be a regular review of the program, examining whether we have any new risks that are not in the register. The latter meeting will initially be every month but should move out after a few meetings. It is essential that we start to manage the risks proactively.

☐ The day moved on to the regular meetings, tracking progress against plan. Again I stressed the importance of having the risk mitigations in the plans so that we could achieve a fully balanced position, mapping the risk mitigations against our ability to resource and deliver them. As usual, people started to talk about the progress on one of the mitigation actions that has kicked in, and to discuss the potential solution to this risk, which is now larger than originally thought (many times larger).

The meeting then moved on to how we could get away with this, but it was agreed that we must inform the business ASAP in order to get their buy-in and support to the considerable additional funding that we will now need. We discussed this for 15 minutes, including the impact in financial terms if the risk is allowed to come into effect. The answer came back that we must not let this risk happen, because this would mean not meeting the service level agreement (SLA) for one particular measure.

When we asked what this measure was and whether it was important, we were told merely that it is important because it makes up the SLA! It turns out that it is only a minor measure, with negligible implications, albeit that it compromises the SLA. Put in financial terms, we're looking at an impact of $20k per year. 'Fine,' we said. 'You guys want to spend $1m solving a problem that will cost us $20k – do you think this makes sense?' Silence followed. So we looked at the issue from a new perspective, and made it the commercial manager's responsibility to try and renegotiate this measure in the SLA. If this fails, we have agreed we should have a discussion with the business, and inform them that this measure will not be hit. We will also look for another mitigation that costs less than $20k per year.

SUMMARY

1 If enough thought is put into it, risk management should be a successful enterprise. The trouble is, that as much as we try to make this a science, there are too many factors involved for it to be that simple. A framework will help provide structure, but this is only effective if the people involved in the program have a clear grasp of the risks they face, their responsibilities for these risks and how they will deal with them if they arise.

2 The situation is a little like that in the manufacturing industry 20 years ago. We are trying to automate process management in IT to gain more efficiencies. The science of risk management is just one part of this. However, we are not there yet and anyone who tries to dehumanize IT program management opens up a whole can of worms.

3 Success in any aspect of program management depends on paying equal attention to people, process and technology factors, and not making the mistake of looking at one or two of these in isolation. Rather than get bogged down worrying about the theory of risk management, take some comfort from the knowledge that common sense, attention to detail and good communication will take you a long way.

4 There will be many possible risks, affecting different parts of the program and different parts of the company. Identify as many as you can, then prioritize these based on potential impact and likelihood of the risk becoming a reality.

5 It is important to ensure that everyone is aware of the potential risks and that responsibility for these is allocated. The business should take just as much responsibility for risk management as the IT department.

6 There should be a formal structure for assessing, monitoring and dealing with risks, which involves the right combinations of people from across the enterprise and includes formal meetings and recording of developments, plans and actions.

7 As well as merely identifying the possible risks to the program, it is essential to have contingency or mitigation plans in place – and a budget dedicated to covering these.

8 Mitigation plans must match the level and scope of the risk, however. There is no point budgeting to spend a vast sum to cover what might be a relatively minor risk to the program in financial terms.

9 Monitoring and measuring risk as the program develops is vital. It is pointless assessing potential risks at the program's outset, only to put the risk log away in a drawer, never to consult it again. New risks may arise as the program progresses, while others may change in status.

CONCLUSION:
THE FUTURE OF
BUSINESS PROCESS

INTRODUCTION

⟨ Change has become a constant, managing it an expanding discipline. ⟩

Queen Elizabeth II's Jubilee speech to Parliament, April 30, 2002.

The intense impact of the internet on commerce, market globalization, the increasing volatility of the larger economies and the shockwaves that are still resounding around the international business community following the terrorist attacks on the US on 11 September 2001, are just some of the more tangible contributors to an acceleration of change, which is now felt worldwide.

How organizations respond to this makes for an interesting study and provides inspiration for how others can begin to think about re-engineering their own operations.

While many organizations are coming unstuck because of their inability to adapt to changing market conditions, others appear to thrive in this volatile environment. Examples of success stories include international computer manufacturer Dell, and UK-based airline RyanAir. What is different about these companies is they are adopting new approaches to doing business, which are redefining their industries and creating new competitive dynamics.

Consider Dell, an example explored in more detail below. Following the 2001 terrorist attacks on America, the company reacted quickly, reconfiguring its supply chain to enable it to produce some 300,000 machines to replace those that had been lost by companies affected by the plane crashes. Its competitors, restricted by the stock and production capacity limitations of their regular suppliers, could not respond as quickly and lost out on the business.

In the UK, budget airline RyanAir responded equally quickly to the events in the US, addressing the growing fear about air travel by dropping its fares the following day. It avoided loss of business by making sure that anyone still wanting to fly would choose its fleet for the trip. The result? RyanAir gained market share, at a time when use of airlines dropped to an alarmingly low level.

By contrast, shortly after these events, other airlines increased fares and at a time of decreasing market share for traditional airlines. Why did they do this? Was it some misguided attempt to compensate for a drop in seat sales? Or was it that they had planned the price increases for some time and did not have the flexibility to alter plans. Companies led by older, more rigid business and IT structure were prevented from changing course quickly. RyanAir, a much newer company, was accustomed to changing its fares structures regularly to offer special promotions, having designed the business from the outset to operate in this fashion.

REACTIVE BUSINESS MODELS BEAT PRE-EMPTIVE BUSINESS MODELS

In many areas of business, it is said that being pre-emptive is preferable to reacting to a situation that has already been created. Yet, in today's fast-changing commercial world, it is almost impossible to predict what the challenges and opportunities of tomorrow will be. For business managers and IT specialists alike, this presents something of a problem – how can they ensure they are ready, if they do not know what it is they are preparing for?

Therefore, the trend is towards being able to generate new business processes in real time, driving any latency out of business operation since, as 11 September 2001 taught the world, there will always be events that organizations cannot foresee. The organizations that will prosper in the long term will be those able to react the fastest to new circumstances.

These 'events' need not be large-scale disasters. Business is affected by many factors and organizations may simply need to react to new opportunities as they present themselves. As the world gets smaller and technology development cycles get ever shorter, being able to predict the next big opportunity is getting harder and harder.

The internet has taught enterprises that speed to market is everything. Coming up with innovative ways of trading or new value-added customer services is one thing, but if it takes your business 12 months to turn these visions into a reality, by the time you are geared up to exploit the opportunity, it may have been exploited by someone else or have passed altogether.

It has become clear that organizations, which depend too heavily on inflexible, pre-defined business processes, and the IT systems that support these, will soon lose their competitive edge. Adaptability – the ability to adapt in real time to new events – is everything.

BUSINESS MODELS NEED TO BE EXTENDED AS WELL AS ADAPTABLE

As well as needing to adopt dynamic business models, organizations will also increasingly need to deploy extended business models that collaborate with other businesses to exploit the benefits of this dynamism up and down the supply chain, maximizing business efficiencies. When organizations begin to see the bigger picture and integration on an enterprise-wide scale (and beyond) becomes easier through adoption of web services, for example, they will become less restricted by the limitations of traditional business processes, non-integrated, proprietary technologies and unconsolidated islands of corporate data. This will enable organizations to react to what is happening in the market by creating new business processes on the fly, rather than trying to predict the future, or worse – ignore it.

Commercial pressures and technological innovations are forcing more organizations to acquire extended business models where they use alliance partners or sub-contractors for elements of the business, which are important to the customer, but where these are not a core element of their organization's portfolio of skills or services. By collapsing the supply chain and creating virtual enterprises, through innovative use of the internet and web services, organizations can turn their energies to the art of managing relationships, instead of trying to do everything themselves.

However, what does this all mean in practice? What does an adaptive enterprise look like and how does it differ from a more traditional organization?

CREATING THE CAPABILITY TO RESPOND

The adaptive enterprise continuously exploits events and leverages its ecosystems (external business relationships) to adapt even faster than its marketplace.

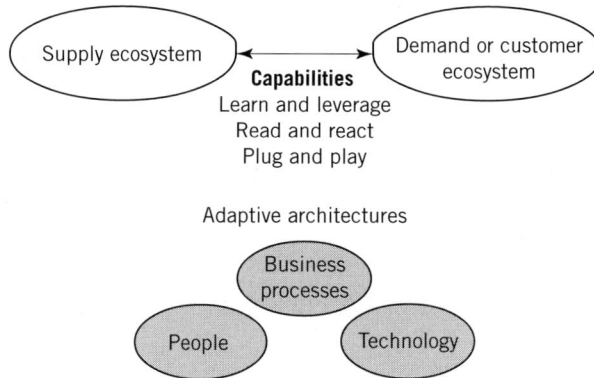

FIGURE 1: Business model innovation

There are three main characteristics that typify an adaptive enterprise, enabling it to respond to events by deploying its capabilities across its whole value chain, both in the supply side and on the demand or customer side. These are the ability to:

1 **Learn and leverage** – If an organization has this characteristic, it is able to continually create the vision and insight into a business challenge. After creating and using the solutions it has designed, it can learn from the experiences and use these to adjust both the vision and the solution. Thus, the organization constantly improves its performance.

2 **Read and react** – The enterprise continuously manages the 'value' portfolio of the company through explicit initiatives, such as the use of dynamic operational models that can adjust to business demand.

3 **Plug and play** – This refers to the acquisition of the ability to support business processes with a technology architecture that has at its heart a common set of standard interfaces and functions. This allows elements to be configured and reconfigured.

A turn around in the way that companies think and operate is needed. The ability to take a new event and respond to it by creating a new business process is a complete reversal of how most businesses are used to functioning. Previously, they have relied upon predicting trends and creating markets.

Consumer goods companies with many hundreds of products, for example, will have hundreds of departments doing hundreds of different tasks to create and manage their activities. This takes a great deal of planning and coordination. Consequently, much of what the organization does – for instance, if it wants to introduce a new product – is governed by what is possible within the confines of its existing business structure, which is typically well established and quite rigid. If a new market opportunity presents itself, the company has to ask itself whether it can respond, rather than how it can respond. In a fast-moving, highly competitive marketplace, this is highly constraining.

Agile, adaptive organizations, on the other hand, are much freer to react to new threats and opportunities. Instead of looking inward at what is or is not possible, these enterprises can look outwards to the market, observe the new themes emerging, for example, in customer behaviour, and answer accordingly.

British drinks company, Diagio, did exactly this when it noticed that consumers were regularly mixing the alcoholic drink Archers with flavoured waters. Spotting an opportunity, the company responded quickly by launching a pre-mixed drink based on the popular combinations it had observed.

Diagio had the right business mind-set and flexible enough IT systems to be driven by an emerging market demand and to turn around a new product launch within a matter of weeks. The market opportunity was used to create a business process and a new product – not the other way round. Launching into a market that is already established avoids the greater part of the launch cost, enabling profitability to be reached in a matter of days, rather than months. Moreover, the amount of capital at risk is much lower, since no big campaign is needed to try to persuade the market of the new idea – a campaign which in less certain circumstances would not necessarily be guaranteed success. Organizations that can exploit this sort of opportunity stand to produce faster business returns (within the same quarter) and are less likely to produce a loss. This allows smaller market niches to be addressed without the need for massive launch cost paybacks.

Dell is another company that exploited, to good effect, the premise that the business process should be designed from the customer need backwards, rather than from a manufacturer's hunch. Dell achieved tremendous success in the global PC market through its strategy of mass customization. Despite the fact that the PC market is now highly commoditized, the organization achieves profitable revenues from PC production by adding unique value for customers, in a way that does not cost the firm dearly. It attains adaptability in its processes and extends its supply chains.

The company uses a just-in-time manufacturing strategy to meet customer demand for individually configured computer systems, which means it does not incur the costs and risks of obsolescence associated with the stockpiling of components and other inventory. It has achieved this by integrating its IT systems with those of its key suppliers, permitting these to respond rapidly to changing demands for stock. If one supplier is unable to deliver the components necessary for Dell to meet a particular customer order, Dell's systems are flexible enough to allow the company to quickly adapt its supply chains, as it did following the terrorist attacks on New York.

Like RyanAir and Diagio, Dell is able to react to the needs of the market. Rather than conduct market research, design a product and then market it to the customer, it has put the customer in the driving seat. The customer has a need, voices this and Dell reacts. And, in turn, the whole supply chain behind Dell reacts too. Products are not pre-planned, nor are component orders. These are generated 'just in time', as the customer requests come in. As a result, the various suppliers are free from the risks of overstocking and can offer a better service to the customer. Profits are maintained because customers perceive a value-added service – one which is not necessarily priced at a premium because of the efficiencies of tight supply chain integration and automation.

LESS RIGIDLY INTEGRATED SYSTEMS HELP CREATE REACTIVE BUSINESS PROCESSES

Dell takes its lead from the customer, rather than telling the customer what it needs and can be thought of as an adaptive or 'event-driven' enterprise. It is not restricted by rigid business structures and its IT systems allow business processes to be changed and improved. These are well integrated to provide an ecosystem, which spans not only the immediate organization, but its business partners too. Data can be released up and down the supply chain to guarantee that each party involved in meeting customer orders has the knowledge required to respond quickly and accurately to each new business need.

Before it opened up its sales order systems to its suppliers, allowing these to answer demand in real time, Dell was taking five days to fulfil custom PC orders, with component orders taking a lengthy 50 days. To ensure that Dell met its commitments to customers, its suppliers had to maintain ten days' worth of inventory in stock and Dell had to keep a day's worth of components at its own factories. To keep this process as accurate and economical as possible, Dell had to predict market trends for PCs and continually issue purchasing forecasts to its suppliers. The company's success depended upon matching market prediction to its contracts with component and material providers.

Today, however, Dell's process works the other way around. The company creates four manufacturing schedules per day based on actual demand (orders received) and publishes these schedules as a web service to its suppliers. Because this service is web-based and uses the XML standard for sharing data, it can be understood by Dell's suppliers' inventory management systems, which, in turn, use the information to deliver the precise requirement for components directly to the assembly lines.

This has allowed Dell to eradicate any need to store significant volumes of components at the factory and enables the company's suppliers to supply only material that is required to fulfil actual sales by Dell. Dell's suppliers are now adopting a similar strategy with the effect of reducing inventory throughout the supply chain.

In Chapter 1, *The Atomic Corporation* by Roger Camrass and Martin Farncombe was referred to. This book argues that giant corporations will eventually die out, to be replaced by networks of smaller, smarter, more adaptable companies, each playing to their own strengths and working in partnership with others, rather than trying to do everything themselves.

Camrass and Farncombe place much emphasis on organizations' ability to think imaginatively and to reinvent themselves as a key factor in determining their chances of survival and prosperity in the long term. They write:

> ‘An innovative organization is one that quickly recognizes significant changes in the external environment and imaginatively reconfigures its resources to exploit them.’ [1]

However, little of this would be possible without IT innovation. The critical element is integration – joining up otherwise separate and diverse IT systems to permit knowledge and related business processes to be constructed and shared from one end of a company, or ideally the entire supply chain, to the other, with as little pre-planning as possible.

[1] Roger Camrass and Martin Farncombe, *The Atomic Corporation, Op. Cit.*

COMPANIES START TO ACHIEVE THE QUALITIES REQUIRED OF ADAPTIVE SYSTEMS

While, in recent years, companies have attempted integration at an application level by either 'hardwiring' these together to share data, or employing Enterprise Application Integration (EAI) tools for internal integration, it is the emergence of web services (discussed in Chapter 11) that gives organizations true freedom in their integration activities. Web services enable more rapid and flexible combinations of systems, both internally and beyond the boundaries of a single enterprise.

One European haulage company, which is using web services at an advanced level, claims some impressive, tangible results from its new found ability to react to customer- or asset-based events in real time.

The company has implemented a web service-based architecture that enables it to respond to events in an adaptive manner across an extended supply chain. It is able to re-route lorries following events such as breakdowns or a customer changing an order. This has increased the company's level of lorry deployment from 70 per cent to 74 per cent, leading to 10 per cent savings on the firm's bottom line.

The swift response is possible because the haulage company's business systems are fully integrated using web services, internally and with those of its suppliers. If an order changes or meets with a problem, the systems up and down the supply chain can reply instantaneously, redirecting another lorry from the fleet.

Looking more closely at the qualities of adaptive systems that this approach facilitates, there is evidence of:

1 **Responsiveness** – The 'system' and the processes are clearly able to respond to events, such as trucks breaking down.

    ☐ **Proactivity** – The system understands how it has reacted in the past and is able to record the effect of previous action in order to optimize its response

    ☐ **Autonomy** – In typical sales automation systems, certain functions, such as sales representatives' territory planning, are carried out by a central processing function that processes large amounts of data in order to match sales outlets to representatives. This reconciles factors like outlet location, accessibility, type of outlet, representative experience or qualification and so on. These systems are typically unable to rapidly adapt to changes of an outlet or a representative. By exploiting adaptive services, which are autonomous, the company in this example has been able to devolve complexity to an agent that represents the truck, which in turn collaborates with other agents rather than centrally processing large amounts of data to redeploy the trucks.

2 **Self-healing** – The web services architecture can respond to bottlenecks caused by failure and reconfigure accordingly. For example, at the hardware level if a processor breaks, the service will be automatically reconfigured onto another processor or system.

3 **Extensible** – The trucking company can bring partners online quickly because of the flexibility provided by web services to connect to the IT systems of new third parties.

The world of web services is one where IT applications, old and new, can be combined and recombined spontaneously, according to the new business need. By providing a standards-based interface, it treats everything behind that interface as a component that can be combined with others to generate new functionality.

To appreciate the difference between this and previous methods of systems integration, consider the example of a retail bank.

Most retail banks now offer their customers online access to their accounts. Customers can activate transactions themselves, such as checking their bank balance, transferring money between accounts or paying bills. All of this can be done automatically, without recourse to a customer services assistant.

Yet, in many cases, this type of internet service has been achieved at great pains and expense to the bank. While the service might mirror that offered by internal branch agents or a telephone-based call centre where the customer asks someone else to handle these transactions on their behalf, more often than not these processes are handled by a different set of systems, using different bespoke application codes.

With web services, on the other hand, the different customer service options would be served by the same application components, requiring minimal redevelopment, incurring relatively low costs and allowing unprecedented speed to market with new services.

Inflexible business processes supported by hot-wired applications, where these are linked together on a point-to-point basis and even integration achieved through EAI, do not offer sufficient levels of flexibility. EAI tools are a major step beyond point-to-point interfaces, but the technology does not offer adaptors for all applications. However 'end-to-end' the supported business processes may be, they will not in themselves provide the requisite agility and responsiveness.

In order to support adaptive business processes, more open, less rigidly integrated IT systems are required, with a rich set of both infrastructure-based services (such as security and transaction services) permitting business services to be built around common components.

Web services enable simpler connections, since they use the internet as an open environment within which to operate. They are the biggest breakthrough in supporting flexible systems integration.

WEB SERVICES ENABLE THE RAPID DEVELOPMENT OF NEW PROCESSES

Due to the speed at which new opportunities and threats can now emerge in the market place, driving latency out of business is no longer enough to maintain a company's competitive edge. Being quick to market with new ideas and having the infrastructure to support new business process and be able to combine and recombine services based on internet technology are critical.

Web services encourage the reuse of existing software functionality in the interests of making applications faster to build. This gives companies speed to market with new business processes and new customer services and paves the way for organizations to reuse the basic software assets of other companies.

While organizations focus their initial deployment of web services to achieve more efficient and flexible applications integration within their internal enterprise and then extend this capability to suppliers, companies are already realizing the potential of sharing web services-based resources with other companies on a commercial basis. This removes the need for multiple organizations to reinvent the wheel each time they need a particular kind of application or service functionality.

Once organizations are more open to sharing standard resources with other enterprises (clearly, they would hold back any web services deemed to give them a competitive edge), it is likely to take place on a business functionality level as well as a purely technological one.

In order to process a finance loan, for instance, banks will be able to access the credit rating services provided by other companies. This will lead some organizations to sell facilities, such as credit rating, as a utility to other financial enterprises and as a chargeable web service. Those buying the services will no longer need to maintain their own credit rating systems.

A further example can be found in online exchanges, where, until recently, a persistent issue has been the ability to handle payments. In early exchanges, manual payment would often be necessary. One global bank with a core competency in electronic payment spotted this opportunity and created a web service to process payments, suitable for use by existing online exchanges.

This business service packages a payment transaction in response to the electronic instruction from the online exchange, which includes all the relevant payment details, such as timing, the seller, the buyer and so forth. The payment is then automatically routed via web services onto the appropriate network and the settlement is made. This innovation has resulted in both settlement times and settlement costs being cut by half.

THE JOINED-UP MESSAGE

Although the role of IT systems is clearly pivotal to achieve adaptability and agility both internally and up and down the supply chain, as continually stressed throughout this book, technology is only one-third of the integration challenge. Alongside technology is the need to change the role and attitude of people and the way that business processes are constructed and supported.

Truly joined-up enterprises will not only strive to implement the latest in web services and associated integration techniques, they will fully understand that the rules of the game have changed forever and they need to make the following adjustments:

☐ It is people, not technology, that deliver change. Organizations must, therefore, grow their own highly skilled, internal change management teams which understand the 'soft' aspects of integration as much as the hard ones.

☐ If continuous change and the ability to remain adaptive is genuinely the company's goal, the business must become its own integrator, adopting best practices for change management, systems integration, risk management and all other aspects of the business re-engineering process, as a central company strategy.

☐ As organizations become more virtual in structure, exploiting relationships with external partners to keep internal costs down while ensuring a complete offering to the customer, the contractual relationship between cooperating companies must change. Client/supplier relationships must be replaced with true partnership arrangements, where all parties are accountable for the job being done or the products and services provided. Instead of instructing suppliers about a particular piece of work to be done, organizations need to involve their partners in their strategic vision if continuous change and general improvements to cost and customer service are to result. Partnerships mean sharing responsibility, risks and rewards, fairly and contractually.

☐ Maintaining a clear vision of measurable, testable goals will be difficult but essential. Reaching them will depend on the use of a flexible game plan, based on architectures, core assets, principles and services.

This book has set out to describe the issues which are being encountered every day and to describe, as lucidly as possible, how these can be approached and how to adapt these methods to face the new challenges as they come along. We leave it for you to judge, by taking and continuously improving the advocated thinking, tools, and techniques, whether our conclusions are correct.

FURTHER READING AND CONTACTS

If you are an organization interested in the ideas of adaptive business and adaptive architectures introduced in this book, and would like to talk to Cap Gemini Ernst & Young about putting these ideas into practice, please contact the Marketing Department on +44 (0)20 7434 2171 or visit www.cgey.com

If you are interested in reading more on some of the topics covered, the following books are a good place to start.

Nancy J Adler, *International Dimensions of Organizational Behaviour*, third edition, South-Western College Publishing, 2001.

Christopher A Bartlett and Sumantra Ghosal, *Transnational Management*, McGraw Hill Education, 1997.

Roger Camrass and Martin Farncombe, *The Atomic Corporation – A Rational Proposal For Uncertain Times*, Capstone Publishing, 2001.

Rene Carayol and David Firth, *Corporate Voodoo – Principles for Business Mavericks and Magicians*, Capstone Publishing, 2001.

Central Computer and Telecommunications Agency, *A Guide to Program Management*, The Stationery Office Books, 1994.

Tom Gilb, *Principles of Software Engineering Management*, Addison Wesley, 1998.

Michael Hammer, *The Agenda*, Random House Business Books, 2001.

Geert Hofstede, *Cultures and Organizations*, McGraw Hill, 1996.

William Perry, *Effective Methods for Testing Software*, John Wiley, 1995.

Bruce Robertson and Valentin Sribar, *The Adaptive Enterprise – IT Infrastructure Strategies to Manage Change and Enable Growth*, Intel Press, 2002.

Dava Sobel, *Longitude*, Fourth Estate, 1996.

WorldWork can be contacted at The WorldWork Partnership, 6 Porter Street, London W1U 6DD. Tel: +44 (0)20 7486 9844.

The subject of this book is vast and fast-moving. There are topics we would have liked to have covered in more detail, but did not have the time or space to do so. If you have a comment or suggestion for how this book might be improved, for any future editions, please send an e-mail to: joinedupsystems@cgey.com